THE LIFE OF CHARLOTTE BRONTË

VOLUME 1

BY

ELIZABETH CLEGHORN GASKELL

First published in 1857

This edition published by Read Books Ltd.
Copyright © 2018 Read Books Ltd.
This book is copyright and may not be
reproduced or copied in any way without
the express permission of the publisher in writing

British Library Cataloguing-in-Publication Data
A catalogue record for this book is available
from the British Library

CONTENTS

CHAPTER I 5
CHAPTER II 13
CHAPTER III. 35
CHAPTER IV. 53
CHAPTER V 69
CHAPTER VI. 84
CHAPTER VII. 105
CHAPTER VIII 123
CHAPTER IX. 166
CHAPTER X 181
CHAPTER XI. 198
CHAPTER XII. 228
CHAPTER XIII 251
CHAPTER XIV 265

CHAPTER I

The Leeds and Skipton railway runs along a deep valley of the Aire; a slow and sluggish stream, compared to the neighbouring river of Wharfe. Keighley station is on this line of railway, about a quarter of a mile from the town of the same name. The number of inhabitants and the importance of Keighley have been very greatly increased during the last twenty years, owing to the rapidly extended market for worsted manufactures, a branch of industry that mainly employs the factory population of this part of Yorkshire, which has Bradford for its centre and metropolis.

Keighley is in process of transformation from a populous, old-fashioned village, into a still more populous and flourishing town. It is evident to the stranger, that as the gable-ended houses, which obtrude themselves corner-wise on the widening street, fall vacant, they are pulled down to allow of greater space for traffic, and a more modern style of architecture. The quaint and narrow shop-windows of fifty years ago, are giving way to large panes and plate-glass. Nearly every dwelling seems devoted to some branch of commerce. In passing hastily through the town, one hardly perceives where the necessary lawyer and doctor can live, so little appearance is there of any dwellings of the professional middle-class, such as abound in our old cathedral towns. In fact, nothing can be more opposed than the state of society, the modes of thinking, the standards of reference on all points of morality, manners, and even politics and religion, in such a new manufacturing place as Keighley in the north, and any stately, sleepy, picturesque cathedral town in the south. Yet the aspect of Keighley promises well for future stateliness, if not picturesqueness. Grey stone abounds; and the rows of houses built of it have a kind of solid grandeur connected with their uniform and enduring lines. The frame-work of the doors, and the lintels of the windows, even in the smallest dwellings, are made of blocks of stone. There is no painted wood to require continual beautifying, or else present a shabby aspect; and the stone is kept scrupulously clean by the notable Yorkshire housewives. Such glimpses into the interior as a passer-by obtains, reveal a rough abundance of the means of living, and diligent and active habits in the women. But the voices of the people are hard, and their tones discordant, promising little of the musical taste that distinguishes the district, and which has already furnished a Carrodus to the musical world. The names over the shops (of which the one just given is a sample) seem strange even to an inhabitant of the neighbouring county, and have a peculiar smack and flavour of the place.

The town of Keighley never quite melts into country on the road to Haworth, although the houses become more sparse as the traveller journeys upwards to the grey round hills that seem to bound his journey in a westerly direction. First come some villas; just sufficiently retired from the road to show that they can scarcely belong to any one liable to be summoned in a hurry, at the call of suffering or danger, from his comfortable fireside; the lawyer, the doctor, and the clergyman, live at hand, and hardly in the suburbs, with a screen of shrubs for concealment.

In a town one does not look for vivid colouring; what there may be of this is furnished by the wares in the shops, not by foliage or atmospheric effects; but in the country some brilliancy and vividness seems to be instinctively expected, and there is consequently a slight feeling of disappointment at the grey neutral tint of every object, near or far off, on the way from Keighley to Haworth. The distance is about four miles; and, as I have said, what with villas, great worsted factories, rows of workmen's houses, with here and there an old-fashioned farmhouse and out-buildings, it can hardly be called "country" any part of the way. For two miles the road passes over tolerably level ground, distant hills on the left, a "beck" flowing through meadows on the right, and furnishing water power, at certain points, to the factories built on its banks. The air is dim and lightless with the smoke from all these habitations and places of business. The soil in the valley (or "bottom," to use the local term) is rich; but, as the road begins to ascend, the vegetation becomes poorer; it does not flourish, it merely exists; and, instead of trees, there are only bushes and shrubs about the dwellings. Stone dykes are everywhere used in place of hedges; and what crops there are, on the patches of arable land, consist of pale, hungry-looking, grey green oats. Right before the traveller on this road rises Haworth village; he can see it for two miles before he arrives, for it is situated on the side of a pretty steep hill, with a back-ground of dun and purple moors, rising and sweeping away yet higher than the church, which is built at the very summit of the long narrow street. All round the horizon there is this same line of sinuous wave-like hills; the scoops into which they fall only revealing other hills beyond, of similar colour and shape, crowned with wild, bleak moors—grand, from the ideas of solitude and loneliness which they suggest, or oppressive from the feeling which they give of being pent-up by some monotonous and illimitable barrier, according to the mood of mind in which the spectator may be.

For a short distance the road appears to turn away from Haworth, as it winds round the base of the shoulder of a hill; but then it crosses a bridge over the "beck," and the ascent through the village begins. The flag-stones with which it is paved are placed end-ways, in order to give a better hold to the horses' feet; and, even with this help, they seem to be in constant danger of slipping backwards. The old stone houses are high compared to the width of the street, which makes an abrupt turn before reaching the more level ground at the head of the village, so that the steep aspect of the place, in one part, is almost like that of a wall. But this surmounted, the church lies a little off the main road on the left; a hundred yards, or so, and the driver relaxes his care, and the horse breathes more easily, as they pass into the quite little by-street that leads to Haworth Parsonage. The churchyard is on one side of this lane, the school-house and the sexton's dwelling (where the curates formerly lodged) on the other.

The parsonage stands at right angles to the road, facing down upon the church; so that, in fact, parsonage, church, and belfried school-house, form three sides of an irregular oblong, of which the fourth is open to the fields and moors that lie beyond. The area of this oblong is filled up by a crowded churchyard, and a small garden or court in front of the clergyman's house. As the entrance to this from the road is at the side, the path goes round the corner into the little plot of ground. Underneath the windows is a narrow flower-border, carefully tended in days of yore, although only the most hardy plants could be made to grow there. Within the stone wall, which keeps out the surrounding churchyard, are bushes of elder and lilac; the rest of the ground is occupied by a square grass-plot and a gravel walk. The house is of grey stone, two stories high, heavily roofed with flags, in order to resist the winds that might strip off a lighter covering. It appears to have been built about a hundred years ago, and to consist of four rooms on each story; the two windows on the right (as the visitor stands with his back to the church, ready to enter in at the front door) belonging to Mr. Brontë's study, the two on the left to the family sitting-room. Everything about the place tells of the most dainty order, the most exquisite cleanliness. The door-steps are spotless; the small old-fashioned window-panes glitter like looking-glass. Inside and outside of that house cleanliness goes up into its essence, purity.

The little church lies, as I mentioned, above most of the houses in the village; and the graveyard rises above the church, and is terribly full of upright tombstones. The chapel or church claims greater antiquity than any other in that part of the kingdom; but there is no appearance of this in the external aspect of the present edifice, unless it be in the two eastern windows, which remain unmodernized, and in the lower part of the steeple. Inside, the character of the pillars shows that they were constructed before the reign of Henry VII. It is probable that there existed on this ground, a "field-kirk," or oratory, in the earliest times; and, from the Archbishop's registry at York, it is ascertained that there was a chapel at Haworth in 1317. The inhabitants refer inquirers concerning the date to the following inscription on a stone in the church tower:—

"Hic fecit Cænobium Monachorum Auteste fundator. A. D. sexcentissimo."

That is to say, before the preaching of Christianity in Northumbria. Whitaker says that this mistake originated in the illiterate copying out, by some modern stone-cutter, of an inscription in the character of Henry the Eighth's time on an adjoining stone:—

"Orate pro bono statu Eutest Tod."

"Now every antiquary knows that the formula of prayer 'bono statu' always refers to the living. I suspect this singular Christian name has been mistaken by the stone-cutter for Austet, a contraction of Eustatius, but the word Tod, which has been mis-read for the Arabic figures 600, is perfectly fair and legible. On the presumption of this foolish claim to antiquity, the people would needs set up for independence, and contest the right of the Vicar of Bradford to nominate a curate at Haworth."

I have given this extract, in order to explain the imaginary groundwork of a commotion which took place in Haworth about five and thirty years ago, to which I shall have occasion to allude again more particularly.

The interior of the church is commonplace; it is neither old enough nor modern enough to compel notice. The pews are of black oak, with high divisions; and the names of those to whom they belong are painted in white letters on the doors. There are neither brasses, nor altar-tombs, nor monuments, but there is a mural tablet on the right-hand side of the communion-table, bearing the following inscription:—

HERE
LIE THE REMAINS OF
MARIA BRONTË, WIFE
OF THE
REV. P. BRONTË, A.B., MINISTER OF HAWORTH.
HER SOUL
DEPARTED TO THE SAVIOUR, SEPT. 15TH, 1821,
IN THE 39TH YEAR OF HER AGE.

"Be ye also ready: for in such an hour as ye think not the Son of Man cometh." MATTHEW xxiv. 44.

ALSO HERE LIE THE REMAINS OF
MARIA BRONTË, DAUGHTER OF THE AFORESAID;
SHE DIED ON THE
6TH OF MAY, 1825, IN THE 12TH YEAR OF HER AGE;
AND OF
ELIZABETH BRONTË, HER SISTER,
WHO DIED JUNE 15TH, 1825, IN THE 11TH YEAR
OF HER AGE.

"Verily I say unto you, Except ye be converted, and become as little children, ye shall not enter into the kingdom of heaven."—MATTHEW xviii. 3.

HERE ALSO LIE THE REMAINS OF
PATRICK BRANWELL BRONTË,
WHO DIED SEPT. 24TH, 1848, AGED 30 YEARS;
AND OF

EMILY JANE BRONTË,
WHO DIED DEC. 19TH, 1848, AGED 29 YEARS,
SON AND DAUGHTER OF THE
REV. P. BRONTË, INCUMBENT.

THIS STONE IS ALSO DEDICATED TO THE
MEMORY OF ANNE BRONTË, {1}
YOUNGEST DAUGHTER OF THE REV. P. BRONTË,
A.B.
SHE DIED, AGED 27 YEARS, MAY 28TH, 1849,
AND WAS BURIED AT THE OLD CHURCH,
SCARBORO.'

At the upper part of this tablet ample space is allowed between the lines of the inscription; when the first memorials were written down, the survivors, in their fond affection, thought little of the margin and verge they were leaving for those who were still living. But as one dead member of the household follows another fast to the grave, the lines are pressed together, and the letters become small and cramped. After the record of Anne's death, there is room for no other.

But one more of that generation—the last of that nursery of six little motherless children—was yet to follow, before the survivor, the childless and widowed father, found his rest. On another tablet, below the first, the following record has been added to that mournful list:—

ADJOINING LIE THE REMAINS OF
CHARLOTTE, WIFE
OF THE
REV. ARTHUR BELL NICHOLLS, A.B.,
AND DAUGHTER OF THE REV. P. BRONTË, A.B.,
INCUMBENT
SHE DIED MARCH 31ST, 1855, IN THE 39TH
YEAR OF HER AGE. {2}

This tablet, which corrects the error in the former tablet as to the age of Anne Brontë, bears the following inscription in Roman letters; the initials, however, being in old English.

CHAPTER II

For a right understanding of the life of my dear friend, Charlotte Brontë, it appears to me more necessary in her case than in most others, that the reader should be made acquainted with the peculiar forms of population and society amidst which her earliest years were passed, and from which both her own and her sisters' first impressions of human life must have been received. I shall endeavour, therefore, before proceeding further with my work, to present some idea of the character of the people of Haworth, and the surrounding districts.

Even an inhabitant of the neighbouring county of Lancaster is struck by the peculiar force of character which the Yorkshiremen display. This makes them interesting as a race; while, at the same time, as individuals, the remarkable degree of self-sufficiency they possess gives them an air of independence rather apt to repel a stranger. I use this expression "self-sufficiency" in the largest sense. Conscious of the strong sagacity and the dogged power of will which seem almost the birthright of the natives of the West Riding, each man relies upon himself, and seeks no help at the hands of his neighbour. From rarely requiring the assistance of others, he comes to doubt the power of bestowing it: from the general success of his efforts, he grows to depend upon them, and to over-esteem his own energy and power. He belongs to that keen, yet short-sighted class, who consider suspicion of all whose honesty is not proved as a sign of wisdom. The practical qualities of a man are held in great respect; but the want of faith in strangers and untried modes of action, extends itself even to the manner in which the virtues are regarded; and if they produce no immediate and tangible result, they are rather put aside as unfit for this busy, striving world; especially if they are more of a passive than an active character. The affections are strong and their foundations lie deep: but they are not—such affections seldom are—wide-spreading; nor do they show themselves on the surface. Indeed, there is little display of any of the amenities of life among this wild, rough population. Their accost is curt; their accent and tone of speech blunt and harsh. Something of this may, probably, be attributed to the freedom of mountain air and of isolated hill-side life; something be derived from their rough Norse ancestry. They have a quick perception of character, and a keen sense of humour; the dwellers among them must be prepared for certain uncomplimentary, though most likely true, observations, pithily expressed. Their feelings are not easily roused, but their duration is lasting. Hence there is much close friendship and faithful service; and for a correct exemplification of the form in which the latter frequently appears, I need only refer the reader of "Wuthering Heights" to the character of "Joseph."

From the same cause come also enduring grudges, in some cases amounting to hatred, which occasionally has been bequeathed from generation to generation. I remember Miss Brontë once telling me that it was a saying round about Haworth, "Keep a stone in thy pocket seven year; turn it, and keep it seven year longer, that it may be ever ready to thine hand when thine enemy draws near."

The West Riding men are sleuth-hounds in pursuit of money. Miss Brontë related to my husband a curious instance illustrative of this eager desire for riches. A man that she knew, who was a small manufacturer, had engaged in many local speculations which had always turned out well, and thereby rendered him a person of some wealth. He was rather past middle age, when he bethought him of insuring his life; and he had only just taken out his policy, when he fell ill of an acute disease which was certain to end fatally in a very few days. The doctor, half-hesitatingly, revealed to him his hopeless state. "By jingo!" cried he, rousing up at once into the old energy, "I shall *do* the insurance company!

I always was a lucky fellow!"

These men are keen and shrewd; faithful and persevering in following out a good purpose, fell in tracking an evil one. They are not emotional; they are not easily made into either friends or enemies; but once lovers or haters, it is difficult to change their feeling. They are a powerful race both in mind and body, both for good and for evil.

The woollen manufacture was introduced into this district in the days of Edward III. It is traditionally said that a colony of Flemings came over and settled in the West Riding to teach the inhabitants what to do with their wool. The mixture of agricultural with manufacturing labour that ensued and prevailed in the West Riding up to a very recent period, sounds pleasant enough at this distance of time, when the classical impression is left, and the details forgotten, or only brought to light by those who explore the few remote parts of England where the custom still lingers. The idea of the mistress and her maidens spinning at the great wheels while the master was abroad ploughing his fields, or seeing after his flocks on the purple moors, is very poetical to look back upon; but when such life actually touches on our own days, and we can hear particulars from the lips of those now living, there come out details of coarseness—of the uncouthness of the rustic mingled with the sharpness of the tradesman—of irregularity and fierce lawlessness—that rather mar the vision of pastoral innocence and simplicity. Still, as it is the exceptional and exaggerated characteristics of any period that leave the most vivid memory behind them, it would be wrong, and in my opinion faithless, to conclude that such and such forms of society and modes of living were not best for the period when they prevailed, although the abuses they may have led into, and the gradual progress of the world, have made it well that such ways and manners should pass away for ever, and as preposterous to attempt to return to them, as it would be for a man to return to the clothes of his childhood.

The patent granted to Alderman Cockayne, and the further

restrictions imposed by James I. on the export of undyed woollen cloths (met by a prohibition on the part of the States of Holland of the import of English-dyed cloths), injured the trade of the West Riding manufacturers considerably. Their independence of character, their dislike of authority, and their strong powers of thought, predisposed them to rebellion against the religious dictation of such men as Laud, and the arbitrary rule of the Stuarts; and the injury done by James and Charles to the trade by which they gained their bread, made the great majority of them Commonwealth men. I shall have occasion afterwards to give one or two instances of the warm feelings and extensive knowledge on subjects of both home and foreign politics existing at the present day in the villages lying west and east of the mountainous ridge that separates Yorkshire and Lancashire; the inhabitants of which are of the same race and possess the same quality of character.

The descendants of many who served under Cromwell at Dunbar, live on the same lands as their ancestors occupied then; and perhaps there is no part of England where the traditional and fond recollections of the Commonwealth have lingered so long as in that inhabited by the woollen manufacturing population of the West Riding, who had the restrictions taken off their trade by the Protector's admirable commercial policy. I have it on good authority that, not thirty years ago, the phrase, "in Oliver's days," was in common use to denote a time of unusual prosperity. The class of Christian names prevalent in a district is one indication of the direction in which its tide of hero-worship sets. Grave enthusiasts in politics or religion perceive not the ludicrous side of those which they give to their children; and some are to be found, still in their infancy, not a dozen miles from Haworth, that will have to go through life as Lamartine, Kossuth, and Dembinsky. And so there is a testimony to what I have said, of the traditional feeling of the district, in the fact that the Old Testament names in general use among the Puritans are yet the prevalent appellations in most Yorkshire families of middle or humble rank, whatever their religious persuasion may be. There are numerous records, too, that show the kindly way in which the ejected ministers were received by the gentry, as well as by the poorer part of the inhabitants, during the persecuting days of Charles II. These little facts all testify to the old hereditary spirit of independence, ready ever to resist authority which was conceived to be unjustly exercised, that distinguishes the people of the West Riding to the present day.

The parish of Halifax touches that of Bradford, in which the chapelry of Haworth is included; and the nature of the ground in the two parishes is much the of the same wild and hilly description. The abundance of coal, and the number of mountain streams in the district, make it highly favourable to manufactures; and accordingly, as I stated, the inhabitants have for centuries been engaged in making cloth, as well as in agricultural pursuits. But the intercourse of trade failed, for a long time, to bring amenity and civilization into these outlying hamlets, or widely scattered dwellings. Mr. Hunter, in his "Life of Oliver Heywood," quotes a sentence out of a memorial of one James Rither, living in the reign of Elizabeth, which is partially true to this day:—

"They have no superior to court, no civilities to practise: a sour and sturdy humour is the consequence, so that a stranger is shocked by a tone of defiance in every voice, and an air of fierceness in every countenance."

Even now, a stranger can hardly ask a question without receiving some crusty reply, if, indeed, he receive any at all. Sometimes the sour rudeness amounts to positive insult. Yet, if the "foreigner" takes all this churlishness good-humouredly, or as a matter of course, and makes good any claim upon their latent kindliness and hospitality, they are faithful and generous, and thoroughly to be relied upon. As a slight illustration of the roughness that pervades all classes in these out-of-the-way villages, I may relate a little adventure which happened to my husband and myself, three years ago, at Addingham—

> From Penigent to Pendle Hill,
> From Linton to Long-*Addingham*
> And all that Craven coasts did tell, &c.—

one of the places that sent forth its fighting men to the famous old battle of Flodden Field, and a village not many miles from Haworth.

We were driving along the street, when one of those ne'er-do-weel lads who seem to have a kind of magnetic power for misfortunes, having jumped into the stream that runs through the place, just where all the broken glass and bottles are thrown, staggered naked and nearly covered with blood into a cottage before us. Besides receiving another bad cut in the arm, he had completely laid open the artery, and was in a fair way of bleeding to death—which, one of his relations comforted him by saying, would be likely to "save a deal o' trouble."

When my husband had checked the effusion of blood with a strap that one of the bystanders unbuckled from his leg, he asked if a surgeon had been sent for.

"Yoi," was the answer; "but we dunna think he'll come."

"Why not?"

"He's owd, yo seen, and asthmatic, and it's up-hill."

My husband taking a boy for his guide, drove as fast as he could to the surgeon's house, which was about three-quarters of a mile off, and met the aunt of the wounded lad leaving it.

"Is he coming?" inquired my husband.

"Well, he didna' say he wouldna' come."

"But, tell him the lad may bleed to death."

"I did."

"And what did he say?"

"Why, only, 'D-n him; what do I care?'"

It ended, however, in his sending one of his sons, who, though not brought up to "the surgering trade," was able to do what was necessary in the way of bandages and plasters. The excuse made for the surgeon was, that "he was near eighty, and getting a bit doited, and had had a matter o' twenty childer."

Among the most unmoved of the lookers-on was the brother of the boy so badly hurt; and while he was lying in a pool of blood on the flag floor, and crying out how much his arm was "warching," his stoical relation stood coolly smoking his bit of black pipe, and uttered not a single word of either sympathy or sorrow.

Forest customs, existing in the fringes of dark wood, which clothed the declivity of the hills on either side, tended to brutalize the population until the middle of the seventeenth century. Execution by beheading was performed in a summary way upon either men or women who were guilty of but very slight crimes; and a dogged, yet in some cases fine, indifference to human life was thus generated. The roads were so notoriously bad, even up to the last thirty years, that there was little communication between one village and another; if the produce of industry could be conveyed at stated times to the cloth market of the district, it was all that could be done; and, in lonely houses on the distant hill-side, or by the small magnates of secluded hamlets, crimes might be committed almost unknown, certainly without any great uprising of popular indignation calculated to bring down the strong arm of the law. It must be remembered that in those days there was no rural constabulary; and the few magistrates left to themselves, and generally related to one another, were most of them inclined to tolerate eccentricity, and to wink at faults too much like their own.

Men hardly past middle life talk of the days of their youth, spent in this part of the country, when, during the winter months, they rode up to the saddle-girths in mud; when absolute business was the only reason for stirring beyond the precincts of home, and when that business was conducted under a pressure of difficulties which they themselves, borne along to Bradford market in a swift first-class carriage, can hardly believe to have been possible. For instance, one woollen manufacturer says that, not five and twenty years ago, he had to rise betimes to set off on a winter's-morning in order to be at Bradford with the great waggon-load of goods manufactured by his father; this load was packed over-night, but in the morning there was a great gathering around it, and flashing of lanterns, and examination of horses' feet, before the ponderous waggon got under way; and then some one had to go groping here and there, on hands and knees, and always sounding with a staff down the long, steep, slippery brow, to find where the horses might tread safely, until they reached the comparative easy-going of the deep-rutted main road. People went on horseback over the upland moors, following the tracks of the pack-horses that carried the parcels, baggage, or goods from one town to another, between which there did not happen to be a highway.

But in winter, all such communication was impossible, by reason of the snow which lay long and late on the bleak high ground. I have known people who, travelling by the mail-coach over Blackstone Edge, had been snowed up for a week or ten days at the little inn near the summit, and obliged to spend both Christmas and New Year's Day there, till the store of provisions laid in for the use of the landlord and his family falling short before the inroads of the unexpected visitors, they had recourse to the turkeys, geese, and Yorkshire pies with which the coach was laden; and even these were beginning to fail, when a fortunate thaw released them from their prison.

Isolated as the hill villages may be, they are in the world, compared with the loneliness of the grey ancestral houses to be seen here and there in the dense hollows of the moors. These dwellings are not large, yet they are solid and roomy enough for the accommodation of those who live in them, and to whom the surrounding estates belong. The land has often been held by one family since the days of the Tudors; the owners are, in fact, the remains of the old yeomanry—small squires—who are rapidly becoming extinct as a class, from one of two causes. Either the possessor falls into idle, drinking habits, and so is obliged eventually to sell his property: or he finds, if more shrewd and adventurous, that the "beck" running down the mountain-side, or the minerals beneath his feet, can be turned into a new source of wealth; and leaving the old plodding life of a landowner with small capital, he turns manufacturer, or digs for coal, or quarries for stone.

Still there are those remaining of this class—dwellers in the lonely houses far away in the upland districts—even at the present day, who sufficiently indicate what strange eccentricity—what wild strength of will—nay, even what unnatural power of crime was fostered by a mode of living in which a man seldom met his fellows, and where public opinion was only a distant and inarticulate echo of some clearer voice sounding behind the sweeping horizon.

A solitary life cherishes mere fancies until they become manias. And the powerful Yorkshire character, which was scarcely tamed into subjection by all the contact it met with in "busy town or crowded mart," has before now broken out into strange wilfulness in the remoter districts. A singular account was recently given me of a landowner (living, it is true, on the Lancashire side of the hills, but of the same blood and nature as the dwellers on the other,) who was supposed to be in the receipt of seven or eight hundred a year, and whose house bore marks of handsome antiquity, as if his forefathers had been for a long time people of consideration. My informant was struck with the appearance of the place, and proposed to the countryman who was accompanying him, to go up to it and take a nearer inspection. The reply was, "Yo'd better not; he'd threap yo' down th' loan. He's let fly at some folk's legs, and let shot lodge in 'em afore now, for going too near to his house." And finding, on closer inquiry, that such was really the inhospitable custom of this moorland squire, the gentleman gave up his purpose. I believe that the savage yeoman is still living.

Another squire, of more distinguished family and larger property—one is thence led to imagine of better education, but that does not always follow—died at his house, not many miles from Haworth, only a few years ago. His great amusement and occupation had been cock-fighting. When he was confined to his chamber with what he knew would be his last illness, he had his cocks brought up there, and watched the bloody battle from his bed. As his mortal disease increased, and it became impossible for him to turn so as to follow the combat, he had looking-glasses arranged in such a manner, around and above him, as he lay, that he could still see the cocks fighting. And in this manner he died.

These are merely instances of eccentricity compared to the tales of positive violence and crime that have occurred in these isolated dwellings, which still linger in the memories of the old people of the district, and some of which were doubtless familiar to the authors of "Wuthering Heights" and "The Tenant of Wildfell Hall."

The amusements of the lower classes could hardly be expected to be more humane than those of the wealthy and better educated. The gentleman, who has kindly furnished me with some of the particulars I have given, remembers the bull-baitings at Rochdale, not thirty years ago. The bull was fastened by a chain or rope to a post in the river. To increase the amount of water, as well as to give their workpeople the opportunity of savage delight, the masters were accustomed to stop their mills on the day when the sport took place. The bull would sometimes wheel suddenly round, so that the rope by which he was fastened swept those who had been careless enough to come within its range down into the water, and the good people of Rochdale had the excitement of seeing one or two of their neighbours drowned, as well as of witnessing the bull baited, and the dogs torn and tossed.

The people of Haworth were not less strong and full of character than their neighbours on either side of the hills. The village lies embedded in the moors, between the two counties, on the old road between Keighley and Colne. About the middle of the last century, it became famous in the religious world as the scene of the ministrations of the Rev. William Grimshaw, curate of Haworth for twenty years. Before this time, it is probable that the curates were of the same order as one Mr. Nicholls, a Yorkshire clergyman, in the days immediately succeeding the Reformation, who was "much addicted to drinking and company-keeping," and used to say to his companions, "You must not heed me but when I am got three feet above the earth," that was, into the pulpit.

Mr. Grimshaw's life was written by Newton, Cowper's friend; and from it may be gathered some curious particulars of the manner in which a rough population were swayed and governed by a man of deep convictions, and strong earnestness of purpose. It seems that he had not been in any way remarkable for religious zeal, though he had led a moral life, and been conscientious in fulfilling his parochial duties, until a certain Sunday in September, 1744, when the servant, rising at five, found her master already engaged in prayer; she stated that, after remaining in his chamber for some time, he went to engage in religious exercises in the house of a parishioner, then home again to pray; thence, still fasting, to the church, where, as he was reading the second lesson, he fell down, and, on his partial recovery, had to be led from the church. As he went out, he spoke to the congregation, and told them not to disperse, as he had something to say to them, and would return presently. He was taken to the clerk's house, and again became insensible. His servant rubbed him, to restore the circulation; and when he was brought to himself "he seemed in a great rapture," and the first words he uttered were, "I have had a glorious vision from the third heaven." He did not say what he had seen, but returned into the church, and began the service again, at two in the afternoon, and went on until seven.

From this time he devoted himself, with the fervour of a Wesley, and something of the fanaticism of a Whitfield, to calling out a religious life among his parishioners. They had been in the habit of playing at foot-ball on Sunday, using stones for this purpose; and giving and receiving challenges from other parishes. There were horse-races held on the moors just above the village, which were periodical sources of drunkenness and profligacy. Scarcely a wedding took place without the rough amusement of foot-races, where the half-naked runners were a scandal to all decent strangers. The old custom of "arvills," or funeral feasts, led to frequent pitched battles between the drunken mourners. Such customs were the outward signs of the kind of people with whom Mr. Grimshaw had to deal. But, by various means, some of the most practical kind, he wrought a great change in his parish. In his preaching he was occasionally assisted by Wesley and Whitfield, and at such times the little church proved much too small to hold the throng that poured in from distant villages, or lonely moorland hamlets; and frequently they were obliged to meet in the open air; indeed, there was not room enough in the church even for the communicants. Mr. Whitfield was once preaching in Haworth, and made use of some such expression, as that he hoped there was no need to say much to this congregation, as they had sat under so pious and godly a minister for so many years; "whereupon Mr. Grimshaw stood up in his place, and said with a loud voice, 'Oh, sir! for God's sake do not speak so. I pray you do not flatter them. I fear the greater part of them are going to hell with their eyes open.'" But if they were so bound, it was not for want of exertion on Mr. Grimshaw's part to prevent them. He used to preach twenty or thirty times a week in private houses. If he perceived any one inattentive to his prayers, he would stop and rebuke the offender, and not go on till he saw every one on their knees. He was very earnest in enforcing the strict observance of Sunday; and would not even allow his parishioners to walk in the fields between services. He sometimes gave out a very long Psalm (tradition says the 119th), and while it was being sung, he left the reading-desk, and taking a horsewhip went into the public-houses, and flogged the loiterers into church. They were swift who could escape the lash of the parson by sneaking out the back way. He had strong health and an active body, and rode far and wide over the hills, "awakening" those who had previously had no sense of religion.

To save time, and be no charge to the families at whose houses he held his prayer-meetings, he carried his provisions with him; all the food he took in the day on such occasions consisting simply of a piece of bread and butter, or dry bread and a raw onion.

The horse-races were justly objectionable to Mr. Grimshaw; they attracted numbers of profligate people to Haworth, and brought a match to the combustible materials of the place, only too ready to blaze out into wickedness. The story is, that he tried all means of persuasion, and even intimidation, to have the races discontinued, but in vain. At length, in despair, he prayed with such fervour of earnestness that the rain came down in torrents, and deluged the ground, so that there was no footing for man or beast, even if the multitude had been willing to stand such a flood let down from above. And so Haworth races were stopped, and have never been resumed to this day. Even now the memory of this good man is held in reverence, and his faithful ministrations and real virtues are one of the boasts of the parish.

But after his time, I fear there was a falling back into the wild rough heathen ways, from which he had pulled them up, as it were, by the passionate force of his individual character. He had built a chapel for the Wesleyan Methodists, and not very long after the Baptists established themselves in a place of worship. Indeed, as Dr. Whitaker says, the people of this district are "strong religionists;" only, fifty years ago, their religion did not work down into their lives. Half that length of time back, the code of morals seemed to be formed upon that of their Norse ancestors. Revenge was handed down from father to son as an hereditary duty; and a great capability for drinking without the head being affected was considered as one of the manly virtues. The games of foot-ball on Sundays, with the challenges to the neighbouring parishes, were resumed, bringing in an influx of riotous strangers to fill the public-houses, and make the more sober-minded inhabitants long for good Mr. Grimshaw's stout arm, and ready horsewhip. The old custom of "arvills" was as prevalent as ever. The sexton, standing at the foot of the open grave, announced that the "arvill" would be held at the Black Bull, or whatever public-house might be fixed upon by the friends of the dead; and thither the mourners and their acquaintances repaired. The origin of the custom had been the necessity of furnishing some refreshment for those who came from a distance, to pay the last mark of respect to a friend. In the life of Oliver Heywood there are two quotations, which show what sort of food was provided for "arvills" in quiet Nonconformist connections in the seventeenth century; the first (from Thoresby) tells of "cold possets, stewed prunes, cake, and cheese," as being the arvill after Oliver Heywood's funeral. The second gives, as rather shabby, according to the notion of the times (1673), "nothing but a bit of cake, draught of wine, piece of rosemary, and pair of gloves."

But the arvills at Haworth were often far more jovial doings. Among the poor, the mourners were only expected to provide a kind of spiced roll for each person; and the expense of the liquors—rum, or ale, or a mixture of both called "dog's nose"— was generally defrayed by each guest placing some money on a plate, set in the middle of the table. Richer people would order a dinner for their friends. At the funeral of Mr. Charnock (the next successor but one to Mr. Grimshaw in the incumbency), above eighty people were bid to the arvill, and the price of the feast was 4s. 6d. per head, all of which was defrayed by the friends of the deceased. As few "shirked their liquor," there were very frequently "up-and-down fights" before the close of the day; sometimes with the horrid additions of "pawsing" and "gouging," and biting.

Although I have dwelt on the exceptional traits in the characteristics of these stalwart West-Ridingers, such as they were in the first quarter of this century, if not a few years later, I have little doubt that in the everyday life of the people so independent, wilful, and full of grim humour, there would be much found even at present that would shock those accustomed only to the local manners of the south; and, in return, I suspect the shrewd, sagacious, energetic Yorkshireman would hold such "foreigners" in no small contempt.

I have said, it is most probable that where Haworth Church now stands, there was once an ancient "field-kirk," or oratory. It occupied the third or lowest class of ecclesiastical structures, according to the Saxon law, and had no right of sepulture, or administration of sacraments. It was so called because it was built without enclosure, and open to the adjoining fields or moors. The founder, according to the laws of Edgar, was bound, without subtracting from his tithes, to maintain the ministering priest out of the remaining nine parts of his income. After the Reformation, the right of choosing their clergyman, at any of those chapels of ease which had formerly been field-kirks, was vested in the freeholders and trustees, subject to the approval of the vicar of the parish. But owing to some negligence, this right has been lost to the freeholders and trustees at Haworth, ever since the days of Archbishop Sharp; and the power of choosing a minister has lapsed into the hands of the Vicar of Bradford. So runs the account, according to one authority.

Mr. Brontë says,—"This living has for its patrons the Vicar of Bradford and certain trustees. My predecessor took the living with the consent of the Vicar of Bradford, but in opposition to the trustees; in consequence of which he was so opposed that, after only three weeks' possession, he was compelled to resign." A Yorkshire gentleman, who has kindly sent me some additional information on this subject since the second edition of my work was published, write, thus:—

> "The sole right of presentation to the incumbency of Haworth is vested in the Vicar of Bradford. He only can present. The funds, however, from which the clergyman's stipend mainly proceeds, are vested in the hands of trustees, who have the power to withhold them, if a nominee is sent of whom they disapprove. On the decease of Mr. Charnock, the Vicar first tendered the preferment to

Mr. Brontë, and he went over to his expected cure. He was told that towards himself they had no personal objection; but as a nominee of the Vicar he would not be received. He therefore retired, with the declaration that if he could not come with the approval of the parish, his ministry could not be useful. Upon this the attempt was made to introduce Mr. Redhead.

"When Mr. Redhead was repelled, a fresh difficulty arose. Some one must first move towards a settlement, but a spirit being evoked which could not be allayed, action became perplexing. The matter had to be referred to some independent arbitrator, and my father was the gentleman to whom each party turned its eye. A meeting was convened, and the business settled by the Vicar's conceding the choice to the trustees, and the acceptance of the Vicar's presentation. That choice forthwith fell on Mr. Brontë, whose promptness and prudence had won their hearts."

In conversing on the character of the inhabitants of the West Riding with Dr. Scoresby, who had been for some time Vicar of Bradford, he alluded to certain riotous transactions which had taken place at Haworth on the presentation of the living to Mr. Redhead, and said that there had been so much in the particulars indicative of the character of the people, that he advised me to inquire into them. I have accordingly done so, and, from the lips of some of the survivors among the actors and spectators, I have learnt the means taken to eject the nominee of the Vicar.

The previous incumbent had been the Mr. Charnock whom I have mentioned as next but one in succession to Mr. Grimshaw. He had a long illness which rendered him unable to discharge his duties without assistance, and Mr. Redhead gave him occasional help, to the great satisfaction of the parishioners, and was highly respected by them during Mr. Charnock's lifetime. But the case was entirely altered when, at Mr. Charnock's death in 1819, they conceived that the trustees had been unjustly deprived of their rights by the Vicar of Bradford, who appointed Mr. Redhead as perpetual curate.

The first Sunday he officiated, Haworth Church was filled even to the aisles; most of the people wearing the wooden clogs of the district. But while Mr. Redhead was reading the second lesson, the whole congregation, as by one impulse, began to leave the church, making all the noise they could with clattering and clumping of clogs, till, at length, Mr. Redhead and the clerk were the only two left to continue the service. This was bad enough, but the next Sunday the proceedings were far worse. Then, as before, the church was well filled, but the aisles were left clear; not a creature, not an obstacle was in the way. The reason for this was made evident about the same time in the reading of the service as the disturbances had begun the previous week. A man rode into the church upon an ass, with his face turned towards the tail, and as many old hats piled on his head as he could possibly carry. He began urging his beast round the aisles, and the screams, and cries, and laughter of the congregation entirely drowned all sound of Mr. Redhead's voice, and, I believe, he was obliged to desist.

Hitherto they had not proceeded to anything like personal violence; but on the third Sunday they must have been greatly irritated at seeing Mr. Redhead, determined to brave their will, ride up the village street, accompanied by several gentlemen from Bradford. They put up their horses at the Black Bull—the little inn close upon the churchyard, for the convenience of arvills as well as for other purposes—and went into church. On this the people followed, with a chimney-sweeper, whom they had employed to clean the chimneys of some out-buildings belonging to the church that very morning, and afterward plied with drink till he was in a state of solemn intoxication. They placed him right before the reading-desk, where his blackened face nodded a drunken, stupid assent to all that Mr. Redhead said. At last, either prompted by some mischief-maker, or from some tipsy impulse, he clambered up the pulpit stairs, and attempted to embrace Mr. Redhead. Then the profane fun grew fast and furious. Some of the more riotous, pushed the soot-covered chimney-sweeper against Mr. Redhead, as he tried to escape. They threw both him and his tormentor down on the ground in the churchyard where the soot-bag had been emptied, and, though, at last, Mr. Redhead escaped into the Black Bull, the doors of which were immediately barred, the people raged without, threatening to stone him and his friends. One of my informants is an old man, who was the landlord of the inn at the time, and he stands to it that such was the temper of the irritated mob, that Mr. Redhead was in real danger of his life. This man, however, planned an escape for his unpopular inmates. The Black Bull is near the top of the long, steep Haworth street, and at the bottom, close by the bridge, on the road to Keighley, is a turnpike. Giving directions to his hunted guests to steal out at the back door (through which, probably, many a ne'er-do-weel has escaped from good Mr. Grimshaw's horsewhip), the landlord and some of the stable-boys rode the horses belonging to the party from Bradford backwards and forwards before his front door, among the fiercely-expectant crowd. Through some opening between the houses, those on the horses saw Mr. Redhead and his friends creeping along behind the street; and then, striking spurs, they dashed quickly down to the turnpike; the obnoxious clergyman and his friends mounted in haste, and had sped some distance before the people found out that their prey had escaped, and came running to the closed turnpike gate.

This was Mr. Redhead's last appearance at Haworth for many years. Long afterwards, he came to preach, and in his sermon to a large and attentive congregation he good-humouredly reminded them of the circumstances which I have described. They gave him a hearty welcome, for they owed him no grudge; although before they had been ready enough to stone him, in order to maintain what they considered to be their rights.

The foregoing account, which I heard from two of the survivors, in the presence of a friend who can vouch for the accuracy of my repetition, has to a certain degree been confirmed by a letter from the Yorkshire gentleman, whose words I have already quoted.

"I am not surprised at your difficulty in authenticating matter-of-fact. I find this in recalling what I have heard, and the authority on which I have heard anything. As to the donkey tale, I believe you are right. Mr. Redhead and Dr. Ramsbotham, his son-in-law, are no strangers to me. Each of them has a niche in my affections.

"I have asked, this day, two persons who lived in Haworth at the time to which you allude, the son and daughter of an acting trustee, and each of them between sixty and seventy years of age, and they assure me that the donkey was introduced. One of them says it was mounted by a half-witted man, seated with his face towards the tail of the beast, and having several hats piled on his head. Neither of my informants was, however, present at these edifying services. I believe that no movement was made in the church on either Sunday, until the whole of the authorised reading-service was gone through, and I am sure that nothing was more remote from the more respectable party than any personal antagonism toward Mr. Redhead. He was one of the most amiable and worthy of men, a man to myself endeared by many ties and obligations. I never heard before your book that the sweep ascended the pulpit steps. He was present, however, in the clerical habiliments of his order . . . I may also add that among the many who were present at those sad Sunday orgies the majority were non-residents, and came from those moorland fastnesses on the outskirts of the parish locally designated as 'ovver th' steyres,' one stage more remote than Haworth from modern civilization.

"To an instance or two more of the rusticity of the inhabitants of the chapelry of Haworth, I may introduce you.

"A Haworth carrier called at the office of a friend of mine to deliver a parcel on a cold winter's day, and stood with the door open. 'Robin! shut the door!' said the recipient. 'Have you no doors in your country?' 'Yoi,' responded Robin, 'we hev, but we nivver steik 'em.' I have frequently remarked the number of doors open even in winter.

"When well directed, the indomitable and independent energies of the natives of this part of the country are invaluable; dangerous when perverted. I shall never forget the fierce actions and utterances of one suffering from delirium tremens. Whether in its wrath, disdain, or its dismay, the countenance was infernal. I called once upon a time on a most respectable yeoman, and I was, in language earnest and homely, pressed to accept the hospitality of the house. I consented. The word to me was, 'Nah, Maister, yah mun stop an hev sum te-ah, yah mun, eah, yah mun.' A bountiful table was soon spread; at all events, time soon went while I scaled the hills to see 't' maire at wor thretty year owd, an't' feil at wor fewer.' On sitting down to the table, a venerable woman officiated, and after filling the cups, she thus addressed me: 'Nah, Maister, yah mun loawze th'taible' (loose the table). The master said, 'Shah meeans yah mun sey t' greyce.' I took the hint, and uttered the blessing.

"I spoke with an aged and tried woman at one time, who, after recording her mercies, stated, among others, her powers of speech, by asserting 'Thank the Lord, ah nivver wor a meilly-meouthed wumman.' I feel particularly at fault in attempting the orthography of the dialect, but must excuse myself by telling you that I once saw a letter in which the word I have just now used (excuse) was written 'ecksqueaize!'

"There are some things, however, which rather tend to soften the idea of the rudeness of Haworth. No rural district has been more markedly the abode of musical taste and acquirement, and this at a period when it was difficult to find them to the same extent apart from towns in advance of their times. I have gone to Haworth and found an orchestra to meet me, filled with local performers, vocal and instrumental, to whom the best works of Handel, Haydn, Mozart, Marcello, &c. &c., were familiar as household words. By knowledge, taste, and voice, they were markedly separate from ordinary village choirs, and have been put in extensive requisition for the solo and chorus of many an imposing festival. One man still survives, who, for fifty years, has had one of the finest tenor voices I ever heard, and with it a refined and cultivated taste. To him and to others many inducements have been offered to migrate; but the loom, the association, the mountain air have had charms enow to secure their continuance at home. I love the recollection of their performance; that recollection extends over more than sixty years. The attachments, the antipathies and the hospitalities of the district are ardent, hearty, and homely. Cordiality in each is the prominent characteristic. As a people, these mountaineers have ever been accessible to gentleness and truth, so far as I have known them; but excite suspicion or resentment, and they give emphatic and not impotent resistance. Compulsion they defy.

"I accompanied Mr. Heap on his first visit to Haworth after his accession to the vicarage of Bradford. It was on Easter day, either 1816 or 1817. His predecessor, the venerable John Crosse, known as the 'blind vicar,' had been inattentive to the vicarial claims. A searching investigation had to be made and enforced, and as it proceeded stout and sturdy utterances were not lacking on the part of the parishioners. To a spectator, though rude, they were amusing, and significant, foretelling what might be expected, and what was afterwards realised, on the advent of a new incumbent, if they deemed him an intruder.

"From their peculiar parochial position and circumstances, the inhabitants of the chapelry have been prompt, earnest, and persevering in their opposition to church-rates. Although ten miles from the mother-church, they were called upon to defray a large proportion of this obnoxious tax,—I believe one fifth.

"Besides this, they had to maintain their own edifice, &c., &c. They resisted, therefore, with energy, that which they deemed to be oppression and injustice. By scores would they wend their way from the hills to attend a vestry meeting at Bradford, and in such service failed not to show less of the *suaviter in modo* than the *fortiter in re*. Happily such occasion for their action has not occurred for many years.

"The use of patronymics has been common in this locality. Inquire for a man by his Christian name and surname, and you may have some difficulty in finding him: ask, however, for 'George o' Ned's,' or 'Dick o' Bob's,' or 'Tom o' Jack's,' as the case may be, and your difficulty is at an end. In many instances the person is designated by his residence. In my early years I had occasion to inquire for Jonathan Whitaker, who owned a considerable farm in the township. I was sent hither and thither, until it occurred to me to ask for 'Jonathan o' th' Gate.' My difficulties were then at an end. Such circumstances arise out of the settled character and isolation of the natives.

"Those who have witnessed a Haworth wedding when the parties were above the rank of labourers, will not easily forget the scene. A levy was made on the horses of the neighbourhood, and a merry cavalcade of mounted men and women, single or double, traversed the way to Bradford church. The inn and church appeared to be in natural connection, and as the labours of the Temperance Society had then to begin, the interests of sobriety were not always consulted. On remounting their steeds they commenced with a race, and not unfrequently an inebriate or unskilful horseman or woman was put *hors de combat*. A race also was frequent at the end. of these wedding expeditions, from the bridge to the toll-bar at Haworth. The race-course you will know to be anything but level."

Into the midst of this lawless, yet not unkindly population, Mr. Brontë brought his wife and six little children, in February, 1820. There are those yet alive who remember seven heavily-laden carts lumbering slowly up the long stone street, bearing the "new parson's" household goods to his future abode.

One wonders how the bleak aspect of her new home—the low, oblong, stone parsonage, high up, yet with a still higher background of sweeping moors—struck on the gentle, delicate wife, whose health even then was failing.

CHAPTER III

The Rev. Patrick Brontë is a native of the County Down in Ireland. His father Hugh Brontë, was left an orphan at an early age. He came from the south to the north of the island, and settled in the parish of Ahaderg, near Loughbrickland. There was some family tradition that, humble as Hugh Brontë's circumstances were, he was the descendant of an ancient family. But about this neither he nor his descendants have cared to inquire. He made an early marriage, and reared and educated ten children on the proceeds of the few acres of land which he farmed. This large family were remarkable for great physical strength, and much personal beauty. Even in his old age, Mr. Brontë is a striking-looking man, above the common height, with a nobly-shaped head, and erect carriage. In his youth he must have been unusually handsome.

He was born on Patrickmas day (March 17), 1777, and early gave tokens of extraordinary quickness and intelligence. He had also his full share of ambition; and of his strong sense and forethought there is a proof in the fact, that, knowing that his father could afford him no pecuniary aid, and that he must depend upon his own exertions, he opened a public school at the early age of sixteen; and this mode of living he continued to follow for five or six years. He then became a tutor in the family of the Rev. Mr. Tighe, rector of Drumgooland parish. Thence he proceeded to St. John's College, Cambridge, where he was entered in July, 1802, being at the time five-and-twenty years of age. After nearly four years' residence, he obtained his B.A. degree, and was ordained to a curacy in Essex, whence he removed into Yorkshire. The course of life of which this is the outline, shows a powerful and remarkable character, originating and pursuing a purpose in a resolute and independent manner. Here is a youth—a boy of sixteen—separating himself from his family, and determining to maintain himself; and that, not in the hereditary manner by agricultural pursuits, but by the labour of his brain.

I suppose, from what I have heard, that Mr. Tighe became strongly interested in his children's tutor, and may have aided him, not only in the direction of his studies, but in the suggestion of an English university education, and in advice as to the mode in which he should obtain entrance there. Mr. Brontë has now no trace of his Irish origin remaining in his speech; he never could have shown his Celtic descent in the straight Greek lines and long oval of his face; but at five-and-twenty, fresh from the only life he had ever known, to present himself at the gates of St. John's proved no little determination of will, and scorn of ridicule.

While at Cambridge, he became one of a corps of volunteers, who were then being called out all over the country to resist the apprehended invasion by the French. I have heard him allude, in late years, to Lord Palmerston as one who had often been associated with him then in the mimic military duties which they had to perform.

We take him up now settled as a curate at Hartshead, in Yorkshire—far removed from his birth-place and all his Irish connections; with whom, indeed, he cared little to keep up any intercourse, and whom he never, I believe, revisited after becoming a student at Cambridge.

Hartshead is a very small village, lying to the east of Huddersfield and Halifax; and, from its high situation—on a mound, as it were, surrounded by a circular basin—commanding a magnificent view. Mr. Brontë resided here for five years; and, while the incumbent of Hartshead, he wooed and married Maria Branwell.

She was the third daughter of Mr. Thomas Branwell, merchant, of Penzance. Her mother's maiden name was Carne:

and, both on father's and mother's side, the Branwell family were sufficiently well descended to enable them to mix in the best society that Penzance then afforded. Mr. and Mrs. Branwell would be living—their family of four daughters and one son, still children—during the existence of that primitive state of society which is well described by Dr. Davy in the life of his brother.

"In the same town, when the population was about 2,000 persons, there was only one carpet, the floors of rooms were sprinkled with sea-sand, and there was not a single silver fork.

"At that time, when our colonial possessions were very limited, our army and navy on a small scale, and there was comparatively little demand for intellect, the younger sons of gentlemen were often of necessity brought up to some trade or mechanical art, to which no discredit, or loss of caste, as it were, was attached. The eldest son, if not allowed to remain an idle country squire, was sent to Oxford or Cambridge, preparatory to his engaging in one of the three liberal professions of divinity, law, or physic; the second son was perhaps apprenticed to a surgeon or apothecary, or a solicitor; the third to a pewterer or watchmaker; the fourth to a packer or mercer, and so on, were there more to be provided for.

"After their apprenticeships were finished, the young men almost invariably went to London to perfect themselves in their respective trade or art: and on their return into the country, when settled in business, they were not excluded from what would now be considered genteel society. Visiting then was conducted differently from what it is at present. Dinner-parties were almost unknown, excepting at the annual feast-time. Christmas, too, was then a season of peculiar indulgence and conviviality, and a round of entertainments was given, consisting of tea and supper. Excepting at these two periods, visiting was almost entirely confined to tea-parties, which assembled at three o'clock, broke up at nine, and the amusement of the evening was commonly some round game at cards, as Pope Joan, or Commerce. The lower class was then extremely ignorant, and all classes were very superstitious; even the belief in witches maintained its ground, and there was an almost unbounded credulity respecting the supernatural and monstrous. There was scarcely a parish in the Mount's Bay that was without a haunted house, or a spot to which some story of supernatural horror was not attached. Even when I was a boy, I remember a house in the best street of Penzance which was uninhabited because it was believed to be haunted, and which young people walked by at night at a quickened pace, and with a beating heart. Amongst the middle and higher classes there was little taste for literature, and still less for science, and their pursuits were rarely of a dignified or intellectual kind. Hunting, shooting, wrestling, cock-fighting, generally ending in drunkenness, were what they most delighted in. Smuggling was carried on to a great extent; and drunkenness, and a low state of morals, were naturally associated with it. Whilst smuggling was the means of acquiring wealth to bold and reckless adventurers, drunkenness and dissipation occasioned the ruin of many respectable families."

I have given this extract because I conceive it bears some reference to the life of Miss Brontë, whose strong mind and vivid imagination must have received their first impressions either from the servants (in that simple household, almost friendly companions during the greater part of the day,) retailing the traditions or the news of Haworth village; or from Mr. Brontë, whose intercourse with his children appears to have been considerably restrained, and whose life, both in Ireland and at Cambridge, had been spent under peculiar circumstances; or from her aunt, Miss Branwell, who came to the parsonage, when Charlotte was only six or seven years old, to take charge of her dead sister's family. This aunt was older than Mrs. Brontë, and had lived longer among the Penzance society, which Dr. Davy describes. But in the Branwell family itself, the violence and irregularity of nature did not exist. They were Methodists, and, as far as I can gather, a gentle and sincere piety gave refinement and purity of character. Mr. Branwell, the father, according to his descendants' account, was a man of musical talent. He and his wife lived to see all their children grown up, and died within a year of each other—he in 1808, she in 1809, when their daughter Maria was twenty-five or twenty-six years of age. I have been permitted to look over a series of nine letters, which were addressed by her to Mr. Brontë, during the brief term of their engagement in 1812. They are full of tender grace of expression and feminine modesty; pervaded by the deep piety to which I have alluded as a family characteristic. I shall make one or two extracts from them, to show what sort of a person was the mother of Charlotte Brontë: but first, I must state the circumstances under which this Cornish lady met the scholar from Ahaderg, near Loughbrickland. In the early summer of 1812, when she would be twenty-nine, she came to visit her uncle, the Reverend John Fennel, who was at that time a clergyman of the Church of England, living near Leeds, but who had previously been a Methodist minister. Mr. Brontë was the incumbent of Hartshead; and had the reputation in the neighbourhood of being a very handsome fellow, full of Irish enthusiasm, and with something of an Irishman's capability of falling easily in love. Miss Branwell was extremely small in person; not pretty, but very elegant, and always dressed with a quiet simplicity of taste, which accorded well with her general character, and of which some of the details call to mind the style of dress preferred by her daughter for her favourite heroines. Mr. Brontë was soon captivated by the little, gentle creature, and this time declared that it was for life. In her first letter to him, dated August 26th, she seems almost surprised to find herself engaged, and alludes to the short time which she has known him. In the rest there are touches reminding one of Juliet's—

"But trust me, gentleman, I'll prove more true,
Than those that have more cunning to be strange."

There are plans for happy pic-nic parties to Kirkstall Abbey, in the glowing September days, when "Uncle, Aunt, and Cousin Jane,"—the last engaged to a Mr. Morgan, another clergyman—were of the party; all since dead, except Mr. Brontë. There was no opposition on the part of any of her friends to her engagement. Mr. and Mrs. Fennel sanctioned it, and her brother and sisters in far-away Penzance appear fully to have approved of it. In a letter dated September 18th, she says:—

"For some years I have been perfectly my own mistress, subject to no control whatever; so far from it, that my sisters, who are many years older than myself, and even my dear mother, used to consult me on every occasion of importance, and scarcely ever doubted the propriety of my opinions and actions: perhaps you will be ready to accuse me of vanity in mentioning this, but you must consider that I do not boast of it. I have many times felt it a disadvantage, and although, I thank God, it has never led me into error, yet, in circumstances of uncertainty and doubt, I have deeply felt the want of a guide and instructor." In the same letter she tells Mr. Brontë, that she has informed her sisters of her engagement, and that she should not see them again so soon as she had intended. Mr. Fennel, her uncle, also writes to them by the same post in praise of Mr. Brontë.

The journey from Penzance to Leeds in those days was both very long and very expensive; the lovers had not much money to spend in unnecessary travelling, and, as Miss Branwell had neither father nor mother living, it appeared both a discreet and seemly arrangement that the marriage should take place from her uncle's house. There was no reason either why the engagement should be prolonged. They were past their first youth; they had means sufficient for their unambitious wants; the living of Hartshead is rated in the Clergy List at 202*l*. per annum, and she was in the receipt of a small annuity (50*l*. I have been told) by the will of her father. So, at the end of September, the lovers began to talk about taking a house, for I suppose that Mr. Brontë up to that time had been in lodgings; and all went smoothly and successfully with a view to their marriage in the ensuing winter, until November, when a misfortune happened, which she thus patiently and prettily describes:—

"I suppose you never expected to be much the richer for me, but I am sorry to inform you that I am still poorer than I thought myself. I mentioned having sent for my books, clothes, &c. On Saturday evening, about the time when you were writing the description of your imaginary shipwreck, I was reading and feeling the effects of a real one, having then received a letter from my sister giving me an account of the vessel in which she had sent my box being stranded on the coast of Devonshire, in consequence of which the box was dashed to pieces with the violence of the sea, and all my little property, with the exception of a very few articles, being swallowed up in the mighty deep. If this should not prove the prelude to something worse I shall think little of it, as it is the first disastrous circumstance which has occurred since I left my home."

The last of these letters is dated December the 5th. Miss Branwell and her cousin intended to set about making the wedding-cake in the following week, so the marriage could not be far off. She had been learning by heart a "pretty little hymn" of Mr. Brontë's composing; and reading Lord Lyttelton's "Advice to a Lady," on which she makes some pertinent and just remarks, showing that she thought as well as read. And so Maria Branwell fades out of sight; we have no more direct intercourse with her; we hear of her as Mrs. Brontë, but it is as an invalid, not far from death; still patient, cheerful, and pious. The writing of these letters is elegant and neat; while there are allusions to household occupations—such as making the wedding-cake; there are also allusions to the books she has read, or is reading, showing a well-cultivated mind. Without having anything of her daughter's rare talents, Mrs. Brontë must have been, I imagine, that unusual character, a well-balanced and consistent woman. The style of the letters is easy and good; as is also that of a paper from the same hand, entitled "The Advantages of Poverty in Religious Concerns," which was written rather later, with a view to publication in some periodical.

She was married from her uncle's house in Yorkshire, on the 29th of December, 1812; the same day was also the wedding-day of her younger sister, Charlotte Branwell, in distant Penzance. I do not think that Mrs. Brontë ever revisited Cornwall, but she has left a very pleasant impression on the minds of those relations who yet survive; they speak of her as "their favourite aunt, and one to whom they, as well as all the family, looked up, as a person of talent and great amiability of disposition;" and, again, as "meek and retiring, while possessing more than ordinary talents, which she inherited from her father, and her piety was genuine and unobtrusive."

Mr. Brontë remained for five years at Hartshead, in the parish of Dewsbury. There he was married, and his two children, Maria and Elizabeth, were born. At the expiration of that period, he had the living of Thornton, in Bradford Parish. Some of those great West Riding parishes are almost like bishoprics for their amount of population and number of churches. Thornton church is a little episcopal chapel of ease, rich in Nonconformist monuments, as of Accepted Lister and his friend Dr. Hall. The neighbourhood is desolate and wild; great tracts of bleak land, enclosed by stone dykes, sweeping up Clayton heights. The church itself looks ancient and solitary, and as if left behind by the great stone mills of a flourishing Independent firm, and the solid square chapel built by the members of that denomination. Altogether not so pleasant a place as Hartshead, with its ample outlook over cloud-shadowed, sun-flecked plain, and hill rising beyond hill to form the distant horizon.

Here, at Thornton, Charlotte Brontë was born, on the 21st of April, 1816. Fast on her heels followed Patrick Branwell, Emily Jane, and Anne. After the birth of this last daughter, Mrs. Brontë's health began to decline. It is hard work to provide for the little tender wants of many young children where the means are but limited. The necessaries of food and clothing are much more easily supplied than the almost equal necessaries of attendance, care, soothing, amusement, and sympathy. Maria Brontë, the eldest of six, could only have been a few months more than six years old, when Mr. Brontë removed to Haworth, on February the 25th, 1820. Those who knew her then, describe her as grave, thoughtful, and quiet, to a degree far beyond her years. Her childhood was no childhood; the cases are rare in which the possessors of great gifts have known the blessings of that careless happy time; *their* unusual powers stir within them, and, instead of the natural life of perception—the objective, as the Germans call it—they begin the deeper life of reflection—the subjective.

Little Maria Brontë was delicate and small in appearance, which seemed to give greater effect to her wonderful precocity of intellect. She must have been her mother's companion and helpmate in many a household and nursery experience, for Mr. Brontë was, of course, much engaged in his study; and besides, he was not naturally fond of children, and felt their frequent appearance on the scene as a drag both on his wife's strength, and as an interruption to the comfort of the household.

Haworth Parsonage is—as I mentioned in the first chapter—an oblong stone house, facing down the hill on which the village stands, and with the front door right opposite to the western door of the church, distant about a hundred yards. Of this space twenty yards or so in depth are occupied by the grassy garden, which is scarcely wider than the house. The graveyard lies on two sides of the house and garden. The house consists of four rooms on each floor, and is two stories high. When the Brontës took possession, they made the larger parlour, to the left of the entrance, the family sitting-room, while that on the right was appropriated to Mr. Brontë as a study. Behind this was the kitchen; behind the former, a sort of flagged store-room. Upstairs were four bed-chambers of similar size, with the addition of a small apartment over the passage, or "lobby" as we call it in the north. This was to the front, the staircase going up right opposite to the entrance. There is the pleasant old fashion of window seats all through the house; and one can see that the parsonage was built in the days when wood was plentiful, as the massive stair-banisters, and the wainscots, and the heavy window-frames testify.

This little extra upstairs room was appropriated to the children. Small as it was, it was not called a nursery; indeed, it had not the comfort of a fire-place in it; the servants—two affectionate, warm-hearted sisters, who cannot now speak of the family without tears—called the room the "children's study." The age of the eldest student was perhaps by this time seven.

The people in Haworth were none of them very poor. Many of them were employed in the neighbouring worsted mills; a few were mill-owners and manufacturers in a small way; there were also some shopkeepers for the humbler and everyday wants; but for medical advice, for stationery, books, law, dress, or dainties, the inhabitants had to go to Keighley. There were several Sunday-schools; the Baptists had taken the lead in instituting them, the Wesleyans had followed, the Church of England had brought up the rear. Good Mr. Grimshaw, Wesley's friend, had built a humble Methodist chapel, but it stood close to the road leading on to the moor; the Baptists then raised a place of worship, with the distinction of being a few yards back from the highway; and the Methodists have since thought it well to erect another and a larger chapel, still more retired from the road. Mr. Brontë was ever on kind and friendly terms with each denomination as a body; but from individuals in the village the family stood aloof, unless some direct service was required, from the first. "They kept themselves very close," is the account given by those who remember Mr. and Mrs. Brontë's coming amongst them. I believe many of the Yorkshiremen would object to the system of parochial visiting; their surly independence would revolt from the idea of any one having a right, from his office, to inquire into their condition, to counsel, or to admonish them. The old hill-spirit lingers in them, which coined the rhyme, inscribed on the under part of one of the seats in the Sedilia of Whalley Abbey, not many miles from Haworth,

"Who mells wi' what another does
Had best go home and shoe his goose."

I asked an inhabitant of a district close to Haworth what sort of a clergyman they had at the church which he attended.

"A rare good one," said he: "he minds his own business, and ne'er troubles himself with ours."

Mr. Brontë was faithful in visiting the sick and all those who sent for him, and diligent in attendance at the schools; and so was his daughter Charlotte too; but, cherishing and valuing privacy themselves, they were perhaps over-delicate in not intruding upon the privacy of others.

From their first going to Haworth, their walks were directed rather out towards the heathery moors, sloping upwards behind the parsonage, than towards the long descending village street. A good old woman, who came to nurse Mrs. Brontë in the illness—an internal cancer—which grew and gathered upon her, not many months after her arrival at Haworth, tells me that at that time the six little creatures used to walk out, hand in hand, towards the glorious wild moors, which in after days they loved so passionately; the elder ones taking thoughtful care for the toddling wee things.

They were grave and silent beyond their years; subdued, probably, by the presence of serious illness in the house; for, at the time which my informant speaks of, Mrs. Brontë was confined to the bedroom from which she never came forth alive. "You would not have known there was a child in the house, they were such still, noiseless, good little creatures. Maria would shut herself up" (Maria, but seven!) "in the children's study with a newspaper, and be able to tell one everything when she came out; debates in Parliament, and I don't know what all. She was as good as a mother to her sisters and brother. But there never were such good children. I used to think them spiritless, they were so different to any children I had ever seen. They were good little creatures. Emily was the prettiest."

Mrs. Brontë was the same patient, cheerful person as we have seen her formerly; very ill, suffering great pain, but seldom if ever complaining; at her better times begging her nurse to raise her in bed to let her see her clean the grate, "because she did it as it was done in Cornwall;" devotedly fond of her husband, who warmly repaid her affection, and suffered no one else to take the night-nursing; but, according to my informant, the mother was not very anxious to see much of her children, probably because the sight of them, knowing how soon they were to be left motherless, would have agitated her too much. So the little things clung quietly together, for their father was busy in his study and in his parish, or with their mother, and they took their meals alone; sat reading, or whispering low, in the "children's study," or wandered out on the hill-side, hand in hand.

The ideas of Rousseau and Mr. Day on education had filtered down through many classes, and spread themselves widely out. I imagine, Mr. Brontë must have formed some of his opinions on the management of children from these two theorists. His practice was not half so wild or extraordinary as that to which an aunt of mine was subjected by a disciple of Mr. Day's. She had been taken by this gentleman and his wife, to live with them as their adopted child, perhaps about five-and-twenty years before the time of which I am writing. They were wealthy people and kind hearted, but her food and clothing were of the very simplest and rudest description, on Spartan principles. A healthy, merry child, she did not much care for dress or eating; but the treatment which she felt as a real cruelty was this. They had a carriage, in which she and the favourite dog were taken an airing on alternate days; the creature whose turn it was to be left at home being tossed in a blanket—an operation which my aunt especially dreaded. Her affright at the tossing was probably the reason why it was persevered in. Dressed-up ghosts had become common, and she did not care for them, so the blanket exercise was to be the next mode of hardening her nerves. It is well known that Mr. Day broke off his intention of marrying Sabrina, the girl whom he had educated for this purpose, because, within a few weeks of the time fixed for the wedding, she was guilty of the frivolity, while on a visit from home, of wearing thin sleeves. Yet Mr. Day and my aunt's relations were benevolent people, only strongly imbued with the crotchet that by a system of training might be educed the hardihood and simplicity of the ideal savage, forgetting the terrible isolation of feelings and habits which their pupils would experience in the future life which they must pass among the corruptions and refinements of civilization.

Mr. Brontë wished to make his children hardy, and indifferent to the pleasures of eating and dress. In the latter he succeeded, as far as regarded his daughters.

His strong, passionate, Irish nature was, in general, compressed down with resolute stoicism; but it was there notwithstanding all his philosophic calm and dignity of demeanour; though he did not speak when he was annoyed or displeased. Mrs. Brontë, whose sweet nature thought invariably of the bright side, would say, "Ought I not to be thankful that he never gave me an angry word?"

Mr. Brontë was an active walker, stretching away over the moors for many miles, noting in his mind all natural signs of wind and weather, and keenly observing all the wild creatures that came and went in the loneliest sweeps of the hills. He has seen eagles stooping low in search of food for their young; no eagle is ever seen on those mountain slopes now.

He fearlessly took whatever side in local or national politics appeared to him right. In the days of the Luddites, he had been for the peremptory interference of the law, at a time when no magistrate could be found to act, and all the property of the West Riding was in terrible danger. He became unpopular then among the millworkers, and he esteemed his life unsafe if he took his long and lonely walks unarmed; so he began the habit, which has continued to this day, of invariably carrying a loaded pistol about with him. It lay on his dressing-table with his watch; with his watch it was put on in the morning; with his watch it was taken off at night.

Many years later, during his residence at Haworth, there was a strike; the hands in the neighbourhood felt themselves aggrieved by the masters, and refused to work: Mr. Brontë thought that they had been unjustly and unfairly treated, and he assisted them by all the means in his power to "keep the wolf from their doors," and avoid the incubus of debt. Several of the more influential inhabitants of Haworth and the neighbourhood were mill-owners; they remonstrated pretty sharply with him, but he believed that his conduct was right and persevered in it.

His opinions might be often both wild and erroneous, his principles of action eccentric and strange, his views of life partial, and almost misanthropical; but not one opinion that he held could be stirred or modified by any worldly motive: he acted up to his principles of action; and, if any touch of misanthropy mingled with his view of mankind in general, his conduct to the individuals who came in personal contact with him did not agree with such view. It is true that he had strong and vehement prejudices, and was obstinate in maintaining them, and that he was not dramatic enough in his perceptions to see how miserable others might be in a life that to him was all-sufficient. But I do not pretend to be able to harmonize points of character, and account for them, and bring them all into one consistent and intelligible whole. The family with whom I have now to do shot their roots down deeper than I can penetrate. I cannot measure them, much less is it for me to judge them. I have named these instances of eccentricity in the father because I hold the knowledge of them to be necessary for a right understanding of the life of his daughter.

Mrs. Brontë died in September, 1821, and the lives of those quiet children must have become quieter and lonelier still. Charlotte tried hard, in after years, to recall the remembrance of her mother, and could bring back two or three pictures of her. One was when, sometime in the evening light, she had been playing with her little boy, Patrick Branwell, in the parlour of

Haworth Parsonage. But the recollections of four or five years old are of a very fragmentary character.

Owing to some illness of the digestive organs, Mr. Brontë was obliged to be very careful about his diet; and, in order to avoid temptation, and possibly to have the quiet necessary for digestion, he had begun, before his wife's death, to take his dinner alone—a habit which he always retained. He did not require companionship, therefore he did not seek it, either in his walks, or in his daily life. The quiet regularity of his domestic hours was only broken in upon by church-wardens, and visitors on parochial business; and sometimes by a neighbouring clergyman, who came down the hills, across the moors, to mount up again to Haworth Parsonage, and spend an evening there. But, owing to Mrs. Brontë's death so soon after her husband had removed into the district, and also to the distances, and the bleak country to be traversed, the wives of these clerical friends did not accompany their husbands; and the daughters grew up out of childhood into girlhood bereft, in a singular manner, of all such society as would have been natural to their age, sex, and station.

But the children did not want society. To small infantine gaieties they were unaccustomed. They were all in all to each other. I do not suppose that there ever was a family more tenderly bound to each other. Maria read the newspapers, and reported intelligence to her younger sisters which it is wonderful they could take an interest in. But I suspect that they had no "children's books," and that their eager minds "browzed undisturbed among the wholesome pasturage of English literature," as Charles Lamb expresses it. The servants of the household appear to have been much impressed with the little Brontës' extraordinary cleverness. In a letter which I had from him on this subject, their father writes:—"The servants often said that they had never seen such a clever little child" (as Charlotte), "and that they were obliged to be on their guard as to what they said and did before her. Yet she and the servants always lived on good terms with each other."

These servants are yet alive; elderly women residing in Bradford. They retain a faithful and fond recollection of Charlotte, and speak of her unvarying kindness from the "time when she was ever such a little child!" when she would not rest till she had got the old disused cradle sent from the parsonage to the house where the parents of one of them lived, to serve for a little infant sister. They tell of one long series of kind and thoughtful actions from this early period to the last weeks of Charlotte Brontë's life; and, though she had left her place many years ago, one of these former servants went over from Bradford to Haworth on purpose to see Mr. Brontë, and offer him her true sympathy, when his last child died. I may add a little anecdote as a testimony to the admirable character of the likeness of Miss Brontë prefixed to this volume. A gentleman who had kindly interested himself in the preparation of this memoir took the first volume, shortly after the publication, to the house of this old servant, in order to show her the portrait. The moment she caught a glimpse of the frontispiece, "There she is," in a minute she exclaimed. "Come, John, look!" (to her husband); and her daughter was equally struck by the resemblance. There might not be many to regard the Brontës with affection, but those who once loved them, loved them long and well.

I return to the father's letter. He says:—

"When mere children, as soon as they could read and write, Charlotte and her brothers and sisters used to invent and act little plays of their own, in which the Duke of Wellington, my daughter Charlotte's hero, was sure to come off conqueror; when a dispute would not unfrequently arise amongst them regarding the comparative merits of him, Buonaparte, Hannibal, and Cæsar. When the argument got warm, and rose to its height, as their mother was then dead, I had sometimes to come in as arbitrator, and settle the dispute according to the best of my judgment. Generally, in the management of these concerns, I frequently thought that I discovered signs of rising talent, which I had seldom or never before seen in any of their age . .

. A circumstance now occurs to my mind which I may as well mention. When my children were very young, when, as far as I can remember, the oldest was about ten years of age, and the youngest about four, thinking that they knew more than I had yet discovered, in order to make them speak with less timidity, I deemed that if they were put under a sort of cover I might gain my end; and happening to have a mask in the house, I told them all to stand and speak boldly from under cover of the mask.

"I began with the youngest (Anne, afterwards Acton Bell), and asked what a child like her most wanted; she answered, 'Age and experience.' I asked the next (Emily, afterwards Ellis Bell), what I had best do with her brother Branwell, who was sometimes a naughty boy; she answered, 'Reason with him, and when he won't listen to reason, whip him.' I asked Branwell what was the best way of knowing the difference between the intellects of man and woman; he answered, 'By considering the difference between them as to their bodies.' I then asked Charlotte what was the best book in the world; she answered, 'The Bible.' And what was the next best; she answered, 'The Book of Nature.' I then asked the next what was the best mode of education for a woman; she answered, 'That which would make her rule her house well.' Lastly, I asked the oldest what was the best mode of spending time; she answered, 'By laying it out in preparation for a happy eternity.' I may not have given precisely their words, but I have nearly done so, as they made a deep and lasting impression on my memory. The substance, however, was exactly what I have stated."

The strange and quaint simplicity of the mode taken by the father to ascertain the hidden characters of his children, and the tone and character of these questions and answers, show the curious education which was made by the circumstances surrounding the Brontës. They knew no other children. They knew no other modes of thought than what were suggested to them by the fragments of clerical conversation which they overheard in the parlour, or the subjects of village and local interest which they heard discussed in the kitchen. Each had their own strong characteristic flavour.

They took a vivid interest in the public characters, and the local and the foreign as well as home politics discussed in the newspapers. Long before Maria Brontë died, at the age of eleven, her father used to say he could converse with her on any of the leading topics of the day with as much freedom and pleasure as with any grown-up person.

CHAPTER IV

About a year after Mrs. Brontë's death, an elder sister, as I have before mentioned, came from Penzance to superintend her brother-in-law's household, and look after his children. Miss Branwell was, I believe, a kindly and conscientious woman, with a good deal of character, but with the somewhat narrow ideas natural to one who had spent nearly all her life in the same place. She had strong prejudices, and soon took a distaste to Yorkshire. From Penzance, where plants which we in the north call greenhouse flowers grow in great profusion, and without any shelter even in the winter, and where the soft warm climate allows the inhabitants, if so disposed, to live pretty constantly in the open air, it was a great change for a lady considerably past forty to come and take up her abode in a place where neither flowers nor vegetables would flourish, and where a tree of even moderate dimensions might be hunted for far and wide; where the snow lay long and late on the moors, stretching bleakly and barely far up from the dwelling which was henceforward to be her home; and where often, on autumnal or winter nights, the four winds of heaven seemed to meet and rage together, tearing round the house as if they were wild beasts striving to find an entrance. She missed the small round of cheerful, social visiting perpetually going on in a country town; she missed the friends she had known from her childhood, some of whom had been her parents' friends before they were hers; she disliked many of the customs of the place, and particularly dreaded the cold damp arising from the flag floors in the passages and parlours of Haworth Parsonage. The stairs, too, I believe, are made of stone; and no wonder, when stone quarries are near, and trees are far to seek. I have heard that Miss Branwell always went about the house in pattens, clicking up and down the stairs, from her dread of catching cold. For the same reason, in the latter years of her life, she passed nearly all her time, and took most of her meals, in her bedroom. The children respected her, and had that sort of affection for her which is generated by esteem; but I do not think they ever freely loved her. It was a severe trial for any one at her time of life to change neighbourhood and habitation so entirely as she did; and the greater her merit.

I do not know whether Miss Branwell taught her nieces anything besides sewing, and the household arts in which Charlotte afterwards was such an adept. Their regular lessons were said to their father; and they were always in the habit of picking up an immense amount of miscellaneous information for themselves. But a year or so before this time, a school had been begun in the North of England for the daughters of clergymen. The place was Cowan Bridge, a small hamlet on the coach-road between Leeds and Kendal, and thus easy of access from Haworth, as the coach ran daily, and one of its stages was at Keighley. The yearly expense for each pupil (according to the entrance-rules given in the Report for 1842, and I believe they had not been increased since the establishment of the schools in 1823) was as follows:

"Rule 1l. The terms for clothing, lodging, boarding, and educating, are 14*l*. a year; half to be paid in advance, when the pupils are sent; and also 1*l*. entrance-money, for the use of books, &c. The system of education comprehends history, geography, the use of the globes, grammar, writing and arithmetic, all kinds of needlework, and the nicer kinds of household work—such as getting up fine linen, ironing, &c. If accomplishments are required, an additional charge of 3*l*. a year is made for music or drawing, each."

Rule 3rd requests that the friends will state the line of education desired in the case of every pupil, having a regard to her future prospects.

Rule 4th states the clothing and toilette articles which a girl is expected to bring with her; and thus concludes: "The pupils all appear in the same dress. They wear plain straw cottage bonnets; in summer white frocks on Sundays, and nankeen on other days; in winter, purple stuff frocks, and purple cloth cloaks. For the sake of uniformity, therefore, they are required to bring 3*l*. in lieu of frocks, pelisse, bonnet, tippet, and frills; making the whole sum which each pupil brings with her to the school—

7*l*. half-year in advance.
1*l*. entrance for books.
1*l*. entrance for clothes.

The 8th rule is,—"All letters and parcels are inspected by the superintendent;" but this is a very prevalent regulation in all young ladies' schools, where I think it is generally understood that the schoolmistress may exercise this privilege, although it is certainly unwise in her to insist too frequently upon it.

There is nothing at all remarkable in any of the other regulations, a copy of which was doubtless in Mr. Brontë's hands when he formed the determination to send his daughters to Cowan Bridge School; and he accordingly took Maria and Elizabeth thither in July, 1824.

I now come to a part of my subject which I find great difficulty in treating, because the evidence relating to it on each side is so conflicting that it seems almost impossible to arrive at the truth. Miss Brontë more than once said to me, that she should not have written what she did of Lowood in "Jane Eyre," if she had thought the place would have been so immediately identified with Cowan Bridge, although there was not a word in her account of the institution but what was true at the time when she knew it; she also said that she had not considered it necessary, in a work of fiction, to state every particular with the impartiality that might be required in a court of justice, nor to seek out motives, and make allowances for human failings, as she might have done, if dispassionately analysing the conduct of those who had the superintendence of the institution. I believe she herself would have been glad of an opportunity to correct the over-strong impression which was made upon the public mind by her vivid picture, though even she, suffering her whole life long, both in heart and body, from the consequences of what happened there, might have been apt, to the last, to take her deep belief in facts for the facts themselves—her conception of truth for the absolute truth.

In some of the notices of the previous editions of this work, it is assumed that I derived the greater part of my information with regard to her sojourn at Cowan Bridge from Charlotte Brontë herself. I never heard her speak of the place but once, and that was on the second day of my acquaintance with her. A little child on that occasion expressed some reluctance to finish eating his piece of bread at dinner; and she, stooping down, and addressing him in a low voice, told him how thankful she should have been at his age for a piece of bread; and when we—though I am not sure if I myself spoke—asked her some question as to the occasion she alluded to, she replied with reserve and hesitation, evidently shying away from what she imagined might lead to too much conversation on one of her books. She spoke of the oat-cake at Cowan Bridge (the clap-bread of Westmorland) as being different to the leaven-raised oat-cake of Yorkshire, and of her childish distaste for it. Some one present made an allusion to a similar childish dislike in the true tale of "The terrible knitters o' Dent" given in Southey's "Common-place Book:" and she smiled faintly, but said that the mere difference in food was not all: that the food itself was spoilt by the dirty carelessness of the cook, so that she and her sisters disliked their meals exceedingly; and she named her relief and gladness when the doctor condemned the meat, and spoke of having seen him spit it out. These are all the details I ever heard from her. She so avoided particularizing, that I think Mr. Carus Wilson's name never passed between us.

I do not doubt the general accuracy of my informants,—of those who have given, and solemnly repeated, the details that follow,—but it is only just to Miss Brontë to say that I have stated above pretty nearly all that I ever heard on the subject from her.

A clergyman, living near Kirby Lonsdale, the Reverend William Carus Wilson, was the prime mover in the establishment of this school. He was an energetic man, sparing no labour for the accomplishment of his ends. He saw that it was an extremely difficult task for clergymen with limited incomes to provide for the education of their children; and he devised a scheme, by which a certain sum was raised annually by subscription, to complete the amount required to furnish a solid and sufficient English education, for which the parent's payment of 14*l.* a year would not have been sufficient. Indeed, that made by the parents was considered to be exclusively appropriated to the expenses of lodging and boarding, and the education provided for by the subscriptions. Twelve trustees were appointed; Mr. Wilson being not only a trustee, but the treasurer and secretary; in fact, taking most of the business arrangements upon himself; a responsibility which appropriately fell to him, as he lived nearer the school than any one else who was interested in it. So his character for prudence and judgment was to a certain degree implicated in the success or failure of Cowan Bridge School; and the working of it was for many years the great object and interest of his life. But he was apparently unacquainted with the prime element in good administration—seeking out thoroughly competent persons to fill each department, and then making them responsible for, and judging them by, the result, without perpetual interference with the details.

So great was the amount of good which Mr. Wilson did, by his constant, unwearied superintendence, that I cannot help feeling sorry that, in his old age and declining health, the errors which he was believed to have committed, should have been brought up against him in a form which received such wonderful force from the touch of Miss Brontë's great genius. No doubt whatever can be entertained of the deep interest which he felt in the success of the school. As I write, I have before me his last words on giving up the secretaryship in 1850: he speaks of the "withdrawal, from declining health, of an eye, which, at all events, has loved to watch over the schools with an honest and anxious interest;"—and again he adds, "that he resigns, therefore, with a desire to be thankful for all that God has been pleased to accomplish through his instrumentality (the infirmities and unworthinesses of which he deeply feels and deplores)."

Cowan Bridge is a cluster of some six or seven cottages, gathered together at both ends of a bridge, over which the high road from Leeds to Kendal crosses a little stream, called the Leck. This high road is nearly disused now; but formerly, when the buyers from the West Riding manufacturing districts had frequent occasion to go up into the North to purchase the wool of the Westmorland and Cumberland farmers, it was doubtless much travelled; and perhaps the hamlet of Cowan Bridge had a more prosperous look than it bears at present. It is prettily situated; just where the Leck-fells swoop into the plain; and by the course of the beck alder-trees and willows and hazel bushes grow. The current of the stream is interrupted by broken pieces of grey rock; and the waters flow over a bed of large round white pebbles, which a flood heaves up and moves on either side out of its impetuous way till in some parts they almost form a wall. By the side of the little, shallow, sparkling, vigorous Leck, run long pasture fields, of the fine short grass common in high land; for though Cowan Bridge is situated on a plain, it is a plain from which there is many a fall and long descent before you and the Leck reach the valley of the Lune. I can hardly understand how the school there came to be so unhealthy, the air all round about was so sweet and thyme-scented, when I visited it last summer. But at this day, every one knows that the site of a building intended for numbers should be chosen with far greater care than that of a private dwelling, from the tendency to illness, both infectious and otherwise, produced by the congregation of people in close proximity.

The house is still remaining that formed part of that occupied by the school. It is a long, bow-windowed cottage, now divided into two dwellings. It stands facing the Leck, between which and it intervenes a space, about seventy yards deep, that was once the school garden. This original house was an old dwelling of the Picard family, which they had inhabited for two generations. They sold it for school purposes, and an additional building was erected, running at right angles from the older part. This new part was devoted expressly to schoolrooms, dormitories, &c.; and after the school was removed to Casterton, it was used for a bobbin-mill connected with the stream, where wooden reels were made out of the alders, which grow profusely in such ground as that surrounding Cowan Bridge. This mill is now destroyed. The present cottage was, at the time of which I write, occupied by the teachers' rooms, the dinner-room and kitchens, and some smaller bedrooms. On going into this building, I found one part, that nearest to the high road, converted into a poor kind of public-house, then to let, and having all the squalid appearance of a deserted place, which rendered it difficult to judge what it would look like when neatly kept up, the broken panes replaced in the windows, and the rough-cast (now cracked and discoloured) made white and whole. The other end forms a cottage, with the low ceilings and stone floors of a hundred years ago; the windows do not open freely and widely; and the passage upstairs, leading to the bedrooms, is narrow and tortuous: altogether, smells would linger about the house, and damp cling to it. But sanitary matters were little understood thirty years ago; and it was a great thing to get a roomy building close to the high road, and not too far from the habitation of Mr. Wilson, the originator of the educational scheme. There was much need of such an institution; numbers of ill-paid clergymen hailed the prospect with joy, and eagerly put down the names of their children as pupils when the establishment should be ready to receive them. Mr. Wilson was, no doubt, pleased by the impatience with which the realisation of his idea was anticipated, and opened the school with less than a hundred pounds in hand, and with pupils, the number of whom varies according to different accounts; Mr. W. W. Carus Wilson, the son of the founder, giving it as seventy; while Mr. Shepheard, the son-in-law, states it to have been only sixteen.

Mr. Wilson felt, most probably, that the responsibility of the whole plan rested upon him. The payment made by the parents was barely enough for food and lodging; the subscriptions did not flow very freely into an untried scheme; and great economy was necessary in all the domestic arrangements. He determined to enforce this by frequent personal inspection; carried perhaps to an unnecessary extent, and leading occasionally to a meddling with little matters, which had sometimes the effect of producing irritation of feeling. Yet, although there was economy in providing for the household, there does not appear to have been any parsimony. The meat, flour, milk, &c., were contracted for, but were of very fair quality; and the dietary, which has been shown to me in manuscript, was neither bad nor unwholesome; nor, on the whole, was it wanting in variety. Oatmeal porridge for breakfast; a piece of oat-cake for those who required luncheon; baked and boiled beef, and mutton, potato-pie, and plain homely puddings of different kinds for dinner. At five o'clock, bread and milk for the younger ones; and one piece of bread (this was the only time at which the food was limited) for the elder pupils, who sat up till a later meal of the same description.

Mr. Wilson himself ordered in the food, and was anxious that it should be of good quality. But the cook, who had much of his confidence, and against whom for a long time no one durst utter a complaint, was careless, dirty, and wasteful. To some children oatmeal porridge is distasteful, and consequently unwholesome, even when properly made; at Cowan Bridge School it was too often sent up, not merely burnt, but with offensive fragments of other substances discoverable in it. The beef, that should have been carefully salted before it was dressed, had often become tainted from neglect; and girls, who were school-fellows with the Brontës, during the reign of the cook of whom I am speaking, tell me that the house seemed to be pervaded, morning, noon, and night, by the odour of rancid fat that steamed out of the oven in which much of their food was prepared. There was the same carelessness in making the puddings; one of those ordered was rice boiled in water, and eaten with a sauce of treacle and sugar; but it was often uneatable, because the water had been taken out of the rain tub, and was strongly impregnated with the dust lodging on the roof, whence it had trickled down into the old wooden cask, which also added its own flavour to that of the original rain water. The milk, too, was often "bingy," to use a country expression for a kind of taint that is far worse than sourness, and suggests the idea that it is caused by want of cleanliness about the milk pans, rather than by the heat of the weather. On Saturdays, a kind of pie, or mixture of potatoes and meat, was served up, which was made of all the fragments accumulated during the week. Scraps of meat from a dirty and disorderly larder, could never be very appetizing; and, I believe, that this dinner was more loathed than any in the early days of Cowan Bridge School. One may fancy how repulsive such fare would be to children whose appetites were small, and who had been accustomed to food, far simpler perhaps, but prepared with a delicate cleanliness that made it both tempting and wholesome. At many a meal the little Brontës went without food, although craving with hunger. They were not strong when they came, having only just recovered from a complication of measles and hooping-cough: indeed, I suspect they had scarcely recovered; for there was some consultation on the part of the school authorities whether Maria and Elizabeth should be received or not, in July 1824. Mr. Brontë came again, in the September of that year, bringing with him Charlotte and Emily to be admitted as pupils.

It appears strange that Mr. Wilson should not have been informed by the teachers of the way in which the food was served up; but we must remember that the cook had been known for some time to the Wilson family, while the teachers were brought together for an entirely different work—that of education. They were expressly given to understand that such was their department; the buying in and management of the provisions rested with Mr. Wilson and the cook. The teachers would, of course, be unwilling to lay any complaints on the subject before him.

There was another trial of health common to all the girls. The path from Cowan Bridge to Tunstall Church, where Mr. Wilson preached, and where they all attended on the Sunday, is more than two miles in length, and goes sweeping along the rise and fall of the unsheltered country, in a way to make it a fresh and exhilarating walk in summer, but a bitter cold one in winter, especially to children like the delicate little Brontës, whose thin blood flowed languidly in consequence of their feeble appetites rejecting the food prepared for them, and thus inducing a half-starved condition. The church was not warmed, there being no means for this purpose. It stands in the midst of fields, and the damp mist must have gathered round the walls, and crept in at the windows. The girls took their cold dinner with them, and ate it between the services, in a chamber over the entrance, opening out of the former galleries. The arrangements for this day were peculiarly trying to delicate children, particularly to those who were spiritless and longing for home, as poor Maria Brontë must have been; for her ill health was increasing, and the old cough, the remains of the hooping-cough, lingered about her.

She was far superior in mind to any of her play-fellows and companions, and was lonely amongst them from that very cause; and yet she had faults so annoying that she was in constant disgrace with her teachers, and an object of merciless dislike to one of them, who is depicted as "Miss Scatcherd" in "Jane Eyre," and whose real name I will be merciful enough not to disclose. I need hardly say, that Helen Burns is as exact a transcript of Maria Brontë as Charlotte's wonderful power of reproducing character could give. Her heart, to the latest day on which we met, still beat with unavailing indignation at the worrying and the cruelty to which her gentle, patient, dying sister had been subjected by this woman. Not a word of that part of "Jane Eyre" but is a literal repetition of scenes between the pupil and the teacher. Those who had been pupils at the same time knew who must have written the book from the force with which Helen Burns' sufferings are described. They had, before that, recognised the description of the sweet dignity and benevolence of Miss Temple as only a just tribute to the merits of one whom all that knew her appear to hold in honour; but when Miss Scatcherd was held up to opprobrium they also recognised in the writer of "Jane Eyre" an unconsciously avenging sister of the sufferer.

One of their fellow-pupils, among other statements even worse, gives me the following:—The dormitory in which Maria slept was a long room, holding a row of narrow little beds on each side, occupied by the pupils; and at the end of this dormitory there was a small bed-chamber opening out of it, appropriated to the use of Miss Scatcherd. Maria's bed stood nearest to the door of this room. One morning, after she had become so seriously unwell as to have had a blister applied to her side (the sore from which was not perfectly healed), when the getting-up bell was heard, poor Maria moaned out that she was so ill, so very ill, she wished she might stop in bed; and some of the girls urged her to do so, and said they would explain it all to Miss Temple, the superintendent. But Miss Scatcherd was close at hand, and her anger would have to be faced before Miss Temple's kind thoughtfulness could interfere; so the sick child began to dress, shivering with cold, as, without leaving her bed, she slowly put on her black worsted stockings over her thin white legs (my informant spoke as if she saw it yet, and her whole face flushed out undying indignation). Just then Miss Scatcherd issued from her room, and, without asking for a word of explanation from the sick and frightened girl, she took her by the arm, on the side to which the blister had been applied, and by one vigorous movement whirled her out into the middle of the floor, abusing her all the time for dirty and untidy habits. There she left her. My informant says, Maria hardly spoke, except to beg some of the more indignant girls to be calm; but, in slow, trembling movements, with many a pause, she went down-stairs at last,—and was punished for being late.

Any one may fancy how such an event as this would rankle in Charlotte's mind. I only wonder that she did not remonstrate against her father's decision to send her and Emily back to Cowan Bridge, after Maria's and Elizabeth's deaths. But frequently children are unconscious of the effect which some of their simple revelations would have in altering the opinions entertained by their friends of the persons placed around them. Besides, Charlotte's earnest vigorous mind saw, at an unusually early age, the immense importance of education, as furnishing her with tools which she had the strength and the will to wield, and she would be aware that the Cowan Bridge education was, in many points, the best that her father could provide for her.

Before Maria Brontë's death, that low fever broke out, in the spring of 1825, which is spoken of in "Jane Eyre." Mr. Wilson was extremely alarmed at the first symptoms of this. He went to a kind motherly woman, who had had some connection with the school—as laundress, I believe—and asked her to come and tell him what was the matter with them. She made herself ready, and drove with him in his gig. When she entered the schoolroom, she saw from twelve to fifteen girls lying about; some resting their aching heads on the table, others on the ground; all heavy-eyed, flushed, indifferent, and weary, with pains in every limb. Some peculiar odour, she says, made her recognise that they were sickening for "the fever;" and she told Mr. Wilson so, and that she could not stay there for fear of conveying the infection to her own children; but he half commanded, and half entreated her to remain and nurse them; and finally mounted his gig and drove away, while she was still urging that she must return to her own house, and to her domestic duties, for which she had provided no substitute. However, when she was left in this unceremonious manner, she determined to make the best of it; and a most efficient nurse she proved: although, as she says, it was a dreary time.

Mr. Wilson supplied everything ordered by the doctors, of the best quality and in the most liberal manner; the invalids were attended by Dr. Batty, a very clever surgeon in Kirby, who had had the medical superintendence of the establishment from the beginning, and who afterwards became Mr. Wilson's brother-in-law. I have heard from two witnesses besides Charlotte Brontë, that Dr. Batty condemned the preparation of the food by the expressive action of spitting out a portion of it. He himself, it is but fair to say, does not remember this circumstance, nor does he speak of the fever itself as either alarming or dangerous. About forty of the girls suffered from this, but none of them died at Cowan Bridge; though one died at her own home, sinking under the state of health which followed it. None of the Brontës had the fever. But the same causes, which affected the health of the other pupils through typhus, told more slowly, but not less surely, upon their constitutions. The principal of these causes was the food.

The bad management of the cook was chiefly to be blamed for this; she was dismissed, and the woman who had been forced against her will to serve as head nurse, took the place of housekeeper; and henceforward the food was so well prepared that no one could ever reasonably complain of it. Of course it cannot be expected that a new institution, comprising domestic and educational arrangements for nearly a hundred persons, should work quite smoothly at the beginning.

All this occurred during the first two years of the establishment, and in estimating its effect upon the character of Charlotte Brontë, we must remember that she was a sensitive thoughtful child, capable of reflecting deeply, if not of analyzing truly; and peculiarly susceptible, as are all delicate and sickly children, to painful impressions. What the healthy suffer from but momentarily and then forget, those who are ailing brood over involuntarily and remember long,—perhaps with no resentment, but simply as a piece of suffering that has been stamped into their very life. The pictures, ideas, and conceptions of character received into the mind of the child of eight years old, were destined to be reproduced in fiery words a quarter of a century afterwards. She saw but one side of Mr. Wilson's character; and many of those who knew him at that time assure me of the fidelity with which this is represented, while at the same time they regret that the delineation should have obliterated, as it were, nearly all that was noble or conscientious. And that there were grand and fine qualities in Mr. Wilson, I have received abundant evidence. Indeed for several weeks past I have received letters almost daily, bearing on the subject of this chapter; some vague, some definite; many full of love and admiration for Mr. Wilson, some as full of dislike and indignation; few containing positive facts. After giving careful consideration to this mass of conflicting evidence, I have made such alterations and omissions in this chapter as seem to me to be required. It is but just to state that the major part of the testimony with which I have been favoured from old pupils is in high praise of Mr. Wilson. Among the letters that I have read, there is one whose evidence ought to be highly respected. It is from the husband of "Miss Temple." She died in 1856, but he, a clergyman, thus wrote in reply to a letter addressed to him on the subject by one of Mr. Wilson's friends:—"Often have I heard my late dear wife speak of her sojourn at Cowan Bridge; always in terms of admiration of Mr. Carus Wilson, his parental love to his pupils, and their love for him; of the food and general treatment, in terms of approval. I have heard her allude to an unfortunate cook, who used at times to spoil the porridge, but who, she said, was soon dismissed."

The recollections left of the four Brontë sisters at this period of their lives, on the minds of those who associated with them, are not very distinct. Wild, strong hearts, and powerful minds, were hidden under an enforced propriety and regularity of demeanour and expression, just as their faces had been concealed by their father, under his stiff, unchanging mask. Maria was delicate, unusually clever and thoughtful for her age, gentle, and untidy. Of her frequent disgrace from this last fault—of her sufferings, so patiently borne—I have already spoken. The only glimpse we get of Elizabeth, through the few years of her short life, is contained in a letter which I have received from "Miss Temple." "The second, Elizabeth, is the only one of the family of whom I have a vivid recollection, from her meeting with a somewhat alarming accident, in consequence of which I had her for some days and nights in my bedroom, not only for the sake of greater quiet, but that I might watch over her myself. Her head was severely cut, but she bore all the consequent suffering with exemplary patience, and by it won much upon my esteem. Of the two younger ones (if two there were) I have very slight recollections, save that one, a darling child, under five years of age, was quite the pet nursling of the school." This last would be Emily. Charlotte was considered the most talkative of the sisters—a "bright, clever, little child." Her great friend was a certain "Mellany Hane" (so Mr. Brontë spells the name), whose brother paid for her schooling, and who had no remarkable talent except for music, which her brother's circumstances forbade her to cultivate. She was "a hungry, good-natured, ordinary girl;" older than Charlotte, and ever ready to protect her from any petty tyranny or encroachments on the part of the elder girls. Charlotte always remembered her with affection and gratitude.

I have quoted the word "bright" in the account of Charlotte. I suspect that this year of 1825 was the last time it could ever be applied to her. In the spring of it, Maria became so rapidly worse that Mr. Brontë was sent for. He had not previously been aware of her illness, and the condition in which he found her was a terrible shock to him. He took her home by the Leeds coach, the girls crowding out into the road to follow her with their eyes over the bridge, past the cottages, and then out of sight for ever. She died a very few days after her arrival at home. Perhaps the news of her death falling suddenly into the life of which her patient existence had formed a part, only a little week or so before, made those who remained at Cowan Bridge look with more anxiety on Elizabeth's symptoms, which also turned out to be consumptive. She was sent home in charge of a confidential servant of the establishment; and she, too, died in the early summer of that year. Charlotte was thus suddenly called into the responsibilities of eldest sister in a motherless family. She remembered how anxiously her dear sister Maria had striven, in her grave earnest way, to be a tender helper and a counsellor to them all; and the duties that now fell upon her seemed almost like a legacy from the gentle little sufferer so lately dead.

Both Charlotte and Emily returned to school after the Midsummer holidays in this fatal year. But before the next winter it was thought desirable to advise their removal, as it was evident that the damp situation of the house at Cowan Bridge did not suit their health. {3}

CHAPTER V

For the reason just stated, the little girls were sent home in the autumn of 1825, when Charlotte was little more than nine years old.

About this time, an elderly woman of the village came to live as servant at the parsonage. She remained there, as a member of the household, for thirty years; and from the length of her faithful service, and the attachment and respect which she inspired, is deserving of mention. Tabby was a thorough specimen of a Yorkshire woman of her class, in dialect, in appearance, and in character. She abounded in strong practical sense and shrewdness. Her words were far from flattery; but she would spare no deeds in the cause of those whom she kindly regarded. She ruled the children pretty sharply; and yet never grudged a little extra trouble to provide them with such small treats as came within her power. In return, she claimed to be looked upon as a humble friend; and, many years later, Miss Brontë told me that she found it somewhat difficult to manage, as Tabby expected to be informed of all the family concerns, and yet had grown so deaf that what was repeated to her became known to whoever might be in or about the house. To obviate this publication of what it might be desirable to keep secret, Miss Brontë used to take her out for a walk on the solitary moors; where, when both were seated on a tuft of heather, in some high lonely place, she could acquaint the old woman, at leisure, with all that she wanted to hear.

Tabby had lived in Haworth in the days when the pack-horses went through once a week, with their tinkling bells and gay worsted adornment, carrying the produce of the country from Keighley over the hills to Colne and Burnley. What is more, she had known the "bottom," or valley, in those primitive days when the fairies frequented the margin of the "beck" on moonlight nights, and had known folk who had seen them. But that was when there were no mills in the valleys; and when all the wool-spinning was done by hand in the farm-houses round. "It wur the factories as had driven 'em away," she said. No doubt she had many a tale to tell of by-gone days of the country-side; old ways of living, former inhabitants, decayed gentry, who had melted away, and whose places knew them no more; family tragedies, and dark superstitious dooms; and in telling these things, without the least consciousness that there might ever be anything requiring to be softened down, would give at full length the bare and simple details.

Miss Branwell instructed the children at regular hours in all she could teach, making her bed-chamber into their schoolroom. Their father was in the habit of relating to them any public news in which he felt an interest; and from the opinions of his strong and independent mind they would gather much food for thought; but I do not know whether he gave them any direct instruction. Charlotte's deep thoughtful spirit appears to have felt almost painfully the tender responsibility which rested upon her with reference to her remaining sisters. She was only eighteen months older than Emily; but Emily and Anne were simply companions and playmates, while Charlotte was motherly friend and guardian to both; and this loving assumption of duties beyond her years, made her feel considerably older than she really was.

Patrick Branwell, their only brother, was a boy of remarkable promise, and, in some ways, of extraordinary precocity of talent. Mr. Brontë's friends advised him to send his son to school; but, remembering both the strength of will of his own youth and his mode of employing it, he believed that Patrick was better at home, and that he himself could teach him well, as he had taught others before. So Patrick, or as his family called him—Branwell, remained at Haworth, working hard for some hours a day with his father; but, when the time of the latter was taken up with his parochial duties, the boy was thrown into chance companionship with the lads of the village—for youth will to youth, and boys will to boys.

Still, he was associated in many of his sisters' plays and amusements. These were mostly of a sedentary and intellectual nature. I have had a curious packet confided to me, containing an immense amount of manuscript, in an inconceivably small space; tales, dramas, poems, romances, written principally by Charlotte, in a hand which it is almost impossible to decipher without the aid of a magnifying glass. No description will give so good an idea of the extreme minuteness of the writing as the annexed facsimile of a page.

Among these papers there is a list of her works, which I copy, as a curious proof how early the rage for literary composition had seized upon her:—

CATALOGUE OF MY BOOKS, WITH THE PERIOD OF THEIR COMPLETION, UP TO AUGUST 3RD, 1830.

Two romantic tales in one volume; viz., The Twelve Adventurers and the Adventures in Ireland, April 2nd, 1829.

The Search after Happiness, a Tale, Aug. 1st, 1829.

Leisure Hours, a Tale, and two Fragments, July 6th 1829.

The Adventures of Edward de Crack, a Tale, Feb. 2nd, 1830.

The Adventures of Ernest Alembert, a Tale, May 26th, 1830.

An interesting Incident in the Lives of some of the most eminent Persons of the Age, a Tale, June 10th, 1830.

Tales of the Islanders, in four volumes. Contents of the 1st Vol.:—1. An Account of their Origin; 2. A Description of Vision Island; 3. Ratten's Attempt; 4. Lord Charles Wellesley and the Marquis of Douro's Adventure; completed June 31st, 1829. 2nd Vol.:—1. The School-rebellion; 2. The strange Incident in the Duke of Wellington's Life; 3. Tale to his Sons; 4. The Marquis of Douro and Lord Charles Wellesley's Tale to his little King and Queen; completed Dec. 2nd, 1829. 3rd Vol.:—1. The Duke of Wellington's Adventure in the Cavern; 2. The Duke of Wellington and the little King's and Queen's visit to the Horse-Guards; completed May 8th, 1830. 4th Vol.:—1. The three old Washer-women of Strathfieldsaye; 2. Lord C. Wellesley's Tale to his Brother; completed July 30th, 1830.

Characters of Great Men of the Present Age, Dec. 17th 1829.

The Young Men's Magazines, in Six Numbers, from August to December, the latter months double number, completed December the 12th, 1829. General index to their contents:—1. A True Story; 2. Causes of the War; 3. A Song; 4. Conversations; 5. A True Story continued; 6. The Spirit of Cawdor; 7. Interior of a Pothouse, a Poem; 8. The Glass Town, a Song; 9. The Silver Cup, a Tale; 10. The Table and Vase in the Desert, a Song; 11. Conversations; 12. Scene on the Great Bridge; 13. Song of the Ancient Britons; 14. Scene in my Tun, a Tale; 15. An American Tale; 16. Lines written on seeing the Garden of a Genius; 17. The Lay of the Glass Town; 18. The Swiss Artist, a Tale; 19. Lines on the Transfer of this Magazine; 20. On the Same, by a different hand; 21. Chief Genii in Council; 22. Harvest in Spain; 23. The Swiss Artists continued; 24. Conversations.

The Poetaster, a Drama, in 2 volumes, July 12th, 1830.

A Book of Rhymes, finished December 17th, 1829. Contents:—1. The Beauty of Nature; 2. A Short Poem; 3. Meditations while Journeying in a Canadian Forest; 4. Song of an Exile; 5. On Seeing the Ruins of the Tower of Babel; 6. *A Thing of* 14 *lines*; 7. Lines written on the Bank of a River one fine Summer Evening; 8. Spring, a Song; 9. Autumn, a Song.

Miscellaneous Poems, finished May 30th, 1830. Contents:—1. The Churchyard; 2. Description of the Duke of Wellington's Palace on the Pleasant Banks of the Lusiva; this article is a small prose tale or incident; 3. Pleasure; 4. Lines written on the Summit of a high Mountain of the North of England; 5. Winter; 6. Two Fragments, namely, 1st, The Vision; 2nd, A Short untitled Poem; the Evening Walk, a Poem, June 23rd, 1830.

Making in the whole twenty-two volumes.

C. BRONTË, *August* 3, 1830

As each volume contains from sixty to a hundred pages, and the size of the page lithographed is rather less than the average, the amount of the whole seems very great, if we remember that it was all written in about fifteen months. So much for the quantity; the quality strikes me as of singular merit for a girl of thirteen or fourteen. Both as a specimen of her prose style at this time, and also as revealing something of the quiet domestic life led by these children, I take an extract from the introduction to "Tales of the Islanders," the title of one of their "Little Magazines:"—

"June the 31st, 1829.

"The play of the 'Islanders' was formed in December, 1827, in the following manner. One night, about the time when the cold sleet and stormy fogs of November are succeeded by the snow-storms, and high piercing night winds of confirmed winter, we were all sitting round the warm blazing kitchen fire, having just concluded a quarrel with Tabby concerning the propriety of lighting a candle, from which she came off victorious, no candle having been produced. A long pause succeeded, which was at last broken by Branwell saying, in a lazy manner, 'I don't know what to do.' This was echoed by Emily and Anne.

"*Tabby.* 'Wha ya may go t' bed.'

"*Branwell.* 'I'd rather do anything than that.'

"*Charlotte.* 'Why are you so glum to-night, Tabby? Oh! suppose we had each an island of our own.'

"*Branwell.* 'If we had I would choose the Island of Man.'

"*Charlotte.* 'And I would choose the Isle of Wight.'

"*Emily.* 'The Isle of Arran for me.'

"*Anne.* 'And mine shall be Guernsey.'

"We then chose who should be chief men in our islands. Branwell chose John Bull, Astley Cooper, and Leigh Hunt; Emily, Walter Scott, Mr. Lockhart, Johnny Lockhart; Anne, Michael Sadler, Lord Bentinck, Sir Henry Halford. I chose the Duke of Wellington and two sons, Christopher North and Co., and Mr. Abernethy. Here our conversation was interrupted by the, to us, dismal sound of the clock striking seven, and we were summoned off to bed. The next day we added many others to our list of men, till we got almost all the chief men of the kingdom. After this, for a long time, nothing worth noticing occurred. In June, 1828, we erected a school on a fictitious island, which was to contain 1,000 children. The manner of the building was as follows. The Island was fifty miles in circumference, and certainly appeared more like the work of enchantment than anything real," &c.

Two or three things strike me much in this fragment; one is the graphic vividness with which the time of the year, the hour of the evening, the feeling of cold and darkness outside, the sound of the night-winds sweeping over the desolate snow-covered moors, coming nearer and nearer, and at last shaking the very door of the room where they were sitting—for it opened out directly on that bleak, wide expanse—is contrasted with the glow, and busy brightness of the cheerful kitchen where these remarkable children are grouped. Tabby moves about in her quaint country-dress, frugal, peremptory, prone to find fault pretty sharply, yet allowing no one else to blame her children, we may feel sure. Another noticeable fact is the intelligent partisanship with which they choose their great men, who are almost all stanch Tories of the time. Moreover, they do not confine themselves to local heroes; their range of choice has been widened by hearing much of what is not usually considered to interest children. Little Anne, aged scarcely eight, picks out the politicians of the day for her chief men.

There is another scrap of paper, in this all but illegible handwriting, written about this time, and which gives some idea of the sources of their opinions.

THE HISTORY OF THE YEAR 1829.

"Once Papa lent my sister Maria a book. It was an old geography-book; she wrote on its blank leaf, 'Papa lent me this book.' This book is a hundred and twenty years old; it is at this moment lying before me. While I write this I am in the kitchen of the Parsonage, Haworth; Tabby, the servant, is washing up the breakfast-things, and Anne, my youngest sister (Maria was my eldest), is kneeling on a chair, looking at some cakes which Tabby has been baking for us. Emily is in the parlour, brushing the carpet. Papa and Branwell are gone to Keighley. Aunt is upstairs in her room, and I am sitting by the table writing this in the kitchen. Keighley is a small town four miles from here. Papa and Branwell are gone for the newspaper, the 'Leeds Intelligencer,' a most excellent Tory newspaper, edited by Mr. Wood, and the proprietor, Mr. Henneman. We take two and see three newspapers a week. We take the 'Leeds Intelligencer,' Tory, and the 'Leeds Mercury,' Whig, edited by Mr. Baines, and his brother, son-in-law, and his two sons, Edward and Talbot. We see the 'John Bull;' it is a high Tory, very violent. Mr. Driver lends us it, as likewise 'Blackwood's Magazine,' the most able periodical there is. The Editor is Mr. Christopher North, an old man seventy-four years of age; the 1st of April is his birth-day; his company are Timothy Tickler, Morgan O'Doherty, Macrabin Mordecai, Mullion, Warnell, and James Hogg, a man of most extraordinary genius, a Scottish shepherd. Our plays were established; 'Young Men,' June, 1826; 'Our Fellows,' July, 1827; 'Islanders,' December, 1827. These are our three great plays, that are not kept secret. Emily's and my best plays were established the 1st of December, 1827; the others March, 1828. Best plays mean secret plays; they are very nice ones. All our plays are very strange ones. Their nature I need not write on paper, for I think I shall always remember them. The 'Young Men's' play took its rise from some wooden soldiers Branwell had: 'Our Fellows' from 'Æsop's Fables;' and the 'Islanders' from several events which happened. I will sketch out the origin of our plays more explicitly if I can. First, 'Young Men.' Papa bought Branwell some wooden soldiers at Leeds; when Papa came home it was night, and we were in bed, so next morning Branwell came to our door with a box of soldiers. Emily and I jumped out of bed, and I snatched up one and exclaimed, 'This is the Duke of Wellington! This shall be the Duke!' When I had said this, Emily likewise took up one and said it should be hers; when Anne came down, she said one should be hers. Mine was the prettiest of the whole, and the tallest, and the most perfect in every part. Emily's was a grave-looking fellow, and we called him 'Gravey.' Anne's was a queer little thing, much like herself, and we called him 'Waiting-Boy.' Branwell chose his, and called him 'Buonaparte.'"

The foregoing extract shows something of the kind of reading in which the little Brontës were interested; but their desire for knowledge must have been excited in many directions, for I find a "list of painters whose works I wish to see," drawn up by Charlotte when she was scarcely thirteen:—

"Guido Reni, Julio Romano, Titian, Raphael, Michael Angelo, Correggio, Annibal Caracci, Leonardo da Vinci, Fra Bartolomeo, Carlo Cignani, Vandyke, Rubens, Bartolomeo Ramerghi."

Here is this little girl, in a remote Yorkshire parsonage, who has probably never seen anything worthy the name of a painting in her life, studying the names and characteristics of the great old Italian and Flemish masters, whose works she longs to see some time, in the dim future that lies before her! There is a paper remaining which contains minute studies of, and criticisms upon, the engravings in "Friendship's Offering for 1829;" showing how she had early formed those habits of close observation, and patient analysis of cause and effect, which served so well in after-life as handmaids to her genius.

The way in which Mr. Brontë made his children sympathise with him in his great interest in politics, must have done much to lift them above the chances of their minds being limited or tainted by petty local gossip. I take the only other remaining personal fragment out of "Tales of the Islanders;" it is a sort of apology, contained in the introduction to the second volume, for their not having been continued before; the writers had been for a long time too busy, and latterly too much absorbed in politics.

"Parliament was opened, and the great Catholic question was brought forward, and the Duke's measures were disclosed, and all was slander, violence, party-spirit, and confusion. Oh, those six months, from the time of the King's speech to the end! Nobody could write, think, or speak on any subject but the Catholic question, and the Duke of Wellington, and Mr. Peel. I remember the day when the Intelligence Extraordinary came with Mr. Peel's speech in it, containing the terms on which the Catholics were to be let in! With what eagerness Papa tore off the cover, and how we all gathered round him, and with what breathless anxiety we listened, as one by one they were disclosed, and explained, and argued upon so ably, and so well! and then when it was all out, how aunt said that she thought it was excellent, and that the Catholics could do no harm with such good security! I remember also the doubts as to whether it would pass the House of Lords, and the prophecies that it would not; and when the paper came which was to decide the question, the anxiety was almost dreadful with which we listened to the whole affair: the opening of the doors; the hush; the royal dukes in their robes, and the great duke in green sash and waistcoat; the rising of all the peeresses when he rose; the reading of his speech—Papa saying that his words were like precious gold; and lastly, the majority of one to four (sic) in favour of the Bill. But this is a digression," &c., &c.

This must have been written when she was between thirteen and fourteen.

It will be interesting to some of my readers to know what was the character of her purely imaginative writing at this period. While her description of any real occurrence is, as we have seen, homely, graphic, and forcible, when she gives way to her powers of creation, her fancy and her language alike run riot, sometimes to the very borders of apparent delirium. Of this wild weird writing, a single example will suffice. It is a letter to the editor of one of the "Little Magazines."

"Sir,—It is well known that the Genii have declared that unless they perform certain arduous duties every year, of a mysterious nature, all the worlds in the firmament will be burnt up, and gathered together in one mighty globe, which will roll in solitary grandeur through the vast wilderness of space, inhabited only by the four high princes of the Genii, till time shall be succeeded by Eternity; and the impudence of this is only to be paralleled by another of their assertions, namely, that by their magic might they can reduce the world to a desert, the purest waters to streams of livid poison, and the clearest lakes to stagnant waters, the pestilential vapours of which shall slay all living creatures, except the blood-thirsty beast of the forest, and the ravenous bird of the rock. But that in the midst of this desolation the palace of the Chief Genii shall rise sparkling in the wilderness, and the horrible howl of their war-cry shall spread over the land at morning, at noontide and night; but that they shall have their annual feast over the bones of the dead, and shall yearly rejoice with the joy of victors. I think, sir, that the horrible wickedness of this needs no remark, and therefore I haste to subscribe myself, &c.

"July 14, 1829."

It is not unlikely that the foregoing letter may have had some allegorical or political reference, invisible to our eyes, but very clear to the bright little minds for whom it was intended. Politics were evidently their grand interest; the Duke of Wellington their demi-god. All that related to him belonged to the heroic age. Did Charlotte want a knight-errant, or a devoted lover, the

Marquis of Douro, or Lord Charles Wellesley, came ready to her hand. There is hardly one of her prose-writings at this time in which they are not the principal personages, and in which their "august father" does not appear as a sort of Jupiter Tonans, or Deus ex Machinâ.

As one evidence how Wellesley haunted her imagination, I copy out a few of the titles to her papers in the various magazines.

"Liffey Castle," a Tale by Lord C. Wellesley.

"Lines to the River Aragua," by the Marquis of Douro.

"An Extraordinary Dream," by Lord C. Wellesley.

"The Green Dwarf, a Tale of the Perfect Tense," by the Lord Charles Albert Florian Wellesley.

"Strange Events," by Lord C. A. F. Wellesley.

Life in an isolated village, or a lonely country-house, presents many little occurrences which sink into the mind of childhood, there to be brooded over. No other event may have happened, or be likely to happen, for days, to push one of these aside, before it has assumed a vague and mysterious importance. Thus, children leading a secluded life are often thoughtful and dreamy: the impressions made upon them by the world without—the unusual sights of earth and sky—the accidental meetings with strange faces and figures (rare occurrences in those out-of-the-way places)—are sometimes magnified by them into things so deeply significant as to be almost supernatural. This peculiarity I perceive very strongly in Charlotte's writings at this time. Indeed, under the circumstances, it is no peculiarity. It has been common to all, from the Chaldean shepherds—"the lonely herdsman stretched on the soft grass through half a summer's day"—the solitary monk—to all whose impressions from without have had time to grow and vivify in the imagination, till they have been received as actual personifications, or supernatural visions, to doubt which would be blasphemy.

To counterbalance this tendency in Charlotte, was the strong common sense natural to her, and daily called into exercise by the requirements of her practical life. Her duties were not merely to learn her lessons, to read a certain quantity, to gain certain ideas; she had, besides, to brush rooms, to run errands up and down stairs, to help in the simpler forms of cooking, to be by turns play-fellow and monitress to her younger sisters and brother, to make and to mend, and to study economy under her careful aunt. Thus we see that, while her imagination received vivid impressions, her excellent understanding had full power to rectify them before her fancies became realities. On a scrap of paper, she has written down the following relation:—

"June 22, 1830, 6 o'clock p.m.

"Haworth, near Bradford.

"The following strange occurrence happened on the 22nd of June, 1830:—At the time Papa was very ill, confined to his bed, and so weak that he could not rise without assistance. Tabby and I were alone in the kitchen, about half-past nine ante-meridian. Suddenly we heard a knock at the door; Tabby rose and opened it. An old man appeared, standing without, who accosted her thus:—

"*Old Man.*—'Does the parson live here?'

"*Tabby.*—'Yes.'

"*Old Man.*—'I wish to see him.'

"*Tabby.*—'He is poorly in bed.'

"*Old Man.*—'I have a message for him.'

"*Tabby.*—'Who from?'

"*Old Man.*—'From the Lord.'

"*Tabby.*—'Who?'

"*Old Man.*—'The Lord. He desires me to say that the Bridegroom is coming, and that we must prepare to meet him; that the cords are about to be loosed, and the golden bowl broken; the pitcher broken at the fountain.'

"Here he concluded his discourse, and abruptly went his way. As Tabby closed the door, I asked her if she knew him. Her reply was, that she had never seen him before, nor any one like him. Though I am fully persuaded that he was some fanatical enthusiast, well meaning perhaps, but utterly ignorant of true piety; yet I could not forbear weeping at his words, spoken so unexpectedly at that particular period."

Though the date of the following poem is a little uncertain, it may be most convenient to introduce it here. It must have been written before 1833, but how much earlier there are no means of determining. I give it as a specimen of the remarkable poetical talent shown in the various diminutive writings of this time; at least, in all of them which I have been able to read.

THE WOUNDED STAG.

    Passing amid the deepest shade
      Of the wood's sombre heart,
    Last night I saw a wounded deer
      Laid lonely and apart.

    Such light as pierced the crowded boughs
      (Light scattered, scant and dim,)

Passed through the fern that formed his couch
And centred full on him.

Pain trembled in his weary limbs,
   Pain filled his patient eye,
Pain-crushed amid the shadowy fern
   His branchy crown did lie.

Where were his comrades? where his mate?
   All from his death-bed gone!
And he, thus struck and desolate,
   Suffered and bled alone.

Did he feel what a man might feel,
   Friend-left, and sore distrest?
Did Pain's keen dart, and Grief's sharp sting
   Strive in his mangled breast?

Did longing for affection lost
   Barb every deadly dart;
Love unrepaid, and Faith betrayed,
   Did these torment his heart?

No! leave to man his proper doom!
   These are the pangs that rise
Around the bed of state and gloom,
   Where Adam's offspring dies!

CHAPTER VI

This is perhaps a fitting time to give some personal description of Miss Brontë. In 1831, she was a quiet, thoughtful girl, of nearly fifteen years of age, very small in figure—"stunted" was the word she applied to herself,—but as her limbs and head were in just proportion to the slight, fragile body, no word in ever so slight a degree suggestive of deformity could properly be applied to her; with soft, thick, brown hair, and peculiar eyes, of which I find it difficult to give a description, as they appeared to me in her later life. They were large and well shaped; their colour a reddish brown; but if the iris was closely examined, it appeared to be composed of a great variety of tints. The usual expression was of quiet, listening intelligence; but now and then, on some just occasion for vivid interest or wholesome indignation, a light would shine out, as if some spiritual lamp had been kindled, which glowed behind those expressive orbs. I never saw the like in any other human creature. As for the rest of her features, they were plain, large, and ill set; but, unless you began to catalogue them, you were hardly aware of the fact, for the eyes and power of the countenance over-balanced every physical defect; the crooked mouth and the large nose were forgotten, and the whole face arrested the attention, and presently attracted all those whom she herself would have cared to attract. Her hands and feet were the smallest I ever saw; when one of the former was placed in mine, it was like the soft touch of a bird in the middle of my palm. The delicate long fingers had a peculiar fineness of sensation, which was one reason why all her handiwork, of whatever kind—writing, sewing, knitting—was so clear in its minuteness. She was remarkably neat in her whole personal attire; but she was dainty as to the fit of her shoes and gloves.

I can well imagine that the grave serious composure, which, when I knew her, gave her face the dignity of an old Venetian portrait, was no acquisition of later years, but dated from that early age when she found herself in the position of an elder sister to motherless children. But in a girl only just entered on her teens, such an expression would be called (to use a country phrase) "old-fashioned;" and in 1831, the period of which I now write, we must think of her as a little, set, antiquated girl, very quiet in manners, and very quaint in dress; for besides the influence exerted by her father's ideas concerning the simplicity of attire befitting the wife and daughters of a country clergyman, her aunt, on whom the duty of dressing her nieces principally devolved, had never been in society since she left Penzance, eight or nine years before, and the Penzance fashions of that day were still dear to her heart.

In January, 1831, Charlotte was sent to school again. This time she went as a pupil to Miss W---, who lived at Roe Head, a cheerful roomy country house, standing a little apart in a field, on the right of the road from Leeds to Huddersfield. Three tiers of old-fashioned semicircular bow windows run from basement to roof; and look down upon a long green slope of pasture-land, ending in the pleasant woods of Kirklees, Sir George Armitage's park. Although Roe Head and Haworth are not twenty miles apart, the aspect of the country is as totally dissimilar as if they enjoyed a different climate. The soft curving and heaving landscape round the former gives a stranger the idea of cheerful airiness on the heights, and of sunny warmth in the broad green valleys below. It is just such a neighbourhood as the monks loved, and traces of the old Plantagenet times are to be met with everywhere, side by side with the manufacturing interests of the West Riding of to-day. There is the park of Kirklees, full of sunny glades, speckled with black shadows of immemorial yew-trees; the grey pile of building, formerly a "House of professed Ladies;" the mouldering stone in the depth of the wood, under which Robin Hood is said to lie; close outside the park, an old stonegabled house, now a roadside inn, but which bears the name of the "Three Nuns," and has a pictured sign to correspond. And this quaint old inn is frequented by fustian-dressed mill-hands from the neighbouring worsted factories, which strew the high road from Leeds to Huddersfield, and form the centres round which future villages gather. Such are the contrasts of modes of living, and of times and seasons, brought before the traveller on the great roads that traverse the West Riding. In no other part of England, I fancy, are the centuries brought into such close, strange contact as in the district in which Roe Head is situated. Within six miles of Miss W---'s house—on the left of the road, coming from Leeds—lie the remains of Howley Hall, now the property of Lord Cardigan, but formerly belonging to a branch of the Saviles. Near to it is Lady Anne's well; "Lady Anne," according to tradition, having been worried and eaten by wolves as she sat at the well, to which the indigo-dyed factory people from Birstall and Batley woollen mills would formerly repair on Palm Sunday, when the waters possess remarkable medicinal efficacy; and it is still believed by some that they assume a strange variety of colours at six o'clock on the morning of that day.

All round the lands held by the farmer who lives in the remains of Howley Hall are stone houses of to-day, occupied by the people who are making their living and their fortunes by the woollen mills that encroach upon and shoulder out the proprietors of the ancient halls. These are to be seen in every direction, picturesque, many-gabled, with heavy stone carvings of coats of arms for heraldic ornament; belonging to decayed families, from whose ancestral lands field after field has been shorn away, by the urgency of rich manufacturers pressing hard upon necessity.

A smoky atmosphere surrounds these old dwellings of former Yorkshire squires, and blights and blackens the ancient trees that overshadow them; cinder-paths lead up to them; the ground round about is sold for building upon; but still the neighbours, though they subsist by a different state of things, remember that their forefathers lived in agricultural dependence upon the owners of these halls; and treasure up the traditions connected with the stately households that existed centuries ago. Take Oakwell Hall, for instance. It stands in a pasture-field, about a quarter of a mile from the high road. It is but that distance from the busy whirr of the steam-engines employed in the woollen mills at Birstall; and if you walk to it from Birstall Station about meal-time, you encounter strings of mill-hands, blue with woollen dye, and cranching in hungry haste over the cinder-paths bordering the high road. Turning off from this to the right, you ascend through an old pasture-field, and enter a short by-road, called the "Bloody Lane"—a walk haunted by the ghost of a certain Captain Batt, the reprobate proprietor of an old hall close by, in the days of the Stuarts. From the "Bloody Lane," overshadowed by trees, you come into the field in which Oakwell Hall is situated. It is known in the neighbourhood to be the place described as "Field Head," Shirley's residence. The enclosure in front, half court, half garden; the panelled hall, with the gallery opening into the bed-chambers running round; the barbarous peach-coloured drawing-room; the bright look-out through the garden-door upon the grassy lawns and terraces behind, where the soft-hued pigeons still love to coo and strut in the sun,—are described in "Shirley." The scenery of that fiction lies close around; the real events which suggested it took place in the immediate neighbourhood.

They show a bloody footprint in a bed-chamber of Oakwell Hall, and tell a story connected with it, and with the lane by which the house is approached. Captain Batt was believed to be far away; his family was at Oakwell; when in the dusk, one winter evening, he came stalking along the lane, and through the hall, and up the stairs, into his own room, where he vanished. He had been killed in a duel in London that very same afternoon of December 9th, 1684.

The stones of the Hall formed part of the more ancient vicarage, which an ancestor of Captain Batt's had seized in the troublous times for property which succeeded the Reformation. This Henry Batt possessed himself of houses and money without scruple; and, at last, stole the great bell of Birstall Church, for which sacrilegious theft a fine was imposed on the land, and has to be paid by the owner of the Hall to this day.

But the Oakwell property passed out of the hands of the Batts at the beginning of the last century; collateral descendants succeeded, and left this picturesque trace of their having been. In the great hall hangs a mighty pair of stag's horns, and dependent from them a printed card, recording the fact that, on the 1st of September, 1763, there was a great hunting-match, when this stag was slain; and that fourteen gentlemen shared in the chase, and dined on the spoil in that hall, along with Fairfax Fearneley, Esq., the owner. The fourteen names are given, doubtless "mighty men of yore;" but, among them all, Sir Fletcher Norton, Attorney-General, and Major-General Birch were the only ones with which I had any association in 1855. Passing on from Oakwell there lie houses right and left, which were well known to Miss Brontë when she lived at Roe Head, as the hospitable homes of some of her school-fellows. Lanes branch off for three or four miles to heaths and commons on the higher ground, which formed pleasant walks on holidays, and then comes the white gate into the field-path leading to Roe Head itself.

One of the bow-windowed rooms on the ground floor with the pleasant look-out I have described was the drawing-room; the other was the schoolroom. The dining-room was on one side of the door, and faced the road.

The number of pupils, during the year and a half Miss Brontë was there, ranged from seven to ten; and as they did not require the whole of the house for their accommodation, the third story was unoccupied, except by the ghostly idea of a lady, whose rustling silk gown was sometimes heard by the listeners at the foot of the second flight of stairs.

The kind motherly nature of Miss W---, and the small number of the girls, made the establishment more like a private family than a school. Moreover, she was a native of the district immediately surrounding Roe Head, as were the majority of her pupils. Most likely Charlotte Brontë, in coming from Haworth, came the greatest distance of all. "E.'s" home was five miles away; two other dear friends (the Rose and Jessie Yorke of "Shirley") lived still nearer; two or three came from Huddersfield; one or two from Leeds.

I shall now quote from a valuable letter which I have received from "Mary," one of these early friends; distinct and graphic in expression, as becomes a cherished associate of Charlotte Brontë's. The time referred to is her first appearance at Roe Head, on January 19th, 1831.

"I first saw her coming out of a covered cart, in very old-fashioned clothes, and looking very cold and miserable. She was coming to school at Miss W---'s. When she appeared in the schoolroom, her dress was changed, but just as old. She looked a little old woman, so short-sighted that she always appeared to be seeking something, and moving her head from side to side to catch a sight of it. She was very shy and nervous, and spoke with a strong Irish accent. When a book was given her, she dropped her head over it till her nose nearly touched it, and when she was told to hold her head up, up went the book after it, still close to her nose, so that it was not possible to help laughing."

This was the first impression she made upon one of those whose dear and valued friend she was to become in after-life. Another of the girls recalls her first sight of Charlotte, on the day she came, standing by the schoolroom window, looking out on the snowy landscape, and crying, while all the rest were at play. "E." was younger than she, and her tender heart was touched by the apparently desolate condition in which she found the oddly-dressed, odd-looking little girl that winter morning, as "sick for home she stood in tears," in a new strange place, among new strange people. Any over-demonstrative kindness would have scared the wild little maiden from Haworth; but "E." (who is shadowed forth in the Caroline Helstone of "Shirley") managed to win confidence, and was allowed to give sympathy.

To quote again from "Mary's" letter:—

"We thought her very ignorant, for she had never learnt grammar at all, and very little geography."

This account of her partial ignorance is confirmed by her other school-fellows. But Miss W--- was a lady of remarkable intelligence and of delicate tender sympathy. She gave a proof of this in her first treatment of Charlotte. The little girl was well-read, but not well-grounded. Miss W--- took her aside and told her she was afraid that she must place her in the second class for some time till she could overtake the girls of her own age in the knowledge of grammar, &c.; but poor Charlotte received this announcement with so sad a fit of crying, that Miss W---'s kind heart was softened, and she wisely perceived that, with such a girl, it would be better to place her in the first class, and allow her to make up by private study in those branches where she was deficient.

"She would confound us by knowing things that were out of our range altogether. She was acquainted with most of the short pieces of poetry that we had to learn by heart; would tell us the authors, the poems they were taken from, and sometimes repeat a page or two, and tell us the plot. She had a habit of writing in italics (printing characters), and said she had learnt it by writing in their magazine. They brought out a 'magazine' once a month, and wished it to look as like print as possible. She told us a tale out of it. No one wrote in it, and no one read it, but herself, her brother, and two sisters. She promised to show me some of these magazines, but retracted it afterwards, and would never be persuaded to do so. In our play hours she sate, or stood still, with a book, if possible. Some of us once urged her to be on our side in a game at ball. She said she had never played, and could not play. We made her try, but soon found that she could not see the ball, so we put her out. She took all our proceedings with pliable indifference, and always seemed to need a previous resolution to say 'No' to anything. She used to go and stand under the trees in the play-ground, and say it was pleasanter. She endeavoured to explain this, pointing out the shadows, the peeps of sky, &c. We understood but little of it. She said that at Cowan Bridge she used to stand in the burn, on a stone, to watch the water flow by. I told her she should have gone fishing; she said she never wanted. She always showed physical feebleness in everything. She ate no animal food at school. It was about this time I told her she was very ugly. Some years afterwards, I told her I thought I had been very impertinent. She replied, 'You did me a great deal of good, Polly, so don't repent of it.' She used to draw much better, and more quickly, than anything we had seen before, and knew much about celebrated pictures and painters. Whenever an opportunity offered of examining a picture or cut of any kind, she went over it piecemeal, with her eyes close to the paper, looking so long that we used to ask her 'what she saw in it.' She could always see plenty, and explained it very well. She made poetry and drawing at least exceedingly interesting to me; and then I got the habit, which I have yet, of referring mentally to her opinion on all matters of that kind, along with many more, resolving to describe such and such things to her, until I start at the recollection that I never shall."

To feel the full force of this last sentence—to show how steady and vivid was the impression which Miss Brontë made on those fitted to appreciate her—I must mention that the writer of this letter, dated January 18th, 1856, in which she thus speaks of constantly referring to Charlotte's opinion has never seen her for eleven years, nearly all of which have been passed among strange scenes, in a new continent, at the antipodes.

"We used to be furious politicians, as one could hardly help being in 1832. She knew the names of the two ministries; the one that resigned, and the one that succeeded and passed the Reform Bill. She worshipped the Duke of Wellington, but said that Sir Robert Peel was not to be trusted; he did not act from principle like the rest, but from expediency. I, being of the furious radical party, told her 'how could any of them trust one another; they were all of them rascals!' Then she would launch out into praises of the Duke of Wellington, referring to his actions; which I could not contradict, as I knew nothing about him. She said she had taken interest in politics ever since she was five years old. She did not get her opinions from her father—that is, not directly—but from the papers, &c., he preferred."

In illustration of the truth of this, I may give an extract from a letter to her brother, written from Roe Head, May 17th, 1832:—"Lately I had begun to think that I had lost all the interest which I used formerly to take in politics; but the extreme pleasure I felt at the news of the Reform Bill's being thrown out by the House of Lords, and of the expulsion, or resignation of Earl Grey, &c., convinced me that I have not as yet lost all my penchant for politics. I am extremely glad that aunt has consented to take in 'Fraser's Magazine;' for, though I know from your description of its general contents it will be rather uninteresting when compared with 'Blackwood,' still it will be better than remaining the whole year without being able to obtain a sight of any periodical whatever; and such would assuredly be our case, as, in the little wild moorland village where we reside, there would be no possibility of borrowing a work of that description from a circulating library. I hope with you that the present delightful weather may contribute to the perfect restoration of our dear papa's health; and that it may give aunt pleasant reminiscences of the salubrious climate of her native place," &c.

To return to "Mary's" letter.

"She used to speak of her two elder sisters, Maria and Elizabeth, who died at Cowan Bridge. I used to believe them to have been wonders of talent and kindness. She told me, early one morning, that she had just been dreaming; she had been told that she was wanted in the drawing-room, and it was Maria and Elizabeth. I was eager for her to go on, and when she said there was no more, I said, 'but go on! *Make it out!* I know you can.' She said she would not; she wished she had not dreamed, for it did not go on nicely, they were changed; they had forgotten what they used to care for. They were very fashionably dressed, and began criticising the room, &c.

"This habit of 'making out' interests for themselves that most children get who have none in actual life, was very strong in her. The whole family used to 'make out' histories, and invent characters and events. I told her sometimes they were like growing potatoes in a cellar. She said, sadly, 'Yes! I know we are!'

"Some one at school said she 'was always talking about clever people; Johnson, Sheridan, &c.' She said, 'Now you don't know the meaning of *clever*, Sheridan might be clever; yes, Sheridan was clever,—scamps often are; but Johnson hadn't a spark of cleverality in him.' No one appreciated the opinion; they made some trivial remark about 'cleverality,' and she said no more.

"This is the epitome of her life. At our house she had just as little chance of a patient hearing, for though not school-girlish, we were more intolerant. We had a rage for practicality, and laughed all poetry to scorn. Neither she nor we had any idea but that our opinions were the opinions of all the *sensible* people in the world, and we used to astonish each other at every sentence... Charlotte, at school, had no plan of life beyond what circumstances made for her. She knew that she must provide for herself, and chose her trade; at least chose to begin it once. Her idea of self-improvement ruled her even at school. It was to cultivate her tastes. She always said there was enough of hard practicality and *useful* knowledge forced on us by necessity, and that the thing most needed was to soften and refine our minds. She picked up every scrap of information concerning painting, sculpture, poetry, music, &c., as if it were gold."

What I have heard of her school days from other sources, confirms the accuracy of the details in this remarkable letter. She was an indefatigable student: constantly reading and learning; with a strong conviction of the necessity and value of education, very unusual in a girl of fifteen. She never lost a moment of time, and seemed almost to grudge the necessary leisure for relaxation and play-hours, which might be partly accounted for by the awkwardness in all games occasioned by her shortness of sight. Yet, in spite of these unsociable habits, she was a great favourite with her school-fellows. She was always ready to try and do what they wished, though not sorry when they called her awkward, and left her out of their sports. Then, at night, she was an invaluable story-teller, frightening them almost out of their wits as they lay in bed. On one occasion the effect was such that she was led to scream out aloud, and Miss W---, coming up stairs, found that one of the listeners had been seized with violent palpitations, in consequence of the excitement produced by Charlotte's story.

Her indefatigable craving for knowledge tempted Miss W--- on into setting her longer and longer tasks of reading for examination; and towards the end of the year and a half that she remained as a pupil at Roe Head, she received her first bad mark for an imperfect lesson. She had had a great quantity of Blair's "Lectures on Belles Lettres" to read; and she could not answer some of the questions upon it; Charlotte Brontë had a bad mark. Miss W--- was sorry, and regretted that she had set Charlotte so long a task. Charlotte cried bitterly. But her school-fellows were more than sorry—they were indignant. They declared that the infliction of ever so slight a punishment on Charlotte Brontë was unjust—for who had tried to do her duty like her?—and testified their feeling in a variety of ways, until Miss W---, who was in reality only too willing to pass over her good pupil's first fault, withdrew the bad mark; and the girls all returned to their allegiance except "Mary," who took her own way during the week or two that remained of the half-year, choosing to consider that Miss W---, in giving Charlotte Brontë so long a task, had forfeited her claim to obedience of the school regulations.

The number of pupils was so small that the attendance to certain subjects at particular hours, common in larger schools, was not rigidly enforced. When the girls were ready with their lessons, they came to Miss W--- to say them. She had a remarkable knack of making them feel interested in whatever they had to learn. They set to their studies, not as to tasks or duties to be got through, but with a healthy desire and thirst for knowledge, of which she had managed to make them perceive the relishing savour. They did not leave off reading and learning as soon as the compulsory pressure of school was taken away. They had been taught to think, to analyse, to reject, to appreciate. Charlotte Brontë was happy in the choice made for her of the second school to which she was sent. There was a robust freedom in the out-of-doors life of her companions. They played at merry games in the fields round the house: on Saturday half-holidays they went long scrambling walks down mysterious shady lanes, then climbing the uplands, and thus gaining extensive views over the country, about which so much had to be told, both of its past and present history.

Miss W--- must have had in great perfection the French art, "conter," to judge from her pupil's recollections of the tales she related during these long walks, of this old house, or that new mill, and of the states of society consequent on the changes involved by the suggestive dates of either building. She remembered the times when watchers or wakeners in the night heard the distant word of command, and the measured tramp of thousands of sad desperate men receiving a surreptitious military training, in preparation for some great day which they saw in their visions, when right should struggle with might and come off victorious: when the people of England, represented by the workers of Yorkshire, Lancashire, and Nottinghamshire, should make their voice heard in a terrible slogan, since their true and pitiful complaints could find no hearing in parliament. We forget, now-a-days, so rapid have been the changes for the better, how cruel was the condition of numbers of labourers at the close of the great Peninsular war. The half-ludicrous nature of some of their grievances has lingered on in tradition; the real intensity of their sufferings has become forgotten. They were maddened and desperate; and the country, in the opinion of many, seemed to be on the verge of a precipice, from which it was only saved by the prompt and resolute decision of a few in authority. Miss W--- spoke of those times; of the mysterious nightly drillings; of thousands on lonely moors; of the muttered threats of individuals too closely pressed upon by necessity to be prudent; of the overt acts, in which the burning of Cartwright's mill took a prominent place; and these things sank deep into the mind of one, at least, among her hearers.

Mr. Cartwright was the owner of a factory called Rawfolds, in Liversedge, not beyond the distance of a walk from Roe Head. He had dared to employ machinery for the dressing of woollen cloth, which was an unpopular measure in 1812, when many other circumstances conspired to make the condition of the mill-hands unbearable from the pressure of starvation and misery. Mr. Cartwright was a very remarkable man, having, as I have been told, some foreign blood in him, the traces of which were very apparent in his tall figure, dark eyes and complexion, and singular, though gentlemanly bearing. At any rate he had been much abroad, and spoke French well, of itself a suspicious circumstance to the bigoted nationality of those days. Altogether he was an unpopular man, even before he took the last step of employing shears, instead of hands, to dress his wool. He was quite aware of his unpopularity, and of the probable consequences. He had his mill prepared for an assault. He took up his lodgings in it; and the doors were strongly barricaded at night. On every step of the stairs there was placed a roller, spiked with barbed points all round, so as to impede the ascent of the rioters, if they succeeded in forcing the doors.

On the night of Saturday the 11th of April, 1812, the assault was made. Some hundreds of starving cloth-dressers assembled in the very field near Kirklees that sloped down from the house which Miss W--- afterwards inhabited, and were armed by their leaders with pistols, hatchets, and bludgeons, many of which had been extorted by the nightly bands that prowled about the country, from such inhabitants of lonely houses as had provided themselves with these means of self-defence. The silent sullen multitude marched in the dead of that spring-night to Rawfolds, and giving tongue with a great shout, roused Mr. Cartwright up to the knowledge that the long-expected attack was come. He was within walls, it is true; but against the fury of hundreds he had only four of his own workmen and five soldiers to assist him. These ten men, however, managed to keep up such a vigorous and well-directed fire of musketry that they defeated all the desperate attempts of the multitude outside to break down the doors, and force a way into the mill; and, after a conflict of twenty minutes, during which two of the assailants were killed and several wounded, they withdrew in confusion, leaving Mr. Cartwright master of the field, but so dizzy and exhausted, now the peril was past, that he forgot the nature of his defences, and injured his leg rather seriously by one of the spiked rollers, in attempting to go up his own staircase. His dwelling was near the factory. Some of the rioters vowed that, if he did not give in, they would leave this, and go to his house, and murder his wife and children. This was a terrible threat, for he had been obliged to leave his family with only one or two soldiers to defend them. Mrs. Cartwright knew what they had threatened; and on that dreadful night, hearing, as she thought, steps approaching, she snatched up her two infant children, and put them in a basket up the great chimney, common in old-fashioned Yorkshire houses. One of the two children who had been thus stowed away used to point out with pride, after she had grown up to woman's estate, the marks of musket shot, and the traces of gunpowder on the walls of her father's mill. He was the first that had offered any resistance to the progress of the "Luddites," who had become by this time so numerous as almost to assume the character of an insurrectionary army. Mr. Cartwright's conduct was so much admired by the neighbouring mill-owners that they entered into a subscription for his benefit which amounted in the end to 3,000*l*.

Not much more than a fortnight after this attack on Rawfolds, another manufacturer who employed the obnoxious machinery was shot down in broad daylight, as he was passing over Crossland Moor, which was skirted by a small plantation in which the murderers lay hidden. The readers of "Shirley" will recognise these circumstances, which were related to Miss Brontë years after they occurred, but on the very spots where they took place, and by persons who remembered full well those terrible times of insecurity to life and property on the one hand, and of bitter starvation and blind ignorant despair on the other.

Mr. Brontë himself had been living amongst these very people in 1812, as he was then clergyman at Hartshead, not three miles from Rawfolds; and, as I have mentioned, it was in these perilous times that he began his custom of carrying a loaded pistol continually about with him. For not only his Tory politics, but his love and regard for the authority of the law, made him despise the cowardice of the surrounding magistrates, who, in their dread of the Luddites, refused to interfere so as to prevent the destruction of property. The clergy of the district were the bravest men by far.

There was a Mr. Roberson of Heald's Hall, a friend of Mr. Brontë's who has left a deep impression of himself on the public mind. He lived near Heckmondwike, a large, straggling, dirty village, not two miles from Roe Head. It was principally inhabited by blanket weavers, who worked in their own cottages; and Heald's Hall is the largest house in the village, of which Mr. Roberson was the vicar. At his own cost, he built a handsome church at Liversedge, on a hill opposite the one on which his house stood, which was the first attempt in the West Riding to meet the wants of the overgrown population, and made many personal sacrifices for his opinions, both religious and political, which were of the true old-fashioned Tory stamp. He hated everything which he fancied had a tendency towards anarchy. He was loyal in every fibre to Church and King; and would have proudly laid down his life, any day, for what he believed to be right and true. But he was a man of an imperial will, and by it he bore down opposition, till tradition represents him as having something grimly demoniac about him. He was intimate with Cartwright, and aware of the attack likely to be made on his mill; accordingly, it is said, he armed himself and his household, and was prepared to come to the rescue, in the event of a signal being given that aid was needed. Thus far is likely enough. Mr. Roberson had plenty of warlike spirit in him, man of peace though he was.

But, in consequence of his having taken the unpopular side, exaggerations of his character linger as truth in the minds of the people; and a fabulous story is told of his forbidding any one to give water to the wounded Luddites, left in the mill-yard, when he rode in the next morning to congratulate his friend Cartwright on his successful defence. Moreover, this stern, fearless clergyman had the soldiers that were sent to defend the neighbourhood billeted at his house; and this deeply displeased the workpeople, who were to be intimidated by the red-coats. Although not a magistrate, he spared no pains to track out the Luddites concerned in the assassination I have mentioned; and was so successful in his acute unflinching energy, that it was believed he had been supernaturally aided; and the country people, stealing into the fields surrounding Heald's Hall on dusky winter evenings, years after this time, declared that through the windows they saw Parson Roberson dancing, in a strange red light, with black demons all whirling and eddying round him. He kept a large boys' school; and made himself both respected and dreaded by his pupils. He added a grim kind of humour to his strength of will; and the former quality suggested to his fancy strange out-of-the-way kinds of punishment for any refractory pupils: for instance, he made them stand on one leg in a corner of the schoolroom, holding a heavy book in each hand; and once, when a boy had run away home, he followed him on horseback, reclaimed him from his parents, and, tying him by a rope to the stirrup of his saddle, made him run alongside of his horse for the many miles they had to traverse before reaching Heald's Hall.

One other illustration of his character may be given. He discovered that his servant Betty had "a follower;" and, watching his time till Richard was found in the kitchen, he ordered him into the dining-room, where the pupils were all assembled. He then questioned Richard whether he had come after Betty; and on his confessing the truth, Mr. Roberson gave the word, "Off with him, lads, to the pump!" The poor lover was dragged to the court-yard, and the pump set to play upon him; and, between every drenching, the question was put to him, "Will you promise not to come after Betty again?" For a long time Richard bravely refused to give in; when "Pump again, lads!" was the order. But, at last, the poor soaked "follower" was forced to yield, and renounce his Betty.

The Yorkshire character of Mr. Roberson would be incomplete if I did not mention his fondness for horses. He lived to be a very old man, dying some time nearer to 1840 than 1830; and even after he was eighty years of age, he took great delight in breaking refractory steeds; if necessary, he would sit motionless on their backs for half-an-hour or more to bring them to. There is a story current that once, in a passion, he shot his wife's favourite horse, and buried it near a quarry, where the ground, some years after, miraculously opened and displayed the skeleton; but the real fact is, that it was an act of humanity to put a poor old horse out of misery; and that, to spare it pain, he shot it with his own hands, and buried it where, the ground sinking afterwards by the working of a coal-pit, the bones came to light. The traditional colouring shows the animus with which his memory is regarded by one set of people. By another, the neighbouring clergy, who remember him riding, in his old age, down the hill on which his house stood, upon his strong white horse—his bearing proud and dignified, his shovel hat bent over and shadowing his keen eagle eyes—going to his Sunday duty like a faithful soldier that dies in harness—who can appreciate his loyalty to conscience, his sacrifices to duty, and his stand by his religion—his memory is venerated. In his extreme old age, a rubric meeting was held, at which his clerical brethren gladly subscribed to present him with a testimonial of their deep respect and regard.

This is a specimen of the strong character not seldom manifested by the Yorkshire clergy of the Established Church. Mr. Roberson was a friend of Charlotte Brontë's father; lived within a couple of miles of Roe Head while she was at school there; and was deeply engaged in transactions, the memory of which was yet recent when she heard of them, and of the part which he had had in them.

I may now say a little on the character of the Dissenting population immediately surrounding Roe Head; for the "Tory and clergyman's daughter," "taking interest in politics ever since she was five years old," and holding frequent discussions with such of the girls as were Dissenters and Radicals, was sure to have made herself as much acquainted as she could with the condition of those to whom she was opposed in opinion.

The bulk of the population were Dissenters, principally Independents. In the village of Heckmondwike, at one end of which Roe Head is situated, there were two large chapels belonging to that denomination, and one to the Methodists, all of which were well filled two or three times on a Sunday, besides having various prayer-meetings, fully attended, on week-days. The inhabitants were a chapel-going people, very critical about the doctrine of their sermons, tyrannical to their ministers, and violent Radicals in politics. A friend, well acquainted with the place when Charlotte Brontë was at school, has described some events which occurred then among them:—

"A scene, which took place at the Lower Chapel at Heckmondwike, will give you some idea of the people at that time. When a newly-married couple made their appearance at chapel, it was the custom to sing the Wedding Anthem, just after the last prayer, and as the congregation was quitting the chapel. The band of singers who performed this ceremony expected to have money given them, and often passed the following night in drinking; at least, so said the minister of the place; and he determined to put an end to this custom. In this he was supported by many members of the chapel and congregation; but so strong was the democratic element, that he met with the most violent opposition, and was often insulted when he went into the street. A bride was expected to make her first appearance, and the minister told the singers not to perform the anthem. On their declaring they would, he had the large pew which they usually occupied locked; they broke it open: from the pulpit he told the congregation that, instead of their singing a hymn, he would read a chapter; hardly had he uttered the first word, before up rose the singers, headed by a tall, fierce-looking weaver, who gave out a hymn, and all sang it at the very top of their voices, aided by those of their friends who were in the chapel. Those who disapproved of the conduct of the singers, and sided with the minister, remained seated till the hymn was finished. Then he gave out the chapter again, read it, and preached. He was just about to conclude with prayer, when up started the singers and screamed forth another hymn. These disgraceful scenes were continued for many weeks, and so violent was the feeling, that the different parties could hardly keep from blows as they came through the chapel-yard. The minister, at last, left the place, and along with him went many of the most temperate and respectable part of the congregation, and the singers remained triumphant.

"I believe that there was such a violent contest respecting the choice of a pastor, about this time, in the Upper Chapel at Heckmondwike, that the Riot Act had to be read at a church-meeting."

Certainly, the *soi-disant* Christians who forcibly ejected Mr. Redhead at Haworth, ten or twelve years before, held a very heathen brotherhood with the *soi-disant* Christians of Heckmondwike; though the one set might be called members of the Church of England and the other Dissenters.

The letter from which I have taken the above extract relates throughout to the immediate neighbourhood of the place where Charlotte Brontë spent her school-days, and describes things as they existed at that very time. The writer says,—"Having been accustomed to the respectful manners of the lower orders in the agricultural districts, I was at first, much disgusted and somewhat alarmed at the great freedom displayed by the working classes of Heckmondwike and Gomersall to those in a station above them. The term 'lass,' was as freely applied to any young lady, as the word 'wench' is in Lancashire. The extremely untidy appearance of the villagers shocked me not a little, though I must do the housewives the justice to say that the cottages themselves were not dirty, and had an air of rough plenty about them (except when trade was bad), that I had not been accustomed to see in the farming districts. The heap of coals on one side of the house-door, and the brewing tubs on the other, and the frequent perfume of malt and hops as you walked along, proved that fire and 'home-brewed' were to be found at almost every man's hearth. Nor was hospitality, one of the main virtues of Yorkshire, wanting. Oat-cake, cheese, and beer were freely pressed upon the visitor.

"There used to be a yearly festival, half-religious, half social, held at Heckmondwike, called 'The Lecture.' I fancy it had come down from the times of the Nonconformists. A sermon was preached by some stranger at the Lower Chapel, on a weekday evening, and the next day, two sermons in succession were delivered at the Upper Chapel. Of course, the service was a very long one, and as the time was June, and the weather often hot, it used to be regarded by myself and my companions as no pleasurable way of passing the morning. The rest of the day was spent in social enjoyment; great numbers of strangers flocked to the place; booths were erected for the sale of toys and gingerbread (a sort of 'Holy Fair'); and the cottages, having had a little extra paint and white-washing, assumed quite a holiday look.

"The village of Gomersall" (where Charlotte Brontë's friend "Mary" lived with her family), "which was a much prettier place than Heckmondwike, contained a strange-looking cottage, built of rough unhewn stones, many of them projecting considerably, with uncouth heads and grinning faces carved upon them; and upon a stone above the door was cut, in large letters, 'SPITE HALL.' It was erected by a man in the village, opposite to the house of his enemy, who had just finished for himself a good house, commanding a beautiful view down the valley, which this hideous building quite shut out."

Fearless—because this people were quite familiar to all of them—amidst such a population, lived and walked the gentle Miss W---'s eight or nine pupils. She herself was born and bred among this rough, strong, fierce set, and knew the depth of goodness and loyalty that lay beneath their wild manners and insubordinate ways. And the girls talked of the little world around them, as if it were the only world that was; and had their opinions and their parties, and their fierce discussions like their elders—possibly, their betters. And among them, beloved and respected by all, laughed at occasionally by a few, but always to her face—lived, for a year and a half, the plain, short-sighted, oddly-dressed, studious little girl they called Charlotte Brontë.

CHAPTER VII

Miss Brontë left Roe Head in 1832, having won the affectionate regard both of her teacher and her school-fellows, and having formed there the two fast friendships which lasted her whole life long; the one with "Mary," who has not kept her letters; the other with "E.," who has kindly entrusted me with a large portion of Miss Brontë's correspondence with her. This she has been induced to do by her knowledge of the urgent desire on the part of Mr. Brontë that the life of his daughter should be written, and in compliance with a request from her husband that I should be permitted to have the use of these letters, without which such a task could be but very imperfectly executed. In order to shield this friend, however, from any blame or misconstruction, it is only right to state that, before granting me this privilege, she throughout most carefully and completely effaced the names of the persons and places which occurred in them; and also that such information as I have obtained from her bears reference solely to Miss Brontë and her sisters, and not to any other individuals whom I may find it necessary to allude to in connection with them.

In looking over the earlier portion of this correspondence, I am struck afresh by the absence of hope, which formed such a strong characteristic in Charlotte. At an age when girls, in general, look forward to an eternal duration of such feelings as they or their friends entertain, and can therefore see no hindrance to the fulfilment of any engagements dependent on the future state of the affections, she is surprised that "E." keeps her promise to write. In after-life, I was painfully impressed with the fact, that Miss Brontë never dared to allow herself to look forward with hope; that she had no confidence in the future; and I thought, when I heard of the sorrowful years she had passed through, that it had been this this pressure of grief which had crushed all buoyancy of expectation out of her. But it appears from the letters, that it must have been, so to speak, constitutional; or, perhaps, the deep pang of losing her two elder sisters combined with a permanent state of bodily weakness in producing her hopelessness. If her trust in God had been less strong, she would have given way to unbounded anxiety, at many a period of her life. As it was, we shall see, she made a great and successful effort to leave "her times in His hands."

After her return home, she employed herself in teaching her sisters, over whom she had had superior advantages. She writes thus, July 21st, 1832, of her course of life at the parsonage:—

"An account of one day is an account of all. In the morning, from nine o'clock till half-past twelve, I instruct my sisters, and draw; then we walk till dinner-time. After dinner I sew till tea-time, and after tea I either write, read, or do a little fancy-work, or draw, as I please. Thus, in one delightful, though somewhat monotonous course, my life is passed. I have been only out twice to tea since I came home. We are expecting company this afternoon, and on Tuesday next we shall have all the female teachers of the Sunday-school to tea."

I may here introduce a quotation from a letter which I have received from "Mary" since the publication of the previous editions of this memoir.

"Soon after leaving school she admitted reading something of Cobbett's. 'She did not like him,' she said; 'but all was fish that came to her net.' At this time she wrote to me that reading and drawing were the only amusements she had, and that her supply of books was very small in proportion to her wants. She never spoke of her aunt. When I saw Miss Branwell she was a very precise person, and looked very odd, because her dress, &c., was so utterly out of fashion. She corrected one of us once for using the word 'spit' or 'spitting.' She made a great favourite of Branwell. She made her nieces sew, with purpose or without, and as far as possible discouraged any other culture. She used to keep the girls sewing charity clothing, and maintained to me that it was not for the good of the recipients, but of the sewers. 'It was proper for them to do it,' she said. Charlotte never was 'in wild excitement' that I know of. When in health she used to talk better, and indeed when in low spirits never spoke at all. She needed her best spirits to say what was in her heart, for at other times she had not courage. She never gave decided opinions at such times...

"Charlotte said she could get on with any one who had a bump at the top of their heads (meaning conscientiousness). I found that I seldom differed from her, except that she was far too tolerant of stupid people, if they had a grain of kindness in them."

It was about this time that Mr. Brontë provided his children with a teacher in drawing, who turned out to be a man of considerable talent, but very little principle. Although they never attained to anything like proficiency, they took great interest in acquiring this art; evidently, from an instinctive desire to express their powerful imaginations in visible forms. Charlotte told me, that at this period of her life, drawing, and walking out with her sisters, formed the two great pleasures and relaxations of her day.

The three girls used to walk upwards toward the "purple-black" moors, the sweeping surface of which was broken by here and there a stone-quarry; and if they had strength and time to go far enough, they reached a waterfall, where the beck fell over some rocks into the "bottom." They seldom went downwards through the village. They were shy of meeting even familiar faces, and were scrupulous about entering the house of the very poorest uninvited. They were steady teachers at the Sunday-School, a habit which Charlotte kept up very faithfully, even after she was left alone; but they never faced their kind voluntary, and always preferred the solitude and freedom of the moors.

* * * * *

In the September of this year, Charlotte went to pay her first visit to her friend "E." It took her into the neighbourhood of Roe Head, and brought her into pleasant contact with many of her old school-fellows. After this visit she and her friend seem to have agreed to correspond in French, for the sake of improvement in the language. But this improvement could not be great, when it could only amount to a greater familiarity with dictionary words, and when there was no one to explain to them that a verbal translation of English idioms hardly constituted French composition; but the effort was laudable, and of itself shows how willing they both were to carry on the education which they had begun under Miss W-. I will give an extract which, whatever may be thought of the language, is graphic enough, and presents us with a happy little family picture; the eldest sister returning home to the two younger, after a fortnight's absence.

"J'arrivait à Haworth en parfaite sauveté sans le moindre accident ou malheur. Mes petites sœurs couraient hors de la maison pour me rencontrer aussitôt que la voiture se fit voir, et elles m'embrassaient avec autant d'empressement et de plaisir comme si j'avais été absente pour plus d'an. Mon Papa, ma Tante, et le monsieur dent men frère avoit parlé, furent tous assemblés dans le Salon, et en peu de temps je m'y rendis aussi. C'est souvent l'ordre du Ciel que quand on a perdu un plaisir il y en a un autre prêt à prendre sa place. Ainsi je venois de partir de très-chers amis, mais tout à l'heure je revins à des parens aussi chers et bon dans le moment. Même que vous me perdiez (ose-je croire que mon départ vous était un chagrin?) vous attendites l'arrivée de votre frère, et de votre sœur. J'ai donné à mes sœurs les pommes que vous leur envoyiez avec tant de bonté; elles disent qu'elles sont sûr que Mademoiselle E. est très-aimable et bonne; l'une et l'autre sont extrêmement impatientes de vous voir; j'espère qu'en peu de mois elles auront ce plaisir."

But it was some time yet before the friends could meet, and meanwhile they agreed to correspond once a month. There were no events to chronicle in the Haworth letters. Quiet days, occupied in reaching, and feminine occupations in the house, did not present much to write about; and Charlotte was naturally driven to criticise books.

Of these there were many in different plights, and according to their plight, kept in different places. The well-bound were ranged in the sanctuary of Mr. Brontë's study; but the purchase of books was a necessary luxury to him, but as it was often a choice between binding an old one, or buying a new one, the familiar volume, which had been hungrily read by all the members of the family, was sometimes in such a condition that the bedroom shelf was considered its fitting place. Up and down the house were to be found many standard works of a solid kind. Sir Walter Scott's writings, Wordsworth's and Southey's poems were among the lighter literature; while, as having a character of their own—earnest, wild, and occasionally fanatical—may be named some of the books which came from the Branwell side of the family—from the Cornish followers of the saintly John Wesley—and which are touched on in the account of the works to which Caroline Helstone had access in "Shirley:"—"Some venerable Lady's Magazines, that had once performed a voyage with their owner, and undergone a storm"—(possibly part of the relics of Mrs. Brontë's possessions, contained in the ship wrecked on the coast of Cornwall)—"and whose pages were stained with salt water; some mad Methodist Magazines full of miracles and apparitions, and preternatural warnings, ominous dreams, and frenzied fanaticisms; and the equally mad letters of Mrs. Elizabeth Rowe from the Dead to the Living."

Mr. Brontë encouraged a taste for reading in his girls; and though Miss Branwell kept it in due bounds, by the variety of household occupations, in which she expected them not merely to take a part, but to become proficients, thereby occupying regularly a good portion of every day, they were allowed to get books from the circulating library at Keighley; and many a happy walk, up those long four miles, must they have had, burdened with some new book, into which they peeped as they hurried home. Not that the books were what would generally be called new; in the beginning of 1833, the two friends seem almost simultaneously to have fallen upon "Kenilworth," and Charlotte writes as follows about it:—

"I am glad you like 'Kenilworth;' it is certainly more resembling a romance than a novel: in my opinion, one of the most interesting works that ever emanated from the great Sir Walter's pen. Varney is certainly the personification of consummate villainy; and in the delineation of his dark and profoundly artful mind, Scott exhibits a wonderful knowledge of human nature, as well as a surprising skill in embodying his perceptions, so as to enable others to become participators in that knowledge."

Commonplace as this extract may seem, it is noteworthy on two or three accounts: in the first place, instead of discussing the plot or story, she analyses the character of Varney; and next, she, knowing nothing of the world, both from her youth and her isolated position, has yet been so accustomed to hear "human nature" distrusted, as to receive the notion of intense and artful villainy without surprise.

What was formal and set in her way of writing to "E." diminished as their personal acquaintance increased, and as each came to know the home of the other; so that small details concerning people and places had their interest and their significance. In the summer of 1833, she wrote to invite her friend to come and pay her a visit. "Aunt thought it would be better" (she says) "to defer it until about the middle of summer, as the winter, and even the spring seasons, are remarkably cold and bleak among our mountains."

The first impression made on the visitor by the sisters of her school-friend was, that Emily was a tall, long-armed girl, more fully grown than her elder sister; extremely reserved in manner. I distinguish reserve from shyness, because I imagine shyness would please, if it knew how; whereas, reserve is indifferent whether it pleases or not. Anne, like her eldest sister, was shy; Emily was reserved.

Branwell was rather a handsome boy, with "tawny" hair, to use Miss Brontë's phrase for a more obnoxious colour. All were very clever, original, and utterly different to any people or family "E." had ever seen before. But, on the whole, it was a happy visit to all parties. Charlotte says, in writing to "E.," just after her return home—"Were I to tell you of the impression you have made on every one here, you would accuse me of flattery. Papa and aunt are continually adducing you as an example for me to shape my actions and behaviour by. Emily and Anne say 'they never saw any one they liked so well as you.' And Tabby, whom you have absolutely fascinated, talks a great deal more nonsense about your ladyship than I care to repeat. It is now so dark that, notwithstanding the singular property of seeing in the night-time, which the young ladies at Roe Head used to attribute to me, I can scribble no longer."

To a visitor at the parsonage, it was a great thing to have Tabby's good word. She had a Yorkshire keenness of perception into character, and it was not everybody she liked.

Haworth is built with an utter disregard of all sanitary conditions: the great old churchyard lies above all the houses, and it is terrible to think how the very water-springs of the pumps below must be poisoned. But this winter of 1833-4 was particularly wet and rainy, and there were an unusual number of deaths in the village. A dreary season it was to the family in the parsonage: their usual walks obstructed by the spongy state of the moors—the passing and funeral bells so frequently tolling, and filling the heavy air with their mournful sound— and, when they were still, the "chip, chip," of the mason, as he cut the grave-stones in a shed close by. In many, living, as it were, in a churchyard, and with all the sights and sounds connected with the last offices to the dead things of everyday occurrence, the very familiarity would have bred indifference. But it was otherwise with Charlotte Brontë. One of her friends says:—"I have seen her turn pale and feel faint when, in Hartshead church, some one accidentally remarked that we were walking over graves.

Charlotte was certainly afraid of death. Not only of dead bodies, or dying people. She dreaded it as something horrible. She thought we did not know how long the 'moment of dissolution' might really be, or how terrible. This was just such a terror as only hypochondriacs can provide for themselves. She told me long ago that a misfortune was often preceded by the dream frequently repeated which she gives to 'Jane Eyre,' of carrying a little wailing child, and being unable to still it. She described herself as having the most painful sense of pity for the little thing, lying *inert*, as sick children do, while she walked about in some gloomy place with it, such as the aisle of Haworth Church. The misfortunes she mentioned were not always to herself. She thought such sensitiveness to omens was like the cholera, present to susceptible people,—some feeling more, some less."

About the beginning of 1834, "E." went to London for the first time. The idea of her friend's visit seems to have stirred Charlotte strangely. She appears to have formed her notions of its probable consequences from some of the papers in the "British Essayists," "The Rambler," "The Mirror," or "The Lounger," which may have been among the English classics on the parsonage bookshelves; for she evidently imagines that an entire change of character for the worse is the usual effect of a visit to "the great metropolis," and is delighted to find that "E." is "E." still. And, as her faith in her friend's stability is restored, her own imagination is deeply moved by the idea of what great wonders are to be seen in that vast and famous city.

"Haworth, February 20th, 1834.

"Your letter gave me real and heartfelt pleasure, mingled with no small share of astonishment. Mary had previously informed me of your departure for London, and I had not ventured to calculate on any communication from you while surrounded by the splendours and novelties of that great city, which has been called the mercantile metropolis of Europe. Judging from human nature, I thought that a little country girl, for the first time in a situation so well calculated to excite curiosity, and to distract attention, would lose all remembrance, for a time at least, of distant and familiar objects, and give herself up entirely to the fascination of those scenes which were then presented to her view. Your kind, interesting, and most welcome epistle showed me, however, that I had been both mistaken and uncharitable in these suppositions. I was greatly amused at the tone of nonchalance which you assumed, while treating of London and its wonders. Did you not feel awed while gazing at St. Paul's and Westminster Abbey? Had you no feeling of intense and ardent interest, when in St. James's you saw the palace where so many of England's kings have held their courts, and beheld the representations of their persons on the walls? You should not be too much afraid of appearing *country-bred*; the magnificence of London has drawn exclamations of astonishment from travelled men, experienced in the world, its wonders and beauties. Have you yet seen anything of the great personages whom the sitting of Parliament now detains in London—the Duke of Wellington, Sir Robert Peel, Earl Grey, Mr. Stanley, Mr. O'Connell? If I were you, I would not be too anxious to spend my time in reading whilst in town. Make use of your own eyes for the purposes of observation now, and, for a time at least, lay aside the spectacles with which authors would furnish us."

In a postscript she adds:—

"Will you be kind enough to inform me of the number of performers in the King's military band?"

And in something of the same strain she writes on

"June 19th.

"My own Dear E.,

"I may rightfully and truly call you so now. You *have* returned or *are* returning from London—from the great city which is to me as apocryphal as Babylon, or Nineveh, or ancient Rome. You are withdrawing from the world (as it is called), and bringing with you—if your letters enable me to form a correct judgment—a heart as unsophisticated, as natural, as true, as that you carried there. I am slow, *very* slow, to believe the protestations of another; I know my own sentiments, I can read my own mind, but the minds of the rest of man and woman kind are to me sealed volumes, hieroglyphical scrolls, which I cannot easily either unseal or decipher. Yet time, careful study, long acquaintance, overcome most difficulties; and, in your case, I think they have succeeded well in bringing to light and construing that hidden language, whose turnings, windings, inconsistencies, and obscurities, so frequently baffle the researches of the honest observer of human nature . . . I am truly grateful for your mindfulness of so obscure a person as myself, and I hope the pleasure is not altogether selfish; I trust it is partly derived from the consciousness that my friend's character is of a higher, a more steadfast order than I was once perfectly aware of. Few girls would have done as you have done—would have beheld the glare, and glitter, and dazzling display of London with dispositions so unchanged, heart so uncontaminated. I see no affectation in your letters, no trifling, no frivolous contempt of plain, and weak admiration of showy persons and things."

In these days of cheap railway trips, we may smile at the idea of a short visit to London having any great effect upon the character, whatever it may have upon the intellect. But her London—her great apocryphal city—was the "town" of a century before, to which giddy daughters dragged unwilling papas, or went with injudicious friends, to the detriment of all their better qualities, and sometimes to the ruin of their fortunes; it was the Vanity Fair of the "Pilgrim's Progress" to her.

But see the just and admirable sense with which she can treat a subject of which she is able to overlook all the bearings.

"Haworth, July 4th, 1834.

"In your last, you request me to tell you of your faults. Now, really, how can you be so foolish! I *won't* tell you of your faults, because I don't know them. What a creature would that be, who, after receiving an affectionate and kind letter from a beloved friend, should sit down and write a catalogue of defects by way of answer! Imagine me doing so, and then consider what epithets you would bestow on me. Conceited, dogmatical, hypocritical, little humbug, I should think, would be the mildest. Why, child! I've neither time nor inclination to reflect on your *faults* when you are so far from me, and when, besides, kind letters and presents, and so forth, are continually bringing forth your goodness in the most prominent light. Then, too, there are judicious relations always round you, who can much better discharge that unpleasant office. I have no doubt their advice is completely at your service; why then should I intrude mine? If you will not hear them, it will be vain though one should rise from the dead to instruct you. Let us have no more nonsense, if you love me. Mr. --- is going to be married, is he? Well, his wife elect appeared to me to be a clever and amiable lady, as far as I could judge from the little I saw of her, and from your account. Now to that flattering sentence must I tack on a list of her faults? You say it is in contemplation for you to leave ---. I am sorry for it.

--- is a pleasant spot, one of the old family halls of England, surrounded by lawn and woodland, speaking of past times, and suggesting (to me at least) happy feelings. M. thought you grown less, did she? I am not grown a bit, but as short and dumpy as ever. You ask me to recommend you some books for your perusal. I will do so in as few words as I can. If you like poetry, let it be first-rate; Milton, Shakspeare, Thomson, Goldsmith, Pope (if you will, though I don't admire him), Scott, Byron, Campbell, Wordsworth, and Southey. Now don't be startled at the names of Shakspeare and Byron. Both these were great men, and their works are like themselves. You will know how to choose the good, and to avoid the evil; the finest passages are always the purest, the bad are invariably revolting; you will never wish to read them over twice. Omit the comedies of Shakspeare, and the Don Juan, perhaps the Cain, of Byron, though the latter is a magnificent poem, and read the rest fearlessly; that must indeed be a depraved mind which can gather evil from Henry VIII., from Richard III., from Macbeth, and Hamlet, and Julius Cæsar. Scott's sweet, wild, romantic poetry can do you no harm. Nor can Wordsworth's, nor Campbell's, nor Southey's—the greatest part at least of his; some is certainly objectionable. For history, read Hume, Rollin, and the Universal History, if you can; I never did. For fiction, read Scott alone; all novels after his are worthless. For biography, read Johnson's Lives of the Poets, Boswell's Life of Johnson, Southey's Life of Nelson, Lockhart's Life of Burns, Moore's Life of Sheridan, Moore's Life of Byron, Wolfe's Remains. For natural history, read Bewick and Audubon, and Goldsmith and White's history of Selborne. For divinity, your brother will advise you there. I can only say, adhere to standard authors, and avoid novelty."

From this list, we see that she must have had a good range

of books from which to choose her own reading. It is evident, that the womanly consciences of these two correspondents were anxiously alive to many questions discussed among the stricter religionists. The morality of Shakspeare needed the confirmation of Charlotte's opinion to the sensitive "E.;" and a little later, she inquired whether dancing was objectionable, when indulged in for an hour or two in parties of boys and girls. Charlotte replies, "I should hesitate to express a difference of opinion from Mr. ---, or from your excellent sister, but really the matter seems to me to stand thus. It is allowed on all hands, that the sin of dancing consists not in the mere action of 'shaking the shanks' (as the Scotch say), but in the consequences that usually attend it; namely, frivolity and waste of time; when it is used only, as in the case you state, for the exercise and amusement of an hour among young people (who surely may without any breach of God's commandments be allowed a little light-heartedness), these consequences cannot follow. Ergo (according to my manner of arguing), the amusement is at such times perfectly innocent."

Although the distance between Haworth and B--- was but seventeen miles, it was difficult to go straight from the one to the other without hiring a gig or vehicle of some kind for the journey. Hence a visit from Charlotte required a good deal of pre-arrangement. The Haworth gig was not always to be had; and Mr. Brontë was often unwilling to fall into any arrangement for meeting at Bradford or other places, which would occasion trouble to others. The whole family had an ample share of that sensitive pride which led them to dread incurring obligations, and to fear "outstaying their welcome" when on any visit. I am not sure whether Mr. Brontë did not consider distrust of others as a part of that knowledge of human nature on which he piqued himself. His precepts to this effect, combined with Charlotte's lack of hope, made her always fearful of loving too much; of wearying the objects of her affection; and thus she was often trying to restrain her warm feelings, and was ever chary of that presence so invariably welcome to her true friends. According to this mode of acting, when she was invited for a month, she stayed but a fortnight amidst "E.'s" family, to whom every visit only endeared her the more, and by whom she was received with that kind of quiet gladness with which they would have greeted a sister.

She still kept up her childish interest in politics. In March, 1835, she writes: "What do you think of the course politics are taking? I make this enquiry, because I now think you take a wholesome interest in the matter; formerly you did not care greatly about it. B., you see, is triumphant. Wretch! I am a hearty hater, and if there is any one I thoroughly abhor, it is that man. But the Opposition is divided, Red-hots, and Luke-warms; and the Duke (par excellence *the* Duke) and Sir Robert Peel show no signs of insecurity, though they have been twice beat; so 'Courage, mon amie,' as the old chevaliers used to say, before they joined battle."

In the middle of the summer of 1835, a great family plan was mooted at the parsonage. The question was, to what trade or profession should Branwell be brought up? He was now nearly eighteen; it was time to decide. He was very clever, no doubt; perhaps to begin with, the greatest genius in this rare family. The sisters hardly recognised their own, or each others' powers, but they knew *his*. The father, ignorant of many failings in moral conduct, did proud homage to the great gifts of his son; for Branwell's talents were readily and willingly brought out for the entertainment of others. Popular admiration was sweet to him. And this led to his presence being sought at "arvills" and all the great village gatherings, for the Yorkshiremen have a keen relish for intellect; and it likewise procured him the undesirable distinction of having his company recommended by the landlord of the Black Bull to any chance traveller who might happen to feel solitary or dull over his liquor. "Do you want some one to help you with your bottle, sir? If you do, I'll send up for Patrick" (so the villagers called him till the day of his death, though in his own family he was always "Branwell"). And while the messenger went, the landlord entertained his guest with accounts of the wonderful talents of the boy, whose precocious cleverness, and great conversational powers, were the pride of the village. The attacks of ill health to which Mr. Brontë had been subject of late years, rendered it not only necessary that he should take his dinner alone (for the sake of avoiding temptations to unwholesome diet), but made it also desirable that he should pass the time directly succeeding his meals in perfect quiet. And this necessity, combined with due attention to his parochial duties, made him partially ignorant how his son employed himself out of lesson-time. His own youth had been spent among people of the same conventional rank as those into whose companionship Branwell was now thrown; but he had had a strong will, and an earnest and persevering ambition, and a resoluteness of purpose which his weaker son wanted.

It is singular how strong a yearning the whole family had towards the art of drawing. Mr. Brontë had been very solicitous to get them good instruction; the girls themselves loved everything connected with it—all descriptions or engravings of great pictures; and, in default of good ones, they would take and analyse any print or drawing which came in their way, and find out how much thought had gone to its composition, what ideas it was intended to suggest, and what it *did* suggest. In the same spirit, they laboured to design imaginations of their own; they lacked the power of execution, not of conception. At one time, Charlotte had the notion of making her living as an artist, and wearied her eyes in drawing with pre-Raphaelite minuteness, but not with pre-Raphaelite accuracy, for she drew from fancy rather than from nature.

But they all thought there could be no doubt about Branwell's talent for drawing. I have seen an oil painting of his, done I know not when, but probably about this time. It was a group of his sisters, life-size, three-quarters' length; not much better than sign-painting, as to manipulation; but the likenesses were, I should think, admirable. I could only judge of the fidelity with which the other two were depicted, from the striking resemblance which Charlotte, upholding the great frame of canvas, and consequently standing right behind it, bore to her own representation, though it must have been ten years and more since the portraits were taken. The picture was divided, almost in the middle, by a great pillar. On the side of the column which was lighted by the sun, stood Charlotte, in the womanly dress of that day of gigot sleeves and large collars. On the deeply shadowed side, was Emily, with Anne's gentle face resting on her shoulder. Emily's countenance struck me as full of power; Charlotte's of solicitude; Anne's of tenderness. The two younger seemed hardly to have attained their full growth, though Emily was taller than Charlotte; they had cropped hair, and a more girlish dress. I remember looking on those two sad, earnest, shadowed faces, and wondering whether I could trace the mysterious expression which is said to foretell an early death. I had some fond superstitious hope that the column divided their fates from hers, who stood apart in the canvas, as in life she survived. I liked to see that the bright side of the pillar was towards *her*—that the light in the picture fell on *her*: I might more truly have sought in her presentment—nay, in her living face—for the sign of death—in her prime. They were good likenesses, however badly executed. From thence I should guess his family augured truly that, if Branwell had but the opportunity, and, alas! had but the moral qualities, he might turn out a great painter.

The best way of preparing him to become so appeared to be to send him as a pupil to the Royal Academy. I dare say he longed and yearned to follow this path, principally because it would lead him to that mysterious London—that Babylon the great—which seems to have filled the imaginations and haunted the minds of all the younger members of this recluse family. To Branwell it was more than a vivid imagination, it was an impressed reality. By dint of studying maps, he was as well acquainted with it, even down to its by-ways, as if he had lived there. Poor misguided fellow! this craving to see and know London, and that stronger craving after fame, were never to be satisfied. He was to die at the end of a short and blighted life. But in this year of 1835, all his home kindred were thinking how they could best forward his views, and how help him up to the pinnacle where he desired to be. What their plans were, let Charlotte explain. These are not the first sisters who have laid their lives as a sacrifice before their brother's idolized wish. Would to God they might be the last who met with such a miserable return!

"Haworth, July 6th, 1835.

"I had hoped to have had the extreme pleasure of seeing you at Haworth this summer, but human affairs are mutable, and human resolutions must bend to the course of events. We are all about to divide, break up, separate. Emily is going to school, Branwell is going to London, and I am going to be a governess. This last determination I formed myself, knowing that I should have to take the step sometime, 'and better sune as syne,' to use the Scotch proverb; and knowing well that papa would have enough to do with his limited income, should Branwell be placed at the Royal Academy, and Emily at Roe Head. Where am I going to reside? you will ask. Within four miles of you, at a place neither of us is unacquainted with, being no other than the identical Roe Head mentioned above. Yes! I am going to teach in the very school where I was myself taught. Miss W--- made me the offer, and I preferred it to one or two proposals of private governess-ship, which I had before received. I am sad—very sad—at the thoughts of leaving home; but duty—necessity—these are stern mistresses, who will not be disobeyed. Did I not once say you ought to be thankful for your independence? I felt what I said at the time, and I repeat it now with double earnestness; if anything would cheer me, it is the idea of being so near you. Surely, you and Polly will come and see me; it would be wrong in me to doubt it; you were never unkind yet. Emily and I leave home on the 27th of this month; the idea of being together consoles us both somewhat, and, truth, since I must enter a situation, 'My lines have fallen in pleasant places.' I both love and respect Miss W-."

CHAPTER VIII

On the 29th of July, 1835, Charlotte, now a little more than nineteen years old, went as teacher to Miss W---'s. Emily accompanied her as a pupil; but she became literally ill from home-sickness, and could not settle to anything, and after passing only three months at Roe Head, returned to the parsonage and the beloved moors.

Miss Brontë gives the following reasons as those which prevented Emily's remaining at school, and caused the substitution of her younger sister in her place at Miss W---'s:—

"My sister Emily loved the moors. Flowers brighter than the rose bloomed in the blackest of the heath for her;—out of a sullen hollow in a livid hill-side, her mind could make an Eden. She found in the bleak solitude many and dear delights; and not the least and best-loved was—liberty. Liberty was the breath of Emily's nostrils; without it she perished. The change from her own home to a school, and from her own very noiseless, very secluded, but unrestricted and unartificial mode of life, to one of disciplined routine (though under the kindest auspices), was what she failed in enduring. Her nature proved here too strong for her fortitude. Every morning, when she woke, the vision of home and the moors rushed on her, and darkened and saddened the day that lay before her. Nobody knew what ailed her but me. I knew only too well. In this struggle her health was quickly broken: her white face, attenuated form, and failing strength, threatened rapid decline. I felt in my heart she would die, if she did not go home, and with this conviction obtained her recall. She had only been three months at school; and it was some years before the experiment of sending her from home was again ventured on."

This physical suffering on Emily's part when absent from Haworth, after recurring several times under similar circumstances, became at length so much an acknowledged fact, that whichever was obliged to leave home, the sisters decided that Emily must remain there, where alone she could enjoy anything like good health. She left it twice again in her life; once going as teacher to a school in Halifax for six months, and afterwards accompanying Charlotte to Brussels for ten. When at home, she took the principal part of the cooking upon herself, and did all the household ironing; and after Tabby grew old and infirm, it was Emily who made all the bread for the family; and any one passing by the kitchen-door, might have seen her studying German out of an open book, propped up before her, as she kneaded the dough; but no study, however interesting, interfered with the goodness of the bread, which was always light and excellent. Books were, indeed, a very common sight in that kitchen; the girls were taught by their father theoretically, and by their aunt, practically, that to take an active part in all household work was, in their position, woman's simple duty; but in their careful employment of time, they found many an odd five minutes for reading while watching the cakes, and managed the union of two kinds of employment better than King Alfred.

Charlotte's life at Miss W---'s was a very happy one, until her health failed. She sincerely loved and respected the former schoolmistress, to whom she was now become both companion and friend. The girls were hardly strangers to her, some of them being younger sisters of those who had been her own playmates. Though the duties of the day might be tedious and monotonous, there were always two or three happy hours to look forward to in the evening, when she and Miss W--- sat together—sometimes late into the night—and had quiet pleasant conversations, or pauses of silence as agreeable, because each felt that as soon as a thought or remark occurred which they wished to express, there was an intelligent companion ready to sympathise, and yet they were not compelled to "make talk."

Miss W--- was always anxious to afford Miss Brontë every opportunity of recreation in her power; but the difficulty often was to persuade her to avail herself of the invitations which came, urging her to spend Saturday and Sunday with "E." and "Mary," in their respective homes, that lay within the distance of a walk. She was too apt to consider, that allowing herself a holiday was a dereliction of duty, and to refuse herself the necessary change, from something of an over-ascetic spirit, betokening a loss of healthy balance in either body or mind. Indeed, it is clear that such was the case, from a passage, referring to this time, in the letter of "Mary" from which I have before given extracts.

"Three years after—" (the period when they were at school together)—"I heard that she had gone as teacher to Miss W---'s. I went to see her, and asked how she could give so much for so little money, when she could live without it. She owned that, after clothing herself and Anne, there was nothing left, though she had hoped to be able to save something. She confessed it was not brilliant, but what could she do? I had nothing to answer. She seemed to have no interest or pleasure beyond the feeling of duty, and, when she could get, used to sit alone, and 'make out.' She told me afterwards, that one evening she had sat in the dressing-room until it was quite dark, and then observing it all at once, had taken sudden fright." No doubt she remembered this well when she described a similar terror getting hold upon Jane Eyre. She says in the story, "I sat looking at the white bed and overshadowed walls—occasionally turning a fascinated eye towards the gleaming mirror—I began to recall what I had heard of dead men troubled in their graves . . . I endeavoured to be firm; shaking my hair from my eyes, I lifted my head and tried to look boldly through the dark room; at this moment, a ray from the moon penetrated some aperture in the blind. No! moon light was still, and this stirred . . . prepared as my mind was for horror, shaken as my nerves were by agitation, I thought the swift-darting beam was a herald of some coming vision from another world. My heart beat thick, my head grew hot; a sound filled my ears which I deemed the rustling of wings; something seemed near me." {4}

"From that time," Mary adds, "her imaginations became gloomy or frightful; she could not help it, nor help thinking. She could not forget the gloom, could not sleep at night, nor attend in the day.

"She told me that one night, sitting alone, about this time, she heard a voice repeat these lines:

> "'Come thou high and holy feeling,
> Shine o'er mountain, flit o'er wave,
> Gleam like light o'er dome and shielding.'

"There were eight or ten more lines which I forget. She insisted that she had not made them, that she had heard a voice repeat them. It is possible that she had read them, and unconsciously recalled them. They are not in the volume of poems which the sisters published. She repeated a verse of Isaiah, which she said had inspired them, and which I have forgotten. Whether the lines were recollected or invented, the tale proves such habits of sedentary, monotonous solitude of thought as would have shaken a feebler mind."

Of course, the state of health thus described came on gradually, and is not to be taken as a picture of her condition in 1836. Yet even then there is a despondency in some of her expressions, that too sadly reminds one of some of Cowper's letters. And it is remarkable how deeply his poems impressed her. His words, his verses, came more frequently to her memory, I imagine, than those of any other poet.

"Mary" says: "Cowper's poem, 'The Castaway,' was known to them all, and they all at times appreciated, or almost appropriated it. Charlotte told me once that Branwell had done so; and though his depression was the result of his faults, it was in no other respect different from hers. Both were not mental but physical illnesses. She was well aware of this, and would ask how that mended matters, as the feeling was there all the same, and was not removed by knowing the cause. She had a larger religious toleration than a person would have who had never questioned, and the manner of recommending religion was always that of offering comfort, not fiercely enforcing a duty. One time I mentioned that some one had asked me what religion I was of (with the view of getting me for a partizan), and that I had said that that was between God and me;—Emily (who was lying on the hearth-rug) exclaimed, 'That's right.' This was all I ever heard Emily say on religious subjects. Charlotte was free from religious depression when in tolerable health; when that failed, her depression returned. You have probably seen such instances. They don't get over their difficulties; they forget them, when their stomach (or whatever organ it is that inflicts such misery on sedentary people) will let them. I have heard her condemn Socinianism, Calvinism, and many other 'isms' inconsistent with Church of Englandism. I used to wonder at her acquaintance with such subjects."

"May 10th, 1836.

"I was struck with the note you sent me with the umbrella; it showed a degree of interest in my concerns which I have no right to expect from any earthly creature. I won't play the hypocrite; I won't answer your kind, gentle, friendly questions in the way you wish me to. Don't deceive yourself by imagining I have a bit of real goodness about me. My darling, if I were like you, I should have my face Zion-ward, though prejudice and error might occasionally fling a mist over the glorious vision before me—but I *am not like you*. If you knew my thoughts, the dreams that absorb me, and the fiery imagination that at times eats me up, and makes me feel society, as it is, wretchedly insipid, you would pity and I dare say despise me. But I know the treasures of the *Bible*; I love and adore them. I can *see* the

Well of Life in all its clearness and brightness; but when I stoop down to drink of the pure waters they fly from my lips as if I were Tantalus.

"You are far too kind and frequent in your invitations. You puzzle me. I hardly know how to refuse, and it is still more embarrassing to accept. At any rate, I cannot come this week, for we are in the very thickest melée of the Repetitions. I was hearing the terrible fifth section when your note arrived. But Miss Wooler says I must go to Mary next Friday, as she promised for me on Whit-Sunday; and on Sunday morning I will join you at church, if it be convenient, and stay till Monday. There's a free and easy proposal! Miss W--- has driven me to it. She says her character is implicated."

Good, kind Miss W---! however monotonous and trying were the duties Charlotte had to perform under her roof, there was always a genial and thoughtful friend watching over her, and urging her to partake of any little piece of innocent recreation that might come in her way. And in those Midsummer holidays of 1836, her friend E. came to stay with her at Haworth, so there was one happy time secured.

Here follows a series of letters, not dated, but belonging to the latter portion of this year; and again we think of the gentle and melancholy Cowper.

"My dear dear E.,

"I am at this moment trembling all over with excitement, after reading your note; it is what I never received before—it is the unrestrained pouring out of a warm, gentle, generous heart ... I thank you with energy for this kindness. I will no longer shrink from answering your questions. I *do* wish to be better than I am. I pray fervently sometimes to be made so. I have stings of conscience, visitings of remorse, glimpses of holy, of inexpressible things, which formerly I used to be a stranger to; it may all die away, and I may be in utter midnight, but I implore a merciful Redeemer, that, if this be the dawn of the gospel, it may still brighten to perfect day. Do not mistake me—do not think I am good; I only wish to be so. I only hate my former flippancy and forwardness. Oh! I am no better than ever I was. I am in that state of horrid, gloomy uncertainty that, at this moment, I would submit to be old, grey-haired, to have passed all my youthful days of enjoyment, and to be settling on the verge of the grave, if I could only thereby ensure the prospect of reconciliation to God, and redemption through his Son's merits. I never was exactly careless of these matters, but I have always taken a clouded and repulsive view of them; and now, if possible, the clouds are gathering darker, and a more oppressive despondency weighs on my spirits. You have cheered me, my darling; for one moment, for an atom of time, I thought I might call you my own sister in the spirit; but the excitement is past, and I am now as wretched and hopeless as ever. This very night I will pray as you wish me. May the Almighty hear me compassionately! and I humbly hope he will, for you will strengthen my polluted petitions with your own pure requests. All is bustle and confusion round me, the ladies pressing with their sums and their lessons . . . If you love me, *do, do, do* come on Friday: I shall watch and wait for you, and if you disappoint me I shall weep. I wish you could know the thrill of delight which I experienced, when, as I stood at the dining-room window, I saw ---, as he whirled past, toss your little packet over the wall."

Huddersfield market-day was still the great period for events at Roe Head. Then girls, running round the corner of the house and peeping between tree-stems, and up a shadowy lane, could catch a glimpse of a father or brother driving to market in his gig; might, perhaps, exchange a wave of the hand; or see, as Charlotte Brontë did from the window, a white packet tossed over the avail by come swift strong motion of an arm, the rest of the traveller's body unseen.

"Weary with a day's hard work... I am sitting down to write a few lines to my dear E. Excuse me if I say nothing but nonsense, for my mind is exhausted and dispirited. It is a stormy evening, and the wind is uttering a continual moaning sound, that makes me feel very melancholy. At such times—in such moods as these—it is my nature to seek repose in some calm tranquil idea, and I have now summoned up your image to give me rest. There you sit, upright and still in your black dress, and white scarf, and pale marble-like face—just like reality. I wish you would speak to me. If we should be separated—if it should be our lot to live at a great distance, and never to see each other again—in old age, how I should conjure up the memory of my youthful days, and what a melancholy pleasure I should feel in dwelling on the recollection of my early friend!... I have some qualities that make me very miserable, some feelings that you can have no participation in—that few, very few, people in the world can at all understand. I don't pride myself on these peculiarities. I strive to conceal and suppress them as much as I can; but they burst out sometimes, and then those who see the explosion despise me, and I hate myself for days afterwards... I have just received your epistle and what accompanied it. I can't tell what should induce you and your sisters to waste your kindness on such a one as me. I'm obliged to them, and I hope you'll tell them so. I'm obliged to you also, more for your note than for your present. The first gave me pleasure, the last something like pain."

* * * * *

The nervous disturbance, which is stated to have troubled her while she was at Miss W---'s, seems to have begun to distress her about this time; at least, she herself speaks of her irritable condition, which was certainly only a temporary ailment.

"You have been very kind to me of late, and have spared me all those little sallies of ridicule, which, owing to my miserable and wretched touchiness of character, used formerly to make me wince, as if I had been touched with a hot iron; things that nobody else cares for, enter into my mind and rankle there like venom. I know these feelings are absurd, and therefore I try to hide them, but they only sting the deeper for concealment."

Compare this state of mind with the gentle resignation with which she had submitted to be put aside as useless, or told of her ugliness by her school-fellows, only three years before.

"My life since I saw you has passed as monotonously and unbroken as ever; nothing but teach, teach, teach, from morning till night. The greatest variety I ever have is afforded by a letter from you, or by meeting with a pleasant new book. The 'Life of Oberlin,' and 'Leigh Richmond's Domestic Portraiture,' are the last of this description. The latter work strongly attracted and strangely fascinated my attention. Beg, borrow, or steal it without delay; and read the 'Memoir of Wilberforce,'—that short record of a brief uneventful life; I shall never forget it; it is beautiful, not on account of the language in which it is written, not on account of the incidents it details, but because of the simple narrative it gives of a young talented sincere Christian."

* * * * *

About this time Miss W--- removed her school from the fine, open, breezy situation of Roe Head, to Dewsbury Moor, only two or three miles distant. Her new residence was on a lower site, and the air was less exhilarating to one bred in the wild hill-village of Haworth. Emily had gone as teacher to a school at Halifax, where there were nearly forty pupils.

"I have had one letter from her since her departure," writes Charlotte, on October 2nd, 1836: "it gives an appalling account of her duties; hard labour from six in the morning to eleven at night, with only one half-hour of exercise between. This is slavery. I fear she can never stand it."

* * * * *

When the sisters met at home in the Christmas holidays, they talked over their lives, and the prospect which they afforded of employment and remuneration. They felt that it was a duty to relieve their father of the burden of their support, if not entirely, or that of all three, at least that of one or two; and, naturally, the lot devolved upon the elder ones to find some occupation which would enable them to do this. They knew that they were never likely to inherit much money. Mr. Brontë had but a small stipend, and was both charitable and liberal. Their aunt had an annuity of 50*l*., but it reverted to others at her death, and her nieces had no right, and were the last persons in the world to reckon upon her savings. What could they do? Charlotte and Emily were trying teaching, and, as it seemed, without much success. The former, it is true, had the happiness of having a friend for her employer, and of being surrounded by those who knew her and loved her; but her salary was too small for her to save out of it; and her education did not entitle her to a larger. The sedentary and monotonous nature of the life, too, was preying upon her health and spirits, although, with necessity "as her mistress," she might hardly like to acknowledge this even to herself. But Emily—that free, wild, untameable spirit, never happy nor well but on the sweeping moors that gathered round her home—that hater of strangers, doomed to live amongst them, and not merely to live but to slave in their service—what Charlotte could have borne patiently for herself, she could not bear for her sister. And yet what to do? She had once hoped that she herself might become an artist, and so earn her livelihood; but her eyes had failed her in the minute and useless labour which she had imposed upon herself with a view to this end.

It was the household custom among these girls to sew till nine o'clock at night. At that hour, Miss Branwell generally went to bed, and her nieces' duties for the day were accounted done. They put away their work, and began to pace the room backwards and forwards, up and down,—as often with the candles extinguished, for economy's sake, as not,—their figures glancing into the firelight, and out into the shadow, perpetually. At this time, they talked over past cares and troubles; they planned for the future, and consulted each other as to their plans. In after years this was the time for discussing together the plots of their novels. And again, still later, this was the time for the last surviving sister to walk alone, from old accustomed habit, round and round the desolate room, thinking sadly upon the "days that were no more." But this Christmas of 1836 was not without its hopes and daring aspirations. They had tried their hands at story-writing, in their miniature magazine, long ago; they all of them "made out" perpetually. They had likewise attempted to write poetry; and had a modest confidence that they had achieved a tolerable success. But they knew that they might deceive themselves, and that sisters' judgments of each other's productions were likely to be too partial to be depended upon. So Charlotte, as the eldest, resolved to write to Southey. I believe (from an expression in a letter to be noticed hereafter), that she also consulted Coleridge; but I have not met with any part of that correspondence.

On December 29th, her letter to Southey was despatched; and from an excitement not unnatural in a girl who has worked herself up to the pitch of writing to a Poet Laureate and asking his opinion of her poems, she used some high-flown expressions which, probably, gave him the idea that she was a romantic young lady, unacquainted with the realities of life.

This, most likely, was the first of those adventurous letters that passed through the little post-office of Haworth. Morning after morning of the holidays slipped away, and there was no answer; the sisters had to leave home, and Emily to return to her distasteful duties, without knowing even whether Charlotte's letter had ever reached its destination.

Not dispirited, however, by the delay, Branwell determined to try a similar venture, and addressed the following letter to Wordsworth. It was given by the poet to Mr. Quillinan in 1850, after the name of Brontë had become known and famous. I have no means of ascertaining what answer was returned by Mr. Wordsworth; but that he considered the letter remarkable may, I think, be inferred both from its preservation, and its recurrence to his memory when the real name of Currer Bell was made known to the public.

"Haworth, near Bradford,
"Yorkshire, January 19, 1837.

"Sir,—I most earnestly entreat you to read and pass your judgment upon what I have sent you, because from the day of my birth to this the nineteenth year of my life, I have lived among secluded hills, where I could neither know what I was, or what I could do. I read for the same reason that I ate or drank; because it was a real craving of nature. I wrote on the same principle as I spoke—out of the impulse and feelings of the mind; nor could I help it, for what came, came out, and there was the end of it. For as to self-conceit, that could not receive food from flattery, since to this hour, not half a dozen people in the world know that I have ever penned a line.

"But a change has taken place now, sir: and I am arrived at an age wherein I must do something for myself: the powers I possess must be exercised to a definite end, and as I don't know them myself I must ask of others what they are worth. Yet there is not one here to tell me; and still, if they are worthless, time will henceforth be too precious to be wasted on them.

"Do pardon me, sir, that I have ventured to come before one whose works I have most loved in our literature, and who most has been with me a divinity of the mind, laying before him one of my writings, and asking of him a judgment of its contents. I must come before some one from whose sentence there is no appeal; and such a one is he who has developed the theory of poetry as well as its practice, and both in such a way as to claim a place in the memory of a thousand years to come.

"My aim, sir, is to push out into the open world, and for this I trust not poetry alone—that might launch the vessel, but could not bear her on; sensible and scientific prose, bold and vigorous efforts in my walk in life, would give a farther title to the notice of the world; and then again poetry ought to brighten and crown that name with glory; but nothing of all this can be ever begun without means, and as I don't possess these, I must in every shape strive to gain them. Surely, in this day, when there is not a *writing* poet worth a sixpence, the field must be open, if a better man can step forward.

"What I send you is the Prefatory Scene of a much longer subject, in which I have striven to develop strong passions and weak principles struggling with a high imagination and acute feelings, till, as youth hardens towards age, evil deeds and short enjoyments end in mental misery and bodily ruin. Now, to send you the whole of this would be a mock upon your patience; what you see, does not even pretend to be more than the description of an imaginative child. But read it, sir; and, as you would hold a light to one in utter darkness—as you value your own kindheartedness—*return* me an *answer*, if but one word, telling me whether I should write on, or write no more. Forgive undue warmth, because my feelings in this matter cannot be cool; and believe me, sir, with deep respect,

"Your really humble servant,

"P. B. Brontë"

The poetry enclosed seems to me by no means equal to parts of the letter; but, as every one likes to judge for himself, I copy the six opening stanzas—about a third of the whole, and certainly not the worst.

> So where he reigns in glory bright,
> Above those starry skies of night,
> Amid his Paradise of light
>   Oh, why may I not be?
>
> Oft when awake on Christmas morn,
> In sleepless twilight laid forlorn,
> Strange thoughts have o'er my mind been borne,
>   How he has died for me.
>
> And oft within my chamber lying,
> Have I awaked myself with crying
> From dreams, where I beheld Him dying
>   Upon the accursed Tree.
>
> And often has my mother said,
> While on her lap I laid my head,
> She feared for time I was not made,
>   But for Eternity.
>
> So "I can read my title clear,
> To mansions in the skies,
> And let me bid farewell to fear,
>   And wipe my weeping eyes."

I'll lay me down on this marble stone,
And set the world aside,
To see upon her ebon throne
   The Moon in glory ride.

Soon after Charlotte returned to Dewsbury Moor, she was distressed by hearing that her friend "E." was likely to leave the neighbourhood for a considerable length of time.

"Feb. 20th.

"What shall I do without you? How long are we likely to be separated? Why are we to be denied each other's society? It is an inscrutable fatality. I long to be with you, because it seems as if two or three days, or weeks, spent in your company would beyond measure strengthen me in the enjoyment of those feelings which I have so lately begun to cherish. You first pointed out to me that way in which I am so feebly endeavouring to travel, and now I cannot keep you by my side, I must proceed sorrowfully alone. Why are we to be divided? Surely, it must be because we are in danger of loving each other too well—of losing sight of the *Creator* in idolatry of the *creature*. At first, I could not say 'Thy will be done!' I felt rebellious, but I knew it was wrong to feel so. Being left a moment alone this morning, I prayed fervently to be enabled to resign myself to *every* decree of God's will, though it should be dealt forth by a far severer hand than the present disappointment; since then I have felt calmer and humbler, and consequently happier. Last Sunday I took up my Bible in a gloomy state of mind: I began to read—a feeling stole over me such as I have not known for many long years—a sweet, placid sensation, like those, I remember, which used to visit me when I was a little child, and, on Sunday evenings in summer, stood by the open window reading the life of a certain French nobleman, who attained a purer and higher degree of sanctity than has been known since the days of the early martyrs."

"E.'s" residence was equally within a walk from Dewsbury Moor as it had been from Roe Head; and on Saturday afternoons both "Mary" and she used to call upon Charlotte, and often endeavoured to persuade her to return with them, and be the guest of one of them till Monday morning; but this was comparatively seldom. Mary says:—"She visited us twice or thrice when she was at Miss W---'s. We used to dispute about politics and religion. She, a Tory and clergyman's daughter, was always in a minority of one in our house of violent Dissent and Radicalism. She used to hear over again, delivered *with authority*, all the lectures I had been used to give her at school on despotic aristocracy, mercenary priesthood, &c. She had not energy to defend herself; sometimes she owned to a *little* truth in it, but generally said nothing. Her feeble health gave her her yielding manner, for she could never oppose any one without gathering up all her strength for the struggle. Thus she would let me advise and patronise most imperiously, sometimes picking out any grain of sense there might be in what I said, but never allowing any one materially to interfere with her independence of thought and action. Though her silence sometimes left one under the impression that she agreed when she did not, she never gave a flattering opinion, and thus her words were golden, whether for praise or blame."

"Mary's" father was a man of remarkable intelligence, but of strong, not to say violent prejudices, all running in favour of Republicanism and Dissent. No other county but Yorkshire could have produced such a man. His brother had been a *détenu* in France, and had afterwards voluntarily taken up his residence there. Mr. T. himself had been much abroad, both on business and to see the great continental galleries of paintings. He spoke French perfectly, I have been told, when need was; but delighted usually in talking the broadest Yorkshire. He bought splendid engravings of the pictures which he particularly admired, and his house was full of works of art and of books; but he rather liked to present his rough side to any stranger or new-comer; he would speak his broadest, bring out his opinions on Church and State in their most startling forms, and, by and by, if he found his hearer could stand the shock, he would involuntarily show his warm kind heart, and his true taste, and real refinement. His family of four sons and two daughters were brought up on Republican principles; independence of thought and action was encouraged; no "shams" tolerated. They are scattered far and wide: Martha, the younger daughter, sleeps in the Protestant cemetery at Brussels; Mary is in New Zealand; Mr. T. is dead. And so life and death have dispersed the circle of "violent Radicals and Dissenters" into which, twenty years ago, the little, quiet, resolute clergyman's daughter was received, and by whom she was truly loved and honoured.

January and February of 1837 had passed away, and still there was no reply from Southey. Probably she had lost expectation and almost hope when at length, in the beginning of March, she received the letter inserted in Mr. C. C. Southey's life of his Father, vol. iv. p. 327.

After accounting for his delay in replying to hers by the fact of a long absence from home, during which his letters had accumulated, whence "it has lain unanswered till the last of a numerous file, not from disrespect or indifference to its contents, but because in truth it is not an easy task to answer it, nor a pleasant one to cast a damp over the high spirits and the generous desires of youth," he goes on to say: "What you are I can only infer from your letter, which appears to be written in sincerity, though I may suspect that you have used a fictitious signature. Be that as it may, the letter and the verses bear the same stamp, and I can well understand the state of mind they indicate.

* * * * *

"It is not my advice that you have asked as to the direction of your talents, but my opinion of them, and yet the opinion may be worth little, and the advice much. You evidently possess, and in no inconsiderable degree, what Wordsworth calls the 'faculty of verse.' I am not depreciating it when I say that in these times it is not rare. Many volumes of poems are now published every year without attracting public attention, any one of which if it had appeared half a century ago, would have obtained a high reputation for its author. Whoever, therefore, is ambitious of distinction in this way ought to be prepared for disappointment.

"But it is not with a view to distinction that you should cultivate this talent, if you consult your own happiness. I, who have made literature my profession, and devoted my life to it, and have never for a moment repented of the deliberate choice, think myself, nevertheless, bound in duty to caution every young man who applies as an aspirant to me for encouragement and advice, against taking so perilous a course. You will say that a woman has no need of such a caution; there can be no peril in it for her. In a certain sense this is true; but there is a danger of which I would, with all kindness and all earnestness, warn you. The day dreams in which you habitually indulge are likely to induce a distempered state of mind; and in proportion as all the ordinary uses of the world seem to you flat and unprofitable, you will be unfitted for them without becoming fitted for anything else. Literature cannot be the business of a woman's life, and it ought not to be. The more she is engaged in her proper duties, the less leisure will she have for it, even as an accomplishment and a recreation. To those duties you have not yet been called, and when you are you will be less eager for celebrity. You will not seek in imagination for excitement, of which the vicissitudes of this life, and the anxieties from which you must not hope to be exempted, be your state what it may, will bring with them but too much.

"But do not suppose that I disparage the gift which you possess; nor that I would discourage you from exercising it. I only exhort you so to think of it, and so to use it, as to render it conducive to your own permanent good. Write poetry for its own sake; not in a spirit of emulation, and not with a view to celebrity; the less you aim at that the more likely you will be to deserve and finally to obtain it. So written, it is wholesome both for the heart and soul; it may be made the surest means, next to religion, of soothing the mind and elevating it. You may embody in it your best thoughts and your wisest feelings, and in so doing discipline and strengthen them.

"Farewell, madam. It is not because I have forgotten that I was once young myself, that I write to you in this strain; but because I remember it. You will neither doubt my sincerity nor my good will; and however ill what has here been said may accord with your present views and temper, the longer you live the more reasonable it will appear to you. Though I may be but an ungracious adviser, you will allow me, therefore, to subscribe myself, with the best wishes for your happiness here and hereafter, your true friend,

"ROBERT SOUTHEY."

* * * * *

I was with Miss Brontë when she received Mr. Cuthbert Southey's note, requesting her permission to insert the foregoing letter in his father's life. She said to me, "Mr. Southey's letter was kind and admirable; a little stringent, but it did me good."

It is partly because I think it so admirable, and partly because it tends to bring out her character, as shown in the following reply, that I have taken the liberty of inserting the foregoing extracts from it.

"Sir, March 16th.

"I cannot rest till I have answered your letter, even though by addressing you a second time I should appear a little intrusive; but I must thank you for the kind and wise advice you have condescended to give me. I had not ventured to hope for such a reply; so considerate in its tone, so noble in its spirit. I must suppress what I feel, or you will think me foolishly enthusiastic.

"At the first perusal of your letter, I felt only shame and regret that I had ever ventured to trouble you with my crude rhapsody; I felt a painful heat rise to my face when I thought of the quires of paper I had covered with what once gave me so much delight, but which now was only a source of confusion; but after I had thought a little and read it again and again, the prospect seemed to clear. You do not forbid me to write; you do not say that what I write is utterly destitute of merit. You only warn me against the folly of neglecting real duties for the sake of imaginative pleasures; of writing for the love of fame; for the selfish excitement of emulation. You kindly allow me to write poetry for its own sake, provided I leave undone nothing which I ought to do, in order to pursue that single, absorbing, exquisite gratification. I am afraid, sir, you think me very foolish. I know the first letter I wrote to you was all senseless trash from beginning to end; but I am not altogether the idle dreaming being it would seem to denote. My father is a clergyman of limited, though competent income, and I am the eldest of his children. He expended quite as much in my education as he could afford in justice to the rest. I thought it therefore my duty, when I left school, to become a governess. In that capacity I find enough to occupy my thoughts all day long, and my head and hands too, without having a moment's time for one dream of the imagination. In the evenings, I confess, I do think, but I never trouble any one else with my thoughts. I carefully avoid any appearance of preoccupation and eccentricity, which might lead those I live amongst to suspect the nature of my pursuits. Following my father's advice—who from my childhood has counselled me, just in the wise and friendly tone of your letter—I have endeavoured not only attentively to observe all the duties a woman ought to fulfil, but to feel deeply interested in them. I don't always succeed, for sometimes when I'm teaching or sewing I would rather be reading or writing; but I try to deny myself; and my father's approbation amply rewarded me for the privation. Once more allow me to thank you with sincere gratitude. I trust I shall never more feel ambitious to see my name in print: if the wish should rise, I'll look at Southey's letter, and suppress it. It is honour enough for me that I have written to him, and received an answer. That letter is consecrated; no one shall ever see it, but papa and my brother and sisters. Again I thank you. This incident, I suppose, will be renewed no more; if I live to be an old woman, I shall remember it thirty years hence as a bright dream. The signature which you suspected of being fictitious is my real name. Again, therefore, I must sign myself,

"C. Brontë.

"P.S.—Pray, sir, excuse me for writing to you a second time; I could not help writing, partly to tell you how thankful I am for your kindness, and partly to let you know that your advice shall not be wasted; however sorrowfully and reluctantly it may be at first followed.

"C. B."

I cannot deny myself the gratification of inserting Southey's reply:—

"Keswick, March 22, 1837.

"Dear Madam,

"Your letter has given me great pleasure, and I should not forgive myself if I did not tell you so. You have received admonition as considerately and as kindly as it was given. Let me now request that, if you ever should come to these Lakes while I am living here, you will let me see you. You would then think of me afterwards with the more goodwill, because you would perceive that there is neither severity nor moroseness in the state of mind to which years and observation have brought me.

"It is, by God's mercy, in our power to attain a degree of self-government, which is essential to our own happiness, and contributes greatly to that of those around us. Take care of over-excitement, and endeavour to keep a quiet mind (even for your health it is the best advice that can be given you): your moral and spiritual improvement will then keep pace with the culture of your intellectual powers.

"And now, madam, God bless you!

"Farewell, and believe me to be your sincere friend,

"ROBERT SOUTHEY.

Of this second letter, also, she spoke, and told me that it contained an invitation for her to go and see the poet if ever she visited the Lakes. "But there was no money to spare," said she, "nor any prospect of my ever earning money enough to have the chance of so great a pleasure, so I gave up thinking of it." At the time we conversed together on the subject we were at the Lakes. But Southey was dead.

This "stringent" letter made her put aside, for a time, all idea of literary enterprise. She bent her whole energy towards the fulfilment of the duties in hand; but her occupation was not sufficient food for her great forces of intellect, and they cried out perpetually, "Give, give," while the comparatively less breezy air of Dewsbury Moor told upon her health and spirits more and more. On August 27, 1837, she writes:—

"I am again at Dewsbury, engaged in the old business,—teach, teach, teach . . . *When will you come home*? Make haste! You have been at Bath long enough for all purposes; by this time you have acquired polish enough, I am sure; if the varnish is laid on much thicker, I am afraid the good wood underneath will be quite concealed, and your Yorkshire friends won't stand that. Come, come. I am getting really tired of your absence. Saturday after Saturday comes round, and I can have no hope of hearing your knock at the door, and then being told that 'Miss E. is come.' Oh, dear! in this monotonous life of mine, that was a pleasant event. I wish it would recur again; but it will take two or three interviews before the stiffness—the estrangement of this long separation—will wear away."

About this time she forgot to return a work-bag she had borrowed, by a messenger, and in repairing her error she says:—"These aberrations of memory warn me pretty intelligibly that I am getting past my prime." AEtat 21! And the same tone of despondency runs through the following letter:—

"I wish exceedingly that I could come to you before Christmas, but it is impossible; another three weeks must elapse before I shall again have my comforter beside me, under the roof of my own dear quiet home. If I could always live with you, and daily read the Bible with you—if your lips and mine could at the same time drink the same draught, from the same pure fountain of mercy—I hope, I trust, I might one day become better, far better than my evil, wandering thoughts, my corrupt heart, cold to the spirit and warm to the flesh, will now permit me to be. I often plan the pleasant life which we might lead together, strengthening each other in that power of self-denial, that hallowed and glowing devotion, which the first saints of God often attained to. My eyes fill with tears when I contrast the bliss of such a state, brightened by hopes of the future, with the melancholy state I now live in, uncertain that I ever felt true contrition, wandering in thought and deed, longing for holiness, which I shall *never, never* obtain, smitten at times to the heart with the conviction that ghastly Calvinistic doctrines are true—darkened, in short, by the very shadows of spiritual death. If Christian perfection be necessary to salvation, I shall never be saved; my heart is a very hotbed for sinful thoughts, and when I decide on an action I scarcely remember to look to my Redeemer for direction. I know not how to pray; I cannot bend my life to the grand end of doing good; I go on constantly seeking my own pleasure, pursuing the gratification of my own desires. I forget God, and will not God forget me? And, meantime, I know the greatness of Jehovah; I acknowledge the perfection of His word; I adore the purity of the Christian faith; my theory is right, my practice horribly wrong."

The Christmas holidays came, and she and Anne returned to the parsonage, and to that happy home circle in which alone their natures expanded; amongst all other people they shrivelled up more or less. Indeed, there were only one or two strangers who could be admitted among the sisters without producing the same result. Emily and Anne were bound up in their lives and interests like twins. The former from reserve, the latter from timidity, avoided all friendships and intimacies beyond their family. Emily was impervious to influence; she never came in contact with public opinion, and her own decision of what was right and fitting was a law for her conduct and appearance, with which she allowed no one to interfere. Her love was poured out on Anne, as Charlotte's was on her. But the affection among all the three was stronger than either death or life.

"E." was eagerly welcomed by Charlotte, freely admitted by Emily, and kindly received by Anne, whenever she could visit them; and this Christmas she had promised to do so, but her coming had to be delayed on account of a little domestic accident detailed in the following letter:—

"Dec. 29, 1837.

"I am sure you will have thought me very remiss in not sending my promised letter long before now; but I have a sufficient and very melancholy excuse in an accident that befell our old faithful Tabby, a few days after my return home. She was gone out into the village on some errand, when, as she was descending the steep street, her foot slipped on the ice, and she fell; it was dark, and no one saw her mischance, till after a time her groans attracted the attention of a passer-by. She was lifted up and carried into the druggist's near; and, after the examination, it was discovered that she had completely shattered and dislocated one leg. Unfortunately, the fracture could not be set till six o'clock the next morning, as no surgeon was to be had before that time, and she now lies at our house in a very doubtful and dangerous state. Of course we are all exceedingly distressed at the circumstance, for she was like one of our own family. Since the event we have been almost without assistance—a person has dropped in now and then to do the drudgery, but we have as yet been able to procure no regular servant; and consequently, the whole work of the house, as well as the additional duty of nursing Tabby, falls on ourselves. Under these circumstances I dare not press your visit here, at least until she is pronounced out of danger; it would be too selfish of me. Aunt wished me to give you this information before, but papa and all the rest were anxious I should delay until we saw whether matters took a more settled aspect, and I myself kept putting it off from day to day, most bitterly reluctant to give up all the pleasure I had anticipated so long. However, remembering what you told me, namely, that you had commended the matter to a higher decision than ours, and that you were resolved to submit with resignation to that decision, whatever it might be, I hold it my duty to yield also, and to be silent; it may be all for the best. I fear, if you had been here during this severe weather, your visit would have been of no advantage to you, for the moors are blockaded with snow, and you would never have been able to get out. After this disappointment, I never dare reckon with certainty on the enjoyment of a pleasure again; it seems as if some fatality stood between you and me. I am not good enough for you, and you must be kept from the contamination of too intimate society. I would urge your visit yet—I would entreat and press it—but the thought comes across me, should Tabby die while you are in the house, I should never forgive myself. No! it must not be, and in a thousand ways the consciousness of that mortifies and disappoints me most keenly, and I am not the only one who is disappointed. All in the house were looking to your visit with eagerness. Papa says he highly approves of my friendship with you, and he wishes me to continue it through life."

A good neighbour of the Brontës—a clever, intelligent Yorkshire woman, who keeps a druggist's shop in Haworth, and from her occupation, her experience, and excellent sense, holds the position of village doctress and nurse, and, as such, has been a friend, in many a time of trial, and sickness, and death, in the households round—told me a characteristic little incident connected with Tabby's fractured leg. Mr. Brontë is truly generous and regardful of all deserving claims. Tabby had lived with them for ten or twelve years, and was, as Charlotte expressed it, "one of the family." But on the other hand, she was past the age for any very active service, being nearer seventy than sixty at the time of the accident; she had a sister living in the village; and the savings she had accumulated, during many years' service, formed a competency for one in her rank of life. Or if, in this time of sickness, she fell short of any comforts which her state rendered necessary, the parsonage could supply them. So reasoned Miss Branwell, the prudent, not to say anxious aunt; looking to the limited contents of Mr. Brontë's purse, and the unprovided-for-future of her nieces; who were, moreover, losing the relaxation of the holidays, in close attendance upon Tabby.

Miss Branwell urged her views upon Mr. Brontë as soon as the immediate danger to the old servant's life was over. He refused at first to listen to the careful advice; it was repugnant to his liberal nature. But Miss Branwell persevered; urged economical motives; pressed on his love for his daughters. He gave way. Tabby was to be removed to her sister's, and there nursed and cared for, Mr. Brontë coming in with his aid when her own resources fell short. This decision was communicated to the girls. There were symptoms of a quiet, but sturdy rebellion, that winter afternoon, in the small precincts of Haworth parsonage. They made one unanimous and stiff remonstrance. Tabby had tended them in their childhood; they, and none other, should tend her in her infirmity and age. At tea-time, they were sad and silent, and the meal went away untouched by any of the three. So it was at breakfast; they did not waste many words on the subject, but each word they did utter was weighty. They "struck" eating till the resolution was rescinded, and Tabby was allowed to remain a helpless invalid entirely dependent upon them. Herein was the strong feeling of Duty being paramount to pleasure, which lay at the foundation of Charlotte's character, made most apparent; for we have seen how she yearned for her friend's company; but it was to be obtained only by shrinking from what she esteemed right, and that she never did, whatever might be the sacrifice.

She had another weight on her mind this Christmas. I have said that the air of Dewsbury Moor did not agree with her, though she herself was hardly aware how much her life there was affecting her health. But Anne had begun to suffer just before the holidays, and Charlotte watched over her younger sisters with the jealous vigilance of some wild creature, that changes her very nature if danger threatens her young. Anne had a slight cough, a pain at her side, a difficulty of breathing. Miss W--- considered it as little more than a common cold; but Charlotte felt every indication of incipient consumption as a stab at her heart, remembering Maria and Elizabeth, whose places once knew them, and should know them no more.

Stung by anxiety for this little sister, she upbraided Miss W--- for her fancied indifference to Anne's state of health. Miss W--- felt these reproaches keenly, and wrote to Mr. Brontë about them. He immediately replied most kindly, expressing his fear that Charlotte's apprehensions and anxieties respecting her sister had led her to give utterance to over-excited expressions of alarm. Through Miss W---'s kind consideration, Anne was a year longer at school than her friends intended. At the close of the half-year Miss W--- sought for the opportunity of an explanation of each other's words, and the issue proved that "the falling out of faithful friends, renewing is of love." And so ended the first, last, and only difference Charlotte ever had with good, kind Miss W ---.

Still her heart had received a shock in the perception of Anne's delicacy; and all these holidays she watched over her with the longing, fond anxiety, which is so full of sudden pangs of fear.

Emily had given up her situation in the Halifax school, at the expiration of six months of arduous trial, on account of her health, which could only be re-established by the bracing moorland air and free life of home. Tabby's illness had preyed on the family resources. I doubt whether Branwell was maintaining himself at this time. For some unexplained reason, he had given up the idea of becoming a student of painting at the Royal Academy, and his prospects in life were uncertain, and had yet to be settled. So Charlotte had quietly to take up her burden of teaching again, and return to her previous monotonous life.

Brave heart, ready to die in harness! She went back to her work, and made no complaint, hoping to subdue the weakness that was gaining ground upon her. About this time, she would turn sick and trembling at any sudden noise, and could hardly repress her screams when startled. This showed a fearful degree of physical weakness in one who was generally so self-controlled; and the medical man, whom at length, through Miss W---'s entreaty, she was led to consult, insisted on her return to the parsonage. She had led too sedentary a life, he said; and the soft summer air, blowing round her home, the sweet company of those she loved, the release, the freedom of life in her own family, were needed, to save either reason or life. So, as One higher than she had overruled that for a time she might relax her strain, she returned to Haworth; and after a season of utter quiet, her father sought for her the enlivening society of her two friends, Mary and Martha T. At the conclusion of the following letter, written to the then absent E., there is, I think, as pretty a glimpse of a merry group of young people as need be; and like all descriptions of doing, as distinct from thinking or feeling, in letters, it saddens one in proportion to the vivacity of the picture of what was once, and is now utterly swept away.

"Haworth, June 9, 1838.

"I received your packet of despatches on Wednesday; it was brought me by Mary and Martha, who have been staying at Haworth for a few days; they leave us to-day. You will be surprised at the date of this letter. I ought to be at Dewsbury Moor, you know; but I stayed as long as I was able, and at length I neither could nor dared stay any longer. My health and spirits had utterly failed me, and the medical man whom I consulted enjoined me, as I valued my life, to go home. So home I went, and the change has at once roused and soothed me; and I am now, I trust, fairly in the way to be myself again.

"A calm and even mind like yours cannot conceive the feelings of the shattered wretch who is now writing to you, when, after weeks of mental and bodily anguish not to be described, something like peace began to dawn again. Mary is far from well. She breathes short, has a pain in her chest, and frequent flushings of fever. I cannot tell you what agony these symptoms give me; they remind me too strongly of my two sisters, whom no power of medicine could save. Martha is now very well; she has kept in a continual flow of good humour during her stay here, and has consequently been very fascinating . . . "

"They are making such a noise about me I cannot write any more. Mary is playing on the piano; Martha is chattering as fast as her little tongue can run; and Branwell is standing before her, laughing at her vivacity."

Charlotte grew much stronger in this quiet, happy period at home. She paid occasional visits to her two great friends, and they in return came to Haworth. At one of their houses, I suspect, she met with the person to whom the following letter refers—some one having a slight resemblance to the character of "St. John," in the last volume of "Jane Eyre," and, like him, in holy orders.

"March 12, 1839.

. . . "I had a kindly leaning towards him, because he is an amiable and well-disposed man. Yet I had not, and could not have, that intense attachment which would make me willing to die for him; and if ever I marry, it must be in that light of adoration that I will regard my husband. Ten to one I shall never have the chance again; but *n'importe*. Moreover, I was aware that he knew so little of me he could hardly be conscious to whom he was writing. Why! it would startle him to see me in my natural home character; he would think I was a wild, romantic enthusiast indeed. I could not sit all day long making a grave face before my husband. I would laugh, and satirize, and say whatever came into my head first. And if he were a clever man, and loved me, the whole world, weighed in the balance against his smallest wish, should be light as air."

So that—her first proposal of marriage—was quietly declined and put on one side. Matrimony did not enter into the scheme of her life, but good, sound, earnest labour did; the question, however, was as yet undecided in what direction she should employ her forces. She had been discouraged in literature; her eyes failed her in the minute kind of drawing which she practised when she wanted to express an idea; teaching seemed to her at this time, as it does to most women at all times, the only way of earning an independent livelihood. But neither she nor her sisters were naturally fond of children. The hieroglyphics of childhood were an unknown language to them, for they had never been much with those younger than themselves. I am inclined to think, too, that they had not the happy knack of imparting information, which seems to be a separate gift from the faculty of acquiring it; a kind of sympathetic tact, which instinctively perceives the difficulties that impede comprehension in a child's mind, and that yet are too vague and unformed for it, with its half-developed powers of expression, to explain by words. Consequently, teaching very young children was anything but a "delightful task" to the three Brontë sisters. With older girls, verging on womanhood, they might have done better, especially if these had any desire for improvement. But the education which the village clergyman's daughters had received, did not as yet qualify them to undertake the charge of advanced pupils. They knew but little French, and were not proficients in music; I doubt whether Charlotte could play at all. But they were all strong again, and, at any rate, Charlotte and Anne must put their shoulders to the wheel. One daughter was needed at home, to stay with Mr. Brontë and Miss Branwell; to be the young and active member in a household of four, whereof three—the father, the aunt, and faithful Tabby—were past middle age. And Emily, who suffered and drooped more than her sisters when away from Haworth, was the one appointed to remain. Anne was the first to meet with a situation.

"April 15th, 1839.

"I could not write to you in the week you requested, as about that time we were very busy in preparing for Anne's departure. Poor child! she left us last Monday; no one went with her; it was her own wish that she might be allowed to go alone, as she thought she could manage better and summon more courage if thrown entirely upon her own resources. We have had one letter from her since she went. She expresses herself very well satisfied, and says that Mrs. --- is extremely kind; the two eldest children alone are under her care, the rest are confined to the nursery, with which and its occupants she has nothing to do . . . I hope she'll do. You would be astonished what a sensible, clever letter she writes; it is only the talking part that I fear. But I do seriously apprehend that Mrs. --- will sometimes conclude that she has a natural impediment in her speech. For my own part, I am as yet 'wanting a situation,' like a housemaid out of place. By the way, I have lately discovered I have quite a talent for cleaning, sweeping up hearths, dusting rooms, making beds, &c.; so, if everything else fails, I can turn my hand to that, if anybody will give me good wages for little labour. I won't be a cook; I hate soothing. I won't be a nurserymaid, nor a lady's-maid, far less a lady's companion, or a mantua-maker, or a straw-bonnet maker, or a taker-in of plain work. I won't be anything but a housemaid . . . With regard to my visit to G., I have as yet received no invitation; but if I should be asked, though I should feel it a great act of self-denial to refuse, yet I have almost made up my mind to do so, though the society of the T.'s is one of the most rousing pleasures I have ever known. Good-bye, my darling E., &c.

"P. S.—Strike out that word 'darling;' it is humbug. Where's the use of protestations? We've known each other, and liked each other, a good while; that's enough."

Not many weeks after this was written, Charlotte also became engaged as a governess. I intend carefully to abstain from introducing the names of any living people, respecting whom I may have to tell unpleasant truths, or to quote severe remarks from Miss Brontë's letters; but it is necessary that the difficulties she had to encounter in her various phases of life, should be fairly and frankly made known, before the force "of what was resisted" can be at all understood. I was once speaking to her about "Agnes Grey"—the novel in which her sister Anne pretty literally describes her own experience as a governess—and alluding more particularly to the account of the stoning of the little nestlings in the presence of the parent birds. She said that none but those who had been in the position of a governess could ever realise the dark side of "respectable" human nature; under no great temptation to crime, but daily giving way to selfishness and ill-temper, till its conduct towards those dependent on it sometimes amounts to a tyranny of which one would rather be the victim than the inflicter. We can only trust in such cases that the employers err rather from a density of perception and an absence of sympathy, than from any natural cruelty of disposition. Among several things of the same kind, which I well remember, she told me what had once occurred to herself. She had been entrusted with the care of a little boy, three or four years old, during the absence of his parents on a day's excursion, and particularly enjoined to keep him out of the stable-yard. His elder brother, a lad of eight or nine, and not a pupil of Miss Brontë's, tempted the little fellow into the forbidden place. She followed, and tried to induce him to come away; but, instigated by his brother, he began throwing stones at her, and one of them hit her so severe a blow on the temple that the lads were alarmed into obedience. The next day, in full family conclave, the mother asked Miss Brontë what occasioned the mark on her forehead. She simply replied, "An accident, ma'am," and no further inquiry was made; but the children (both brothers and sisters) had been present, and honoured her for not "telling tales." From that time, she began to obtain influence over all, more or less, according to their different characters; and as she insensibly gained their affection, her own interest in them was increasing. But one day, at the children's dinner, the small truant of the stable-yard, in a little demonstrative gush, said, putting his hand in hers, "I love 'ou, Miss Brontë." Whereupon, the mother exclaimed, before all the children, "Love the *governess*, my dear!"

"The family into which she first entered was, I believe, that of a wealthy Yorkshire manufacturer. The following extracts from her correspondence at this time will show how painfully the restraint of her new mode of life pressed upon her. The first is from a letter to Emily, beginning with one of the tender expressions in which, in spite of 'humbug,' she indulged herself. 'Mine dear love,' 'Mine-bonnie love,' are her terms of address to this beloved sister.

"June 8th, 1839.

"I have striven hard to be pleased with my new situation. The country, the house and the grounds are, as I have said, divine; but, alack-a-day! there is such a thing as seeing all beautiful around you—pleasant woods, white paths, green lawns, and blue sunshiny sky—and not having a free moment or a free thought left to enjoy them. The children are constantly with me. As for correcting them, I quickly found that was out of the question; they are to do as they like. A complaint to the mother only brings black looks on myself, and unjust, partial excuses to screen the children. I have tried that plan once, and succeeded so notably, I shall try no more. I said in my last letter that Mrs. --- did not know me. I now begin to find she does not intend to know me; that she cares nothing about me, except to contrive how the greatest possible quantity of labour may be got out of me; and to that end she overwhelms me with oceans of needle-work; yards of cambric to hem, muslin nightcaps to make, and, above all things, dolls to dress. I do not think she likes me at all, because I can't help being shy in such an entirely novel scene, surrounded as I have hitherto been by strange and constantly changing faces . . . I used to think I should like to be in the stir of grand folks' society; but I have had enough of it—it is dreary work to look on and listen. I see more clearly than I have ever done before, that a private governess has no existence, is not considered as a living rational being, except as connected with the wearisome duties she has to fulfil . . . One of the pleasantest afternoons I have spent here—indeed, the only one at all pleasant—was when Mr. --- walked out with his children, and I had orders to follow a little behind. As he strolled on through his fields, with his magnificent Newfoundland dog at his side, he looked very like what a frank, wealthy, Conservative gentleman ought to be. He spoke freely and unaffectedly to the people he met, and, though he indulged his children and allowed them to tease himself far too much, he would not suffer them grossly to insult others."

(WRITTEN IN PENCIL TO A FRIEND.)

"July, 1839.

"I cannot procure ink, without going into the drawing-room, where I do not wish to go . . . I should have written to you long since, and told you every detail of the utterly new scene into which I have lately been cast, had I not been daily expecting a letter from yourself, and wondering and lamenting that you did not write; for you will remember it was your turn. I must not bother you too much with my sorrows, of which, I fear, you have heard an exaggerated account. If you were near me, perhaps I might be tempted to tell you all, to grow egotistical, and pour out the long history of a private governess's trials and crosses in her first situation. As it is, I will only ask you to imagine the miseries of a reserved wretch like me, thrown at once into the midst of a large family, at a time when they were particularly gay—when the house was filled with company—all strangers—people whose faces I had never seen before. In this state I had charge given me of a set of pampered, spoilt, turbulent children, whom I was expected constantly to amuse, as well as to instruct. I soon found that the constant demand on my stock of animal spirits reduced them to the lowest state of exhaustion; at times I felt—and, I suppose, seemed—depressed. To my astonishment, I was taken to task on the subject by Mrs. --- with a sternness of manner and a harshness of language scarcely credible; like a fool, I cried most bitterly. I could not help it; my spirits quite failed me at first. I thought I had done my best—strained every nerve to please her; and to be treated in that way, merely because I was shy and sometimes melancholy, was too bad. At first I was for giving all up and going home. But, after a little reflection, I determined to summon what energy I had, and to weather the storm. I said to myself, 'I have never yet quitted a place without gaining a friend; adversity is a good school; the poor are born to labour, and the dependent to endure.' I resolved to be patient, to command my feelings, and to take what came; the ordeal, I reflected, would not last many weeks, and I trusted it would do me good. I recollected the fable of the willow and the oak; I bent quietly, and now, I trust, the storm is blowing over me. Mrs. --- is generally considered an agreeable woman; so she is, I doubt not, in general society. She behaves somewhat more civilly to me now than she did at first, and the children are a little more manageable; but she does not know my character, and she does not wish to know it. I have never had five minutes' conversation with her since I came, except while she was scolding me. I have no wish to be pitied, except by yourself; if I were talking to you I could tell you much more."

(TO EMILY, ABOUT THIS TIME.)

"Mine bonnie love, I was as glad of your letter as tongue can express: it is a real, genuine pleasure to hear from home; a thing to be saved till bedtime, when one has a moment's quiet and rest to enjoy it thoroughly. Write whenever you can. I could like to be at home. I could like to work in a mill. I could like to feel some mental liberty. I could like this weight of restraint to be taken off. But the holidays will come. Coraggio."

Her temporary engagement in this uncongenial family ended in the July of this year; not before the constant strain upon her spirits and strength had again affected her health; but when this delicacy became apparent in palpitations and shortness of breathing, it was treated as affectation—as a phase of imaginary indisposition, which could be dissipated by a good scolding. She had been brought up rather in a school of Spartan endurance than in one of maudlin self-indulgence, and could bear many a pain and relinquish many a hope in silence.

After she had been at home about a week, her friend proposed that she should accompany her in some little excursion, having pleasure alone for its object. She caught at the idea most eagerly at first; but her hope stood still, waned, and had almost disappeared before, after many delays, it was realised. In its fulfilment at last, it was a favourable specimen of many a similar air-bubble dancing before her eyes in her brief career, in which stern realities, rather than pleasures, formed the leading incidents.

"July 26th, 1839.

"Your proposal has almost driven me 'clean daft'—if you don't understand that ladylike expression, you must ask me what it means when I see you. The fact is, an excursion with you anywhere,—whether to Cleathorpe or Canada,—just by ourselves, would be to me most delightful. I should, indeed, like to go; but I can't get leave of absence for longer than a week, and I'm afraid that would not suit you—must I then give it up entirely? I feel as if I *could not*; I never had such a chance of enjoyment before; I do want to see you and talk to you, and be with you. When do you wish to go? Could I meet you at Leeds? To take a gig from Haworth to B., would be to me a very serious increase of expense, and I happen to be very low in cash. Oh! rich people seem to have many pleasures at their command which we are debarred from! However, no repining.

"Say when you go, and I shall be able in my answer to say decidedly whether I can accompany you or not. I must—I will—I'm set upon it—I'll be obstinate and bear down all opposition.

"P.S.—Since writing the above, I find that aunt and papa have determined to go to Liverpool for a fortnight, and take us all with them. It is stipulated, however, that I should give up the Cleathorpe scheme. I yield reluctantly."

I fancy that, about this time, Mr. Brontë found it necessary, either from failing health or the increased populousness of the parish, to engage the assistance of a curate. At least, it is in a letter written this summer that I find mention of the first of a succession of curates, who henceforward revolved round Haworth Parsonage, and made an impression on the mind of one of its inmates which she has conveyed pretty distinctly to the world. The Haworth curate brought his clerical friends and neighbours about the place, and for a time the incursions of these, near the parsonage tea-time, formed occurrences by which the quietness of the life there was varied, sometimes pleasantly, sometimes disagreeably. The little adventure recorded at the end of the following letter is uncommon in the lot of most women, and is a testimony in this case to the unusual power of attraction—though so plain in feature—which Charlotte possessed, when she let herself go in the happiness and freedom of home.

"August 4th, 1839.

"The Liverpool journey is yet a matter of talk, a sort of castle in the air; but, between you and me, I fancy it is very doubtful whether it will ever assume a more solid shape. Aunt—like many other elderly people—likes to talk of such things; but when it comes to putting them into actual execution, she rather falls off. Such being the case, I think you and I had better adhere to our first plan of going somewhere together independently of other people. I have got leave to accompany you for a week—at the utmost a fortnight—but no more. Where do you wish to go? Burlington, I should think, from what M. says, would be as eligible a place as any. When do you set off? Arrange all these things according to your convenience; I shall start no objections. The idea of seeing the sea—of being near it—watching its changes by sunrise, sunset, moonlight, and noon-day—in calm, perhaps in storm—fills and satisfies my mind. I shall be discontented at nothing. And then I am not to be with a set of people with whom I have nothing in common—who would be nuisances and bores: but with you, whom I like and know, and who knows me.

"I have an odd circumstance to relate to you: prepare for a hearty laugh! The other day, Mr. ---, a vicar, came to spend the day with us, bringing with him his own curate. The latter gentleman, by name Mr. B., is a young Irish clergyman, fresh from Dublin University. It was the first time we had any of us seen him, but, however, after the manner of his countrymen, he soon made himself at home. His character quickly appeared in his conversation; witty, lively, ardent, clever too; but deficient in the dignity and discretion of an Englishman. At home, you know, I talk with ease, and am never shy—never weighed down and oppressed by that miserable *mauvaise honte* which torments and constrains me elsewhere. So I conversed with this Irishman, and laughed at his jests; and, though I saw faults in his character, excused them because of the amusement his originality afforded. I cooled a little, indeed, and drew in towards the latter part of the evening, because he began to season his conversation with something of Hibernian flattery, which I did not quite relish. However, they went away, and no more was thought about them. A few days after, I got a letter, the direction of which puzzled me, it being in a hand I was not accustomed to see. Evidently, it was neither from you nor Mary, my only correspondents. Having opened and read it, it proved to be a declaration of attachment and proposal of matrimony, expressed in the ardent language of the sapient young Irishman! I hope you are laughing heartily. This is not like one of my adventures, is it? It more nearly resembles Martha's. I am certainly doomed to be an old maid. Never mind. I made up my mind to that fate ever since I was twelve years old.

"Well! thought I, I have heard of love at first sight, but this beats all! I leave you to guess what my answer would be, convinced that you will not do me the injustice of guessing wrong."

On the 14th of August she still writes from Haworth:—

"I have in vain packed my box, and prepared everything for our anticipated journey. It so happens that I can get no conveyance this week or the next. The only gig let out to hire in Haworth, is at Harrowgate, and likely to remain there, for aught I can hear. Papa decidedly objects to my going by the coach, and walking to B., though I am sure I could manage it. Aunt exclaims against the weather, and the roads, and the four winds of heaven, so I am in a fix, and, what is worse, so are you. On reading over, for the second or third time, your last letter (which, by the by, was written in such hieroglyphics that, at the first hasty perusal, I could hardly make out two consecutive words), I find you intimate that if I leave this journey till Thursday I shall be too late. I grieve that I should have so inconvenienced you; but I need not talk of either Friday or Saturday now, for I rather imagine there is small chance of my ever going at all. The elders of the house have never cordially acquiesced in the measure; and now that impediments seem to start up at every step, opposition grows more open. Papa, indeed, would willingly indulge me, but this very kindness of his makes me doubt whether I ought to draw upon it; so, though I could battle out aunt's discontent, I yield to papa's indulgence. He does not say so, but I know he would rather I stayed at home; and aunt meant well too, I dare say, but I am provoked that she reserved the expression of her decided disapproval till all was settled between you and myself. Reckon on me no more; leave me out in your calculations: perhaps I ought, in the beginning, to have had prudence sufficient to shut my eyes against such a prospect of pleasure, so as to deny myself the hope of it. Be as angry as you please with me for disappointing you. I did not intend it, and have only one thing more to say—if you do not go immediately to the sea, will you come to see us at Haworth? This invitation is not mine only, but papa's and aunt's."

However, a little more patience, a little more delay, and she enjoyed the pleasure she had wished for so much. She and her friend went to Easton for a fortnight in the latter part of September. It was here she received her first impressions of the sea.

"Oct. 24th.

"Have you forgotten the sea by this time, E.? Is it grown dim in your mind? Or can you still see it, dark, blue, and green, and foam-white, and hear it roaring roughly when the wind is high, or rushing softly when it is calm? . . . I am as well as need be, and very fat. I think of Easton very often, and of worthy Mr. H., and his kind-hearted helpmate, and of our pleasant walks to H--- Wood, and to Boynton, our merry evenings, our romps with little Hancheon, &c., &c. If we both live, this period of our lives will long be a theme for pleasant recollection. Did you chance, in your letter to Mr. H., to mention my spectacles? I am sadly inconvenienced by the want of them. I can neither read, write, nor draw with comfort in their absence. I hope Madame won't refuse to give them up . . . Excuse the brevity of this letter, for I have been drawing all day, and my eyes are so tired it is quite a labour to write."

But, as the vivid remembrance of this pleasure died away, an accident occurred to make the actual duties of life press somewhat heavily for a time.

"December 21st, 1839

"We are at present, and have been during the last month, rather busy, as, for that space of time, we have been without a servant, except a little girl to run errands. Poor Tabby became so lame that she was at length obliged to leave us. She is residing with her sister, in a little house of her own, which she bought with her savings a year or two since. She is very comfortable, and wants nothing; as she is near, we see her very often. In the meantime, Emily and I are sufficiently busy, as you may suppose: I manage the ironing, and keep the rooms clean; Emily does the baking, and attends to the kitchen. We are such odd animals, that we prefer this mode of contrivance to having a new face amongst us. Besides, we do not despair of Tabby's return, and she shall not be supplanted by a stranger in her absence. I excited aunt's wrath very much by burning the clothes, the first time I attempted to iron; but I do better now. Human feelings are queer things; I am much happier black-leading the stoves, making the beds, and sweeping the floors at home, than I should be living like a fine lady anywhere else. I must indeed drop my subscription to the Jews, because I have no money to keep it up. I ought to have announced this intention to you before, but I quite forgot I was a subscriber. I intend to force myself to take another situation when I can get one, though I *hate* and *abhor* the very thoughts of governess-ship. But I must do it; and, therefore, I heartily wish I could hear of a family where they need such a commodity as a governess."

CHAPTER IX

The year 1840 found all the Brontës living at home, except Anne. As I have already intimated, for some reason with which I am unacquainted, the plan of sending Branwell to study at the Royal Academy had been relinquished; probably it was found, on inquiry, that the expenses of such a life, were greater than his father's slender finances could afford, even with the help which Charlotte's labours at Miss W---'s gave, by providing for Anne's board and education. I gather from what I have heard, that Branwell must have been severely disappointed when the plan fell through. His talents were certainly very brilliant, and of this he was fully conscious, and fervently desired, by their use, either in writing or drawing, to make himself a name. At the same time, he would probably have found his strong love of pleasure and irregular habits a great impediment in his path to fame; but these blemishes in his character were only additional reasons why he yearned after a London life, in which he imagined he could obtain every stimulant to his already vigorous intellect, while at the same time he would have a license of action to be found only in crowded cities. Thus his whole nature was attracted towards the metropolis; and many an hour must he have spent poring over the map of London, to judge from an anecdote which has been told me. Some traveller for a London house of business came to Haworth for a night; and according to the unfortunate habit of the place, the brilliant "Patrick" was sent for to the inn, to beguile the evening by his intellectual conversation and his flashes of wit. They began to talk of London; of the habits and ways of life there; of the places of amusement; and Branwell informed the Londoner of one or two short cuts from point to point, up narrow lanes or back streets; and it was only towards the end of the evening that the traveller discovered, from his companion's voluntary confession, that he had never set foot in London at all.

At this time the young man seemed to have his fate in his own hands. He was full of noble impulses, as well as of extraordinary gifts; not accustomed to resist temptation, it is true, from any higher motive than strong family affection, but showing so much power of attachment to all about him that they took pleasure in believing that, after a time, he would "right himself," and that they should have pride and delight in the use he would then make of his splendid talents. His aunt especially made him her great favourite. There are always peculiar trials in the life of an only boy in a family of girls. He is expected to act a part in life; to *do*, while they are only to *be*; and the necessity of their giving way to him in some things, is too often exaggerated into their giving way to him in all, and thus rendering him utterly selfish. In the family about whom I am writing, while the rest were almost ascetic in their habits, Branwell was allowed to grow up self-indulgent; but, in early youth, his power of attracting and attaching people was so great, that few came in contact with him who were not so much dazzled by him as to be desirous of gratifying whatever wishes he expressed. Of course, he was careful enough not to reveal anything before his father and sisters of the pleasures he indulged in; but his tone of thought and conversation became gradually coarser, and, for a time, his sisters tried to persuade themselves that such coarseness was a part of manliness, and to blind themselves by love to the fact that Branwell was worse than other young men. At present, though he had, they were aware, fallen into some errors, the exact nature of which they avoided knowing, still he was their hope and their darling; their pride, who should some time bring great glory to the name of Brontë.

He and his sister Charlotte were both slight and small of stature, while the other two were of taller and larger make. I have seen Branwell's profile; it is what would be generally esteemed very handsome; the forehead is massive, the eye well set, and the expression of it fine and intellectual; the nose too is good; but there are coarse lines about the mouth, and the lips, though of handsome shape, are loose and thick, indicating self-indulgence, while the slightly retreating chin conveys an idea of weakness of will. His hair and complexion were sandy. He had enough of Irish blood in him to make his manners frank and genial, with a kind of natural gallantry about them. In a fragment of one of his manuscripts which I have read, there is a justness and felicity of expression which is very striking. It is the beginning of a tale, and the actors in it are drawn with much of the grace of characteristic portrait-painting, in perfectly pure and simple language which distinguishes so many of Addison's papers in the "Spectator." The fragment is too short to afford the means of judging whether he had much dramatic talent, as the persons of the story are not thrown into conversation. But altogether the elegance and composure of style are such as one would not have expected from this vehement and ill-fated young man. He had a stronger desire for literary fame burning in his heart, than even that which occasionally flashed up in his sisters'. He tried various outlets for his talents. He wrote and sent poems to Wordsworth and Coleridge, who both expressed kind and laudatory opinions, and he frequently contributed verses to the *Leeds Mercury*. In 1840, he was living at home, employing himself in occasional composition of various kinds, and waiting till some occupation, for which he might be fitted without any expensive course of preliminary training, should turn up; waiting, not impatiently; for he saw society of one kind (probably what he called "life") at the Black Bull; and at home he was as yet the cherished favourite.

Miss Branwell was unaware of the fermentation of unoccupied talent going on around her. She was not her nieces' confidante—perhaps no one so much older could have been; but their father, from whom they derived not a little of their adventurous spirit, was silently cognisant of much of which she took no note. Next to her nephew, the docile, pensive Anne was her favourite. Of her she had taken charge from her infancy; she was always patient and tractable, and would submit quietly to occasional oppression, even when she felt it keenly. Not so her two elder sisters; they made their opinions known, when roused by any injustice. At such times, Emily would express herself as strongly as Charlotte, although perhaps less frequently. But, in general, notwithstanding that Miss Branwell might be occasionally unreasonable, she and her nieces went on smoothly enough; and though they might now and then be annoyed by petty tyranny, she still inspired them with sincere respect, and not a little affection. They were, moreover, grateful to her for many habits she had enforced upon them, and which in time had become second nature: order, method, neatness in everything; a perfect knowledge of all kinds of household work; an exact punctuality, and obedience to the laws of time and place, of which no one but themselves, I have heard Charlotte say, could tell the value in after-life; with their impulsive natures, it was positive repose to have learnt implicit obedience to external laws. People in Haworth have assured me that, according to the hour of day—nay, the very minute—could they have told what the inhabitants of the parsonage were about. At certain times the girls would be sewing in their aunt's bedroom—the chamber which, in former days, before they had outstripped her in their learning, had served them as a schoolroom; at certain (early) hours they had their meals; from six to eight, Miss Branwell read aloud to Mr. Brontë; at punctual eight, the household assembled to evening prayers in his study; and by nine he, the aunt, and Tabby, were all in bed,—the girls free to pace up and down (like restless wild animals) in the parlour, talking over plans and projects, and thoughts of what was to be their future life.

At the time of which I write, the favourite idea was that of keeping a school. They thought that, by a little contrivance, and a very little additional building, a small number of pupils, four or six, might be accommodated in the parsonage. As teaching seemed the only profession open to them, and as it appeared that

Emily at least could not live away from home, while the others also suffered much from the same cause, this plan of school-keeping presented itself as most desirable. But it involved some outlay; and to this their aunt was averse. Yet there was no one to whom they could apply for a loan of the requisite means, except Miss Branwell, who had made a small store out of her savings, which she intended for her nephew and nieces eventually, but which she did not like to risk. Still, this plan of school-keeping remained uppermost; and in the evenings of this winter of 1839-40, the alterations that would be necessary in the house, and the best way of convincing their aunt of the wisdom of their project, formed the principal subject of their conversation.

This anxiety weighed upon their minds rather heavily, during the months of dark and dreary weather. Nor were external events, among the circle of their friends, of a cheerful character. In January, 1840, Charlotte heard of the death of a young girl who had been a pupil of hers, and a schoolfellow of Anne's, at the time when the sisters were together at Roe Head; and had attached herself very strongly to the latter, who, in return, bestowed upon her much quiet affection. It was a sad day when the intelligence of this young creature's death arrived. Charlotte wrote thus on January 12th, 1840:—

> "Your letter, which I received this morning, was one of painful interest. Anne C., it seems, is *dead*; when I saw her last, she was a young, beautiful, and happy girl; and now 'life's fitful fever' is over with her, and she 'sleeps well.' I shall never see her again. It is a sorrowful thought; for she was a warm-hearted, affectionate being, and I cared for her. Wherever I seek for her now in this world, she cannot be found, no more than a flower or a leaf which withered twenty years ago. A bereavement of this kind gives one a glimpse of the feeling those must have who have seen all drop round them, friend after friend, and are left to end their pilgrimage alone. But tears are fruitless, and I try not

to repine."

During this winter, Charlotte employed her leisure hours in writing a story. Some fragments of the manuscript yet remain, but it is in too small a hand to be read without great fatigue to the eyes; and one cares the less to read it, as she herself condemned it, in the preface to the "Professor," by saying that in this story she had got over such taste as she might once have had for the "ornamental and redundant in composition." The beginning, too, as she acknowledges, was on a scale commensurate with one of Richardson's novels, of seven or eight volumes. I gather some of these particulars from a copy of a letter, apparently in reply to one from Wordsworth, to whom she had sent the commencement of the story, sometime in the summer of 1840.

"Authors are generally very tenacious of their productions, but I am not so much attached to this but that I can give it up without much distress. No doubt, if I had gone on, I should have made quite a Richardsonian concern of it . . . I had materials in my head for half-a-dozen volumes . . . Of course, it is with considerable regret I relinquish any scheme so charming as the one I have sketched. It is very edifying and profitable to create a world out of your own brains, and people it with inhabitants, who are so many Melchisedecs, and have no father nor mother but your own imagination . . . I am sorry I did not exist fifty or sixty years ago, when the 'Ladies' Magazine' was flourishing like a green bay-tree. In that case, I make no doubt, my aspirations after literary fame would have met with due encouragement, and I should have had the pleasure of introducing Messrs. Percy and West into the very best society, and recording all their sayings and doings in double-columned close-printed pages . . . I recollect, when I was a child, getting hold of some antiquated volumes, and reading them by stealth with the most exquisite pleasure. You give a correct description of the patient Grisels of those days. My aunt was one of them; and to this day she thinks the tales of the 'Ladies' Magazine' infinitely superior to any trash of modern literature. So do I; for I read them in childhood, and childhood has a very strong faculty of admiration, but a very weak one of criticism . . . I am pleased that you cannot quite decide whether I am an attorney's clerk or a novel-reading dress-maker. I will not help you at all in the discovery; and as to my handwriting, or the ladylike touches in my style and imagery, you must not draw any conclusion from that—I may employ an amanuensis. Seriously, sir, I am very much obliged to you for your kind and candid letter. I almost wonder you took the trouble to read and notice the novelette of an anonymous scribe, who had not even the manners to tell you whether he was a man or a woman, or whether his 'C. T.' meant Charles Timms or Charlotte Tomkins."

There are two or three things noticeable in the letter from which these extracts are taken. The first is the initials with which she had evidently signed the former one to which she alludes. About this time, to her more familiar correspondents, she occasionally calls herself "Charles Thunder," making a kind of pseudonym for herself out of her Christian name, and the meaning of her Greek surname. In the next place, there is a touch of assumed smartness, very different from the simple, womanly, dignified letter which she had written to Southey, under nearly similar circumstances, three years before. I imagine the cause of this difference to be twofold. Southey, in his reply to her first letter, had appealed to the higher parts of her nature, in calling her to consider whether literature was, or was not, the best course for a woman to pursue. But the person to whom she addressed this one had evidently confined himself to purely literary criticisms, besides which, her sense of humour was tickled by the perplexity which her correspondent felt as to whether he was addressing a man or a woman. She rather wished to encourage the former idea; and, in consequence, possibly, assumed something of the flippancy which very probably existed in her brother's style of conversation, from whom she would derive her notions of young manhood, not likely, as far as refinement was concerned, to be improved by the other specimens she had seen, such as the curates whom she afterwards represented in "Shirley."

These curates were full of strong, High-Church feeling. Belligerent by nature, it was well for their professional character that they had, as clergymen, sufficient scope for the exercise of their warlike propensities. Mr. Brontë, with all his warm regard for Church and State, had a great respect for mental freedom; and, though he was the last man in the world to conceal his opinions, he lived in perfect amity with all the respectable part of those who differed from him. Not so the curates. Dissent was schism, and schism was condemned in the Bible. In default of turbaned Saracens, they entered on a crusade against Methodists in broadcloth; and the consequence was that the Methodists and Baptists refused to pay the church-rates. Miss Brontë thus describes the state of things at this time:—

"Little Haworth has been all in a bustle about church-rates, since you were here. We had a stirring meeting in the schoolroom. Papa took the chair, and Mr. C. and Mr. W. acted as his supporters, one on each side. There was violent opposition, which set Mr. C.'s Irish blood in a ferment, and if papa had not kept him quiet, partly by persuasion and partly by compulsion, he would have given the Dissenters their kale through the reek—a Scotch proverb, which I will explain to you another time. He and Mr. W. both bottled up their wrath for that time, but it was only to explode with redoubled force at a future period. We had two sermons on dissent, and its consequences, preached last Sunday—one in the afternoon by Mr. W., and one in the evening by Mr. C. All the Dissenters were invited to come and hear, and they actually shut up their chapels, and came in a body; of course the church was crowded. Mr. W. delivered a noble, eloquent, High-Church, Apostolical-Succession discourse, in which he banged the Dissenters most fearlessly and unflinchingly. I thought they had got enough for one while, but it was nothing to the dose that was thrust down their throats in the evening. A keener, cleverer, bolder, and more heart-stirring harangue than that which Mr. C. delivered from Haworth pulpit, last Sunday evening, I never heard. He did not rant; he did not cant; he did not whine; he did not sniggle; he just got up and spoke with the boldness of a man who was impressed with the truth of what he was saying, who has no fear of his enemies, and no dread of consequences. His sermon lasted an hour, yet I was sorry when it was done. I do not say that I agree either with him, or with Mr. W., either in all or in half their opinions. I consider them bigoted, intolerant, and wholly unjustifiable on the ground of common sense. My conscience will not let me be either a Puseyite or a Hookist; *mais*, if I were a Dissenter, I would have taken the first opportunity of kicking, or of horse-whipping both the gentlemen for their stern, bitter attack on my religion and its teachers. But in spite of all this, I admired the noble integrity which could dictate so fearless an opposition against so strong an antagonist.

"P.S.—Mr. W. has given another lecture at the Keighley Mechanics' Institution, and papa has also given a lecture; both are spoken of very highly in the newspapers, and it is mentioned as a matter of wonder that such displays of intellect should emanate from the village of Haworth, 'situated among the bogs and mountains, and, until very lately, supposed to be in a state of semi-barbarism.' Such are the words of the newspaper."

To fill up the account of this outwardly eventless year, I may add a few more extracts from the letters entrusted to me.

"May 15th, 1840.

"Do not be over-persuaded to marry a man you can never respect—I do not say *love*; because, I think, if you can respect a person before marriage, moderate love at least will come after; and as to intense *passion*, I am convinced that that is no desirable feeling. In the first place, it seldom or never meets with a requital; and, in the second place, if it did, the feeling would be only temporary: it would last the honeymoon, and then, perhaps, give place to disgust, or indifference, worse, perhaps, than disgust. Certainly this would be the case on the man's part; and on the woman's— God help her, if she is left to love passionately and alone.

"I am tolerably well convinced that I shall never marry at all. Reason tells me so, and I am not so utterly the slave of feeling but that I can *occasionally hear* her voice."

"June 2nd, 1840.

"M. is not yet come to Haworth; but she is to come on the condition that I first go and stay a few days there. If all be well, I shall go next Wednesday. I may stay at G--- until Friday or Saturday, and the early part of the following week I shall pass with you, if you will have me—which last sentence indeed is nonsense, for as I shall be glad to see you, so I know you will be glad to see me. This arrangement will not allow much time, but it is the only practicable one which, considering all the circumstances, I can effect. Do not urge me to stay more than two or three days, because I shall be obliged to refuse you. I intend to walk to Keighley, there to take the coach as far as B---, then to get some one to carry my box, and to walk the rest of the way to G-. If I manage this, I think I shall contrive very well. I shall reach B. by about five o'clock, and then I shall have the cool of the evening for the walk. I have communicated the whole arrangement to M. I desire exceedingly to see both her and you. Good-bye.

C. B.

"If you have any better plan to suggest I am open to conviction, provided your plan is practicable."

"August 20th, 1840.

"Have you seen anything of Miss H. lately? I wish they, or somebody else, would get me a situation. I have answered advertisements without number, but my applications have met with no success.

"I have got another bale of French books from G. containing upwards of forty volumes. I have read about half. They are like the rest, clever, wicked, sophistical, and immoral. The best of it is, they give one a thorough idea of France and Paris, and are the best substitute for French conversation that I have met with.

"I positively have nothing more to say to you, for I am in a stupid humour. You must excuse this letter not being quite as long as your own. I have written to you soon, that you might not look after the postman in vain. Preserve this writing as a curiosity in caligraphy—I think it is exquisite—all brilliant black blots, and utterly illegible letters. 'CALIBAN.'

"'The wind bloweth where it listeth. Thou hearest the

sound thereof, but canst not tell whence it cometh, nor whither it goeth.' That, I believe, is Scripture, though in what chapter or book, or whether it be correctly quoted, I can't possibly say. However, it behoves me to write a letter to a young woman of the name of E., with whom I was once acquainted, 'in life's morning march, when my spirit was young.' This young woman wished me to write to her some time since, though I have nothing to say—I e'en put it off, day by day, till at last, fearing that she will 'curse me by her gods,' I feel constrained to sit down and tack a few lines together, which she may call a letter or not as she pleases. Now if the young woman expects sense in this production, she will find herself miserably disappointed. I shall dress her a dish of salmagundi—I shall cook a hash—compound a stew—toss up an *omelette soufflèe à la Française*, and send it her with my respects. The wind, which is very high up in our hills of Judea, though, I suppose, down in the Philistine flats of B. parish it is nothing to speak of, has produced the same effects on the contents of my knowledge-box that a quaigh of usquebaugh does upon those of most other bipeds. I see everything *couleur de rose*, and am strongly inclined to dance a jig, if I knew how. I think I must partake of the nature of a pig or an ass—both which animals are strongly affected by a high wind. From what quarter the wind blows I cannot tell, for I never could in my life; but I should very much like to know how the great brewing-tub of Bridlington Bay works, and what sort of yeasty froth rises just now on the waves.

"A woman of the name of Mrs. B., it seems, wants a teacher. I wish she would have me; and I have written to Miss W. to tell her so. Verily, it is a delightful thing to live here at home, at full liberty to do just what one pleases. But I recollect some scrubby old fable about grasshoppers and ants, by a scrubby old knave yclept Æsop; the grasshoppers sang all the summer, and starved all the winter.

"A distant relation of mine, one Patrick Branwell, has set off to seek his fortune in the wild, wandering, adventurous, romantic, knight-errant-like capacity of clerk on the Leeds and Manchester Railroad. Leeds and Manchester—where are they? Cities in the wilderness, like Tadmor, alias Palmyra—are they not?

"There is one little trait respecting Mr. W. which lately came to my knowledge, which gives a glimpse of the better side of his character. Last Saturday night he had been sitting an hour in the parlour with Papa; and, as he went away, I heard Papa say to him 'What is the matter with you? You seem in very low spirits to-night.' 'Oh, I don't know. I've been to see a poor young girl, who, I'm afraid, is dying.' 'Indeed; what is her name?' 'Susan Bland, the daughter of John Bland, the superintendent.' Now Susan Bland is my oldest and best scholar in the Sunday-school; and, when I heard that, I thought I would go as soon as I could to see her. I did go on Monday afternoon, and found her on her way to that 'bourn whence no traveller returns.' After sitting with her some time, I happened to ask her mother, if she thought a little port wine would do her good. She replied that the doctor had recommended it, and that when Mr. W. was last there, he had brought them a bottle of wine and jar of preserves. She added, that he was always good-natured to poor folks, and seemed to have a deal of feeling and kindheartedness about him. No doubt, there are defects in his character, but there are also good qualities . . . God bless him! I wonder who, with his advantages, would be without his faults. I know many of his faulty actions, many of his weak points; yet, where I am, he shall always find rather a defender than an accuser. To be sure, my opinion will go but a very little way to decide his character; what of that? People should do right as far as their ability extends. You are not to suppose, from all this, that Mr. W. and I are on very amiable terms; we are not at all. We are distant, cold, and reserved. We seldom speak; and when we do, it is only to exchange the most trivial and common-place remarks."

The Mrs. B. alluded to in this letter, as in want of a governess, entered into a correspondence with Miss Brontë, and expressed herself much pleased with the letters she received from her, with the "style and candour of the application," in which Charlotte had taken care to tell her, that if she wanted a showy, elegant, or fashionable person, her correspondent was not fitted for such a situation. But Mrs. B. required her governess to give instructions in music and singing, for which Charlotte was not qualified: and, accordingly, the negotiation fell through. But Miss Brontë was not one to sit down in despair after disappointment. Much as she disliked the life of a private governess, it was her duty to relieve her father of the burden of her support, and this was the only way open to her. So she set to advertising and inquiring with fresh vigour.

In the meantime, a little occurrence took place, described in one of her letters, which I shall give, as it shows her instinctive aversion to a particular class of men, whose vices some have supposed she looked upon with indulgence. The extract tells all that need be known, for the purpose I have in view, of the miserable pair to whom it relates.

"You remember Mr. and Mrs. ---? Mrs. --- came here the other day, with a most melancholy tale of her wretched husband's drunken, extravagant, profligate habits. She asked Papa's advice; there was nothing she said but ruin before them. They owed debts which they could never pay. She expected Mr. ---'s instant dismissal from his curacy; she knew, from bitter experience, that his vices were utterly hopeless. He treated her and her child savagely; with much more to the same effect. Papa advised her to leave him for ever, and go home, if she had a home to go to. She said, this was what she had long resolved to do; and she would leave him directly, as soon as Mr. B. dismissed him. She expressed great disgust and contempt towards him, and did not affect to have the shadow of regard in any way. I do not wonder at this, but I do wonder she should ever marry a man towards whom her feelings must always have been pretty much the same as they are now. I am morally certain no decent woman could experience anything but aversion towards such a man as Mr. ---. Before I knew, or suspected his character, and when I rather wondered at his versatile talents, I felt it in an uncontrollable degree. I hated to talk with him—hated to look at him; though as I was not certain that there was substantial reason for such a dislike, and thought it absurd to trust to mere instinct, I both concealed and repressed the feeling as much as I could; and, on all occasions, treated him with as much civility as I was mistress of. I was struck with Mary's expression of a similar feeling at first sight; she said, when we left him, 'That is a hideous man, Charlotte!' I thought 'He is indeed.'"

CHAPTER X

Early in March, 1841, Miss Brontë obtained her second and last situation as a governess. This time she esteemed herself fortunate in becoming a member of a kind-hearted and friendly household. The master of it, she especially regarded as a valuable friend, whose advice helped to guide her in one very important step of her life. But as her definite acquirements were few, she had to eke them out by employing her leisure time in needlework; and altogether her position was that of "bonne" or nursery governess, liable to repeated and never-ending calls upon her time. This description of uncertain, yet perpetual employment, subject to the exercise of another person's will at all hours of the day, was peculiarly trying to one whose life at home had been full of abundant leisure. *Idle* she never was in any place, but of the multitude of small talks, plans, duties, pleasures, &c., that make up most people's days, her home life was nearly destitute. This made it possible for her to go through long and deep histories of feeling and imagination, for which others, odd as it sounds, have rarely time. This made it inevitable that—later on, in her too short career—the intensity of her feeling should wear out her physical health. The habit of "making out," which had grown with her growth, and strengthened with her strength, had become a part of her nature. Yet all exercise of her strongest and most characteristic faculties was now out of the question. She could not (as while she was at Miss W---'s) feel, amidst the occupations of the day, that when evening came, she might employ herself in more congenial ways. No doubt, all who enter upon the career of a governess have to relinquish much; no doubt, it must ever be a life of sacrifice; but to Charlotte Brontë it was a perpetual attempt to force all her faculties into a direction for which the whole of her previous life had unfitted them. Moreover, the little Brontës had been brought up motherless; and from knowing nothing of the gaiety and the sportiveness of childhood—from never having experienced caresses or fond attentions themselves—they were ignorant of the very nature of infancy, or how to call out its engaging qualities. Children were to them the troublesome necessities of humanity; they had never been drawn into contact with them in any other way. Years afterwards, when Miss Brontë came to stay with us, she watched our little girls perpetually; and I could not persuade her that they were only average specimens of well brought up children. She was surprised and touched by any sign of thoughtfulness for others, of kindness to animals, or of unselfishness on their part: and constantly maintained that she was in the right, and I in the wrong, when we differed on the point of their unusual excellence. All this must be borne in mind while reading the following letters. And it must likewise be borne in mind—by those who, surviving her, look back upon her life from their mount of observation—how no distaste, no suffering ever made her shrink from any course which she believed it to be her duty to engage in.

"March 3rd, 1841.

"I told some time since, that I meant to get a situation, and when I said so my resolution was quite fixed. I felt that however often I was disappointed, I had no intention of relinquishing my efforts. After being severely baffled two or three times,—after a world of trouble, in the way of correspondence and interviews,—I have at length succeeded, and am fairly established in my new place.

* * * * *

"The house is not very large, but exceedingly comfortable and well regulated; the grounds are fine and extensive. In taking the place, I have made a large sacrifice in the way of salary, in the hope of securing comfort,—by which word I do not mean to express good eating and drinking, or warm fire, or a soft bed, but the society of cheerful faces, and minds and hearts not dug out of a lead-mine, or cut from a marble quarry. My salary is not really more than 16*l*. per annum, though it is nominally 20*l*., but the expense of washing will be deducted therefrom. My pupils are two in number, a girl of eight, and a boy of six. As to my employers, you will not expect me to say much about their characters when I tell you that I only arrived here yesterday. I have not the faculty of telling an individual's disposition at first sight. Before I can venture to pronounce on a character, I must see it first under various lights and from various points of view. All I can say therefore is, both Mr. and Mrs. --- seem to me good sort of people. I have as yet had no cause to complain of want of considerateness or civility. My pupils are wild and unbroken, but apparently well-disposed. I wish I may be able to say as much next time I write to you. My earnest wish and endeavour will be to please them. If I can but feel that I am giving satisfaction, and if at the same time I can keep my health, I shall, I hope, be moderately happy. But no one but myself can tell how hard a governess's work is to me—for no one but myself is aware how utterly averse my whole mind and nature are for the employment. Do not think that I fail to blame myself for this, or that I leave any means unemployed to conquer this feeling. Some of my greatest difficulties lie in things that would appear to you comparatively trivial. I find it so hard to repel the rude familiarity of children. I find it so difficult to ask either servants or mistress for anything I want, however much I want it. It is less pain for me to endure the greatest inconvenience than to go into the kitchen to request its removal. I am a fool. Heaven knows I cannot help it!

"Now can you tell me whether it is considered improper for governesses to ask their friends to come and see them. I do not mean, of course, to stay, but just for a call of an hour or two? If it is not absolute treason, I do fervently request that you will contrive, in some way or other, to let me have a sight of your face. Yet I feel, at the same time, that I am making a very foolish and almost impracticable demand; yet this is only four miles from B---!"

* * * * *

"March 21st.

"You must excuse a very short answer to your most welcome letter; for my time is entirely occupied. Mrs. --- expected a good deal of sewing from me. I cannot sew much during the day, on account of the children, who require the utmost attention. I am obliged, therefore, to devote the evenings to this business. Write to me often; very long letters. It will do both of us good. This place is far better than ---, but God knows, I have enough to do to keep a good heart in the matter. What you said has cheered me a little. I wish I could always act according to your advice. Home-sickness affects me sorely. I like Mr. --- extremely. The children are over-indulged, and consequently hard at times to manage. *Do, do,* do come and see me; if it be a breach of etiquette, never mind. If you can only stop an hour, come. Talk no more about my forsaking you; my darling, I could not afford to do it. I find it is not in my nature to get on in this weary world without sympathy and attachment in some quarter; and seldom indeed do we find it. It is too great a treasure to be ever wantonly thrown away when once secured."

Miss Brontë had not been many weeks in her new situation before she had a proof of the kind-hearted hospitality of her employers. Mr. --- wrote to her father, and urgently invited him to come and make acquaintance with his daughter's new home, by spending a week with her in it; and Mrs. --- expressed great regret when one of Miss Brontë's friends drove up to the house to leave a letter or parcel, without entering. So she found that all her friends might freely visit her, and that her father would be received with especial gladness. She thankfully acknowledged this kindness in writing to urge her friend afresh to come and see her; which she accordingly did.

"June, 1841.

"You can hardly fancy it possible, I dare say, that I cannot find a quarter of an hour to scribble a note in; but so it is; and when a note is written, it has to be carried a mile to the post, and that consumes nearly an hour, which is a large portion of the day. Mr. and Mrs. --- have been gone a week. I heard from them this morning. No time is fixed for their return, but I hope it will not be delayed long, or I shall miss the chance of seeing Anne this vacation. She came home, I understand, last Wednesday, and is only to be allowed three weeks' vacation, because the family she is with are going to Scarborough. *I should like to see her*, to judge for myself of the state of her health. I dare not trust any other person's report, no one seems minute enough in their observations. I should very much have liked you to have seen her. I have got on very well with the servants and children so far; yet it is dreary, solitary work. You can tell as well as me the lonely feeling of being without a companion."

Soon after this was written, Mr. and Mrs. --- returned, in time to allow Charlotte to go and look after Anne's health, which, as she found to her intense anxiety, was far from strong. What could she do to nurse and cherish up this little sister, the youngest of them all? Apprehension about her brought up once more the idea of keeping a school. If, by this means, they three could live together, and maintain themselves, all might go well. They would have some time of their own, in which to try again and yet again at that literary career, which, in spite of all baffling difficulties, was never quite set aside as an ultimate object; but far the strongest motive with Charlotte was the conviction that Anne's health was so delicate that it required a degree of tending which none but her sister could give. Thus she wrote during those midsummer holidays.

"Haworth, July 18th, 1841.

"We waited long and anxiously for you, on the Thursday that you promised to come. I quite wearied my eyes with watching from the window, eye-glass in hand, and sometimes spectacles on nose. However, you are not to blame . . . and as to disappointment, why, all must suffer disappointment at some period or other of their lives. But a hundred things I had to say to you will now be forgotten, and never said. There is a project hatching in this house, which both Emily and I anxiously wished to discuss with you. The project is yet in its infancy, hardly peeping from its shell; and whether it will ever come out a fine fullfledged chicken, or will turn addle and die before it cheeps, is one of those considerations that are but dimly revealed by the oracles of futurity. Now, don't be nonplussed by all this metaphorical mystery. I talk of a plain and everyday occurrence, though, in Delphic style, I wrap up the information in figures of speech concerning eggs, chickens etceatera, etcaeterorum. To come to the point: Papa and aunt talk, by fits and starts, of our—id est, Emily, Anne, and myself—commencing a school! I have often, you know, said how much I wished such a thing; but I never could conceive where the capital was to come from for making such a speculation. I was well aware, indeed, that aunt had money, but I always considered that she was the last person who would offer a loan for the purpose in question. A loan, however, she *has* offered, or rather intimates that she perhaps *will* offer in case pupils can be secured, an eligible situation obtained, &c. This sounds very fair, but still there are matters to be considered which throw something of a damp upon the scheme. I do not expect that aunt will sink more than 150*l.* in such a venture; and would it be possible to establish a respectable (not by any means a *showy*) school, and to commence housekeeping with a capital of only that amount? Propound the question to your sister, if you think she can answer it; if not, don't say a word on the subject. As to getting into debt, that is a thing we could none of us reconcile our mind to for a moment. We do not care how modest, how humble our commencement be, so it be made on sure grounds, and have a safe foundation. In thinking of all possible and impossible places where we could establish a school, I have thought of Burlington, or rather of the neighbourhood of Burlington. Do you remember whether there was any other school there besides that of Miss ---? This is, of course, a perfectly crude and random idea. There are a hundred reasons why it should be an impracticable one. We have no connections, no acquaintances there; it is far from home, &c. Still, I fancy the ground in the East Riding is less fully occupied than in the West. Much inquiry and consideration will be necessary, of course, before any place is decided on; and I fear much time will elapse before any plan is executed . . . Write as soon as you can. I shall not leave my present situation till my future prospects assume a more fixed and definite aspect."

A fortnight afterwards, we see that the seed has been sown which was to grow up into a plan materially influencing her future life.

"August 7th, 1841.

"This is Saturday evening; I have put the children to bed; now I am going to sit down and answer your letter. I am again by myself—housekeeper and governess—for Mr. and Mrs. --- are staying at ---. To speak truth, though I am solitary while they are away, it is still by far the happiest part of my time. The children are under decent control, the servants are very observant and attentive to me, and the occasional absence of the master and mistress relieves me from the duty of always endeavouring to seem cheerful and conversable. Martha ---, it appears, is in the way of enjoying great advantages; so is Mary, for you will be surprised to hear that she is returning immediately to the Continent with her brother; not, however, to stay there, but to take a month's tour and recreation. I have had a long letter from Mary, and a packet containing a present of a very handsome black silk scarf, and a pair of beautiful kid gloves, bought at Brussels. Of course, I was in one sense pleased with the gift—pleased that they should think of me so far off, amidst the excitements of one of the most splendid capitals of Europe; and yet it felt irksome to accept it. I should think Mary and Martha have not more than sufficient pocket-money to supply themselves. I wish they had testified their regard by a less expensive token. Mary's letters spoke of some of the pictures and cathedrals she had seen—pictures the most exquisite, cathedrals the most venerable. I hardly know what swelled to my throat as I read her letter: such a vehement impatience of restraint and steady work; such a strong wish for wings—wings such as wealth can furnish; such an urgent thirst to see, to know, to learn; something internal seemed to expand bodily for a minute. I was tantalised by the consciousness of faculties unexercised,—then all collapsed, and I despaired. My dear, I would hardly make that confession to any one but yourself; and to you, rather in a letter than *vivâ voce*. These rebellious and absurd emotions were only momentary; I quelled them in five minutes. I hope they will not revive, for they were acutely painful. No further steps have been taken about the project I mentioned to you, nor probably will be for the present; but Emily, and Anne, and I, keep it in view. It is our polar star, and we look to it in all circumstances of despondency. I begin to suspect I am writing in a strain which will make you think I am unhappy. This is far from being the case; on the contrary, I know my place is a favourable one, for a governess. What dismays and haunts me sometimes, is a conviction that I have no natural knack for my vocation. If teaching only were requisite, it would be smooth and easy; but it is the living in other people's houses—the estrangement from one's real character—the adoption of a cold, rigid, apathetic exterior, that is painful . . . You will not mention our school project at present. A project not actually commenced is always uncertain. Write to me often, my dear Nell; you *know* your letters are valued. Your 'loving child' (as you choose to call me so),

C. B.

"P.S. I am well in health; don't fancy I am not, but I have one aching feeling at my heart (I must allude to it, though I had resolved not to). It is about Anne; she has so much to endure: far, far more than I ever had. When my thoughts turn to her, they always see her as a patient, persecuted stranger. I know what concealed susceptibility is in her nature, when her feelings are wounded. I wish I could be with her, to administer a little balm. She is more lonely—less gifted with the power of making friends, even than I am. 'Drop the subject.'"

She could bear much for herself; but she could not patiently bear the sorrows of others, especially of her sisters; and again, of the two sisters, the idea of the little, gentle, youngest suffering in lonely patience, was insupportable to her. Something must be done. No matter if the desired end were far away; all time was lost in which she was not making progress, however slow, towards it. To have a school, was to have some portion of daily leisure, uncontrolled but by her own sense of duty; it was for the three sisters, loving each other with so passionate an affection, to be together under one roof, and yet earning their own subsistence; above all, it was to have the power of watching over these two whose life and happiness were ever to Charlotte far more than her own. But no trembling impatience should lead her to take an unwise step in haste. She inquired in every direction she could, as to the chances which a new school might have of success. In all there seemed more establishments like the one which the sisters wished to set up than could be supported. What was to be done? Superior advantages must be offered. But how? They themselves abounded in thought, power, and information; but these are qualifications scarcely fit to be inserted in a prospectus. Of French they knew something; enough to read it fluently, but hardly enough to teach it in competition with natives or professional masters. Emily and Anne had some knowledge of music; but here again it was doubtful whether, without more instruction, they could engage to give lessons in it.

Just about this time, Miss W--- was thinking of relinquishing her school at Dewsbury Moor; and offered to give it up in favour of her old pupils, the Brontës. A sister of hers had taken the active management since the time when Charlotte was a teacher; but the number of pupils had diminished; and, if the Brontës undertook it, they would have to try and work it up to its former state of prosperity. This, again, would require advantages on their part which they did not at present possess, but which Charlotte caught a glimpse of. She resolved to follow the clue, and never to rest till she had reached a successful issue. With the forced calm of a suppressed eagerness, that sends a glow of desire through every word of the following letter, she wrote to her aunt thus.

"Dear Aunt,

"Sept. 29th, 1841.

"I have heard nothing of Miss W--- yet since I wrote to her, intimating that I would accept her offer. I cannot conjecture the reason of this long silence, unless some unforeseen impediment has occurred in concluding the bargain. Meantime, a plan has been suggested and approved by Mr. and Mrs. --- " (the father and mother of her pupils) "and others, which I wish now to impart to you. My friends recommend me, if I desire to secure permanent success, to delay commencing the school for six months longer, and by all means to contrive, by hook or by crook, to spend the intervening time in some school on the continent. They say schools in England are so numerous, competition so great, that without some such step towards attaining superiority, we shall probably have a very hard struggle, and may fail in the end. They say, moreover, that the loan of 100*l*., which you have been so kind as to offer us, will, perhaps, not be all required now, as Miss W--- will lend us the furniture; and that, if the speculation is intended to be a good and successful one, half the sum, at least, ought to be laid out in the manner I have mentioned, thereby insuring a more speedy repayment both of interest and principal.

"I would not go to France or to Paris. I would go to Brussels, in Belgium. The cost of the journey there, at the dearest rate of travelling, would be 5*l*.; living is there little more than half as dear as it is in England, and the facilities for education are equal or superior to any other place in Europe. In half a year, I could acquire a thorough familiarity with French. I could improve greatly in Italian, and even get a dash of German, i.e., providing my health continued as good as it is now. Mary is now staying at Brussels, at a first-rate establishment there. I should not think of going to the Château de Kokleberg, where she is resident, as the terms are much too high; but if I wrote to her, she, with the assistance of Mrs. Jenkins, the wife of the British Chaplain, would be able to secure me a cheap, decent residence and respectable protection. I should have the opportunity of seeing her frequently; she would make me acquainted with the city; and, with the assistance of her cousins, I should probably be introduced to connections far more improving, polished, and cultivated, than any I have yet known.

"These are advantages which would turn to real account, when we actually commenced a school; and, if Emily could share them with me, we could take a footing in the world afterwards which we can never do now. I say Emily instead of Anne; for Anne might take her turn at some future period, if our school answered. I feel certain, while I am writing, that you will see the propriety of what I say. You always like to use your money to the best advantage. You are not fond of making shabby purchases; when you do confer a favour, it is often done in style; and depend upon it, 50*l*., or 100*l*., thus laid out, would be well employed.

Of course, I know no other friend in the world to whom I could apply on this subject except yourself. I feel an absolute conviction that, if this advantage were allowed us, it would be the making of us for life. Papa will, perhaps, think it a wild and ambitious scheme; but who ever rose in the world without ambition? When he left Ireland to go to Cambridge University, he was as ambitious as I am now. I want us *all* to get on. I know we have talents, and I want them to be turned to account. I look to you, aunt, to help us. I think you will not refuse. I know, if you consent, it shall not be my fault if you ever repent your kindness."

This letter was written from the house in which she was residing as governess. It was some little time before an answer came. Much had to be talked over between the father and aunt in Haworth Parsonage. At last consent was given. Then, and not till then, she confided her plan to an intimate friend. She was not one to talk over-much about any project, while it remained uncertain—to speak about her labour, in any direction, while its result was doubtful.

"Nov. 2nd, 1841.

"Now let us begin to quarrel. In the first place, I must consider whether I will commence operations on the defensive, or the offensive. The defensive, I think. You say, and I see plainly, that your feelings have been hurt by an apparent want of confidence on my part. You heard from others of Miss W---'s overtures before I communicated them to you myself. This is true. I was deliberating on plans important to my future prospects. I never exchanged a letter with you on the subject. True again. This appears strange conduct to a friend, near and dear, long-known, and never found wanting. Most true. I cannot give you my *excuses* for this behaviour; this word *excuse* implies confession of a fault, and I do not feel that I have been in fault. The plain fact is, I *was* not, I am not now, certain of my destiny. On the contrary, I have been most uncertain, perplexed with contradictory schemes and proposals. My time, as I have often told you, is fully occupied; yet I had many letters to write, which it was absolutely necessary should be written. I knew it would avail nothing to write to you then to say I was in doubt and uncertainty—hoping this, fearing that, anxious, eagerly desirous to do what seemed impossible to be done. When I thought of you in that busy interval, it was to resolve, that you should know all when my way was clear, and my grand end attained. If I could, I would always work in silence and obscurity, and let my efforts be known by their results. Miss W--- did most kindly propose that I should come to Dewsbury Moor and attempt to revive the school her sister had relinquished. She offered me the use of her furniture. At first, I received the proposal cordially, and prepared to do my utmost to bring about success; but a fire was kindled in my very heart, which I could not quench. I so longed to increase my attainments—to become something better than I am; a glimpse of what I felt, I showed to you in one of my former letters—only a glimpse; Mary cast oil upon the flames— encouraged me, and in her own strong, energetic language, heartened me on. I longed to go to Brussels; but how could I get there? I wished for one, at least, of my sisters to share the advantage with me. I fixed on Emily. She deserved the reward, I knew. How could the point be managed? In extreme excitement, I wrote a letter home, which carried the day. I made an appeal to aunt for assistance, which was answered by consent. Things are not settled; yet it is sufficient to say we have a *chance* of going for half a year. Dewsbury Moor is relinquished. Perhaps, fortunately so. In my secret soul, I believe there is no cause to regret it. My plans for the future are bounded to this intention: if I once get to Brussels, and if my health is spared, I will do my best to make the utmost of every advantage that shall come within my reach. When the half-year is expired, I will do what I can.

* * * * *

"Believe me, though I was born in April, the month of cloud and sunshine, I am not changeful. My spirits are unequal, and sometimes I speak vehemently, and sometimes I say nothing at all; but I have a steady regard for you, and if you will let the cloud and shower pass by, be sure the sun is always behind, obscured, but still existing."

At Christmas she left her situation, after a parting with her employers which seems to have affected and touched her greatly. "They only made too much of me," was her remark, after leaving this family; "I did not deserve it."

* * * * *

All four children hoped to meet together at their father's house this December. Branwell expected to have a short leave of absence from his employment as a clerk on the Leeds and Manchester Railway, in which he had been engaged for five months. Anne arrived before Christmas-day. She had rendered herself so valuable in her difficult situation, that her employers vehemently urged her to return, although she had announced her resolution to leave them; partly on account of the harsh treatment she had received, and partly because her stay at home, during her sisters' absence in Belgium, seemed desirable, when the age of the three remaining inhabitants of the parsonage was taken into consideration.

After some correspondence and much talking over plans at home, it seemed better, in consequence of letters which they received from Brussels giving a discouraging account of the schools there, that Charlotte and Emily should go to an institution at Lille, in the north of France, which was highly recommended by Baptist Noel, and other clergymen. Indeed, at the end of January, it was arranged that they were to set off for this place in three weeks, under the escort of a French lady, then visiting in London. The terms were 50*l*. each pupil, for board and French alone, but a separate room was to be allowed for this sum; without this indulgence, it was lower. Charlotte writes:—

"January 20th, 1842.

"I consider it kind in aunt to consent to an extra sum for a separate room. We shall find it a great privilege in many ways. I regret the change from Brussels to Lille on many accounts, chiefly that I shall not see Martha. Mary has been indefatigably kind in providing me with information. She has grudged no labour, and scarcely any expense, to that end. Mary's price is above rubies. I have, in fact, two friends—you and her—staunch and true, in whose faith and sincerity I have as strong a belief as I have in the Bible. I have bothered you both—you especially; but you always get the tongs and heap coals of fire upon my head. I have had letters to write lately to Brussels, to Lille, and to London. I have lots of chemises, nightgowns, pocket-handkerchiefs, and pockets to make; besides clothes to repair. I have been, every week since I came home, expecting to see Branwell, and he has never been able to get over yet. We fully expect him, however, next Saturday. Under these circumstances how can I go visiting? You tantalize me to death with talking of conversations by the fireside. Depend upon it, we are not to have any such for many a long month to come. I get an interesting impression of old age upon my face; and when you see me next I shall certainly wear caps and spectacles."

CHAPTER XI

I am not aware of all the circumstances which led to the relinquishment of the Lille plan. Brussels had had from the first a strong attraction for Charlotte; and the idea of going there, in preference to any other place, had only been given up in consequence of the information received of the second-rate character of its schools. In one of her letters reference has been made to Mrs. Jenkins, the wife of the chaplain of the British Embassy. At the request of his brother—a clergyman, living not many miles from Haworth, and an acquaintance of Mr. Brontë's—she made much inquiry, and at length, after some discouragement in her search, heard of a school which seemed in every respect desirable. There was an English lady who had long lived in the Orleans family, amidst the various fluctuations of their fortunes, and who, when the Princess Louise was married to King Leopold, accompanied her to Brussels, in the capacity of reader. This lady's granddaughter was receiving her education at the pensionnat of Madame Héger; and so satisfied was the grandmother with the kind of instruction given, that she named the establishment, with high encomiums, to Mrs. Jerkins; and, in consequence, it was decided that, if the terms suited, Miss Brontë and Emily should proceed thither. M. Héger informs me that, on receipt of a letter from Charlotte, making very particular inquiries as to the possible amount of what are usually termed "extras," he and his wife were so much struck by the simple earnest tone of the letter, that they said to each other:—"These are the daughters of an English pastor, of moderate means, anxious to learn with an ulterior view of instructing others, and to whom the risk of additional expense is of great consequence. Let us name a specific sum, within which all expenses shall be included."

This was accordingly done; the agreement was concluded, and the Brontës prepared to leave their native county for the first time, if we except the melancholy and memorable residence at Cowan Bridge. Mr. Brontë determined to accompany his daughters. Mary and her brother, who were experienced in foreign travelling, were also of the party. Charlotte first saw London in the day or two they now stopped there; and, from an expression in one of her subsequent letters, they all, I believe, stayed at the Chapter Coffee House, Paternoster Row—a strange, old-fashioned tavern, of which I shall have more to say hereafter.

Mary's account of their journey is thus given.

"In passing through London, she seemed to think our business was and ought to be, to see all the pictures and statues we could. She knew the artists, and know where other productions of theirs were to be found. I don't remember what we saw except St. Paul's. Emily was like her in these habits of mind, but certainly never took her opinion, but always had one to offer . . . I don't know what Charlotte thought of Brussels. We arrived in the dark, and went next morning to our respective schools to see them. We were, of course, much preoccupied, and our prospects gloomy. Charlotte used to like the country round Brussels. 'At the top of every hill you see something.' She took, long solitary walks on the occasional holidays."

Mr. Brontë took his daughters to the Rue d'Isabelle, Brussels; remained one night at Mr. Jenkins'; and straight returned to his wild Yorkshire village.

What a contrast to that must the Belgian capital have presented to those two young women thus left behind! Suffering acutely from every strange and unaccustomed contact—far away from their beloved home, and the dear moors beyond—their indomitable will was their great support. Charlotte's own words, with regard to Emily, are:—

"After the age of twenty, having meantime studied alone

with diligence and perseverance, she went with me to an establishment on the continent. The same suffering and conflict ensued, heightened by the strong recoil of her upright heretic and English spirit from the gentle Jesuitry of the foreign and Romish system. Once more she seemed sinking, but this time she rallied through the mere force of resolution: with inward remorse and shame she looked back on her former failure, and resolved to conquer, but the victory cost her dear. She was never happy till she carried her hard-won knowledge back to the remote English village, the old parsonage-house, and desolate Yorkshire hills."

They wanted learning. They came for learning. They would learn. Where they had a distinct purpose to be achieved in intercourse with their fellows, they forgot themselves; at all other times they were miserably shy. Mrs. Jenkins told me that she used to ask them to spend Sundays and holidays with her, until she found that they felt more pain than pleasure from such visits. Emily hardly ever uttered more than a monosyllable. Charlotte was sometimes excited sufficiently to speak eloquently and well—on certain subjects; but before her tongue was thus loosened, she had a habit of gradually wheeling round on her chair, so as almost to conceal her face from the person to whom she was speaking.

And yet there was much in Brussels to strike a responsive chord in her powerful imagination. At length she was seeing somewhat of that grand old world of which she had dreamed. As the gay crowds passed by her, so had gay crowds paced those streets for centuries, in all their varying costumes. Every spot told an historic tale, extending back into the fabulous ages when Jan and Jannika, the aboriginal giant and giantess, looked over the wall, forty feet high, of what is now the Rue Villa Hermosa, and peered down upon the new settlers who were to turn them out of the country in which they had lived since the deluge. The great solemn Cathedral of St. Gudule, the religious paintings, the striking forms and ceremonies of the Romish Church—all made a deep impression on the girls, fresh from the bare walls and simple worship of Haworth Church. And then they were indignant with themselves for having been susceptible of this impression, and their stout Protestant hearts arrayed themselves against the false Duessa that had thus imposed upon them.

The very building they occupied as pupils, in Madame Héger's pensionnat, had its own ghostly train of splendid associations, marching for ever, in shadowy procession, through and through the ancient rooms, and shaded alleys of the gardens. From the splendour of to-day in the Rue Royale, if you turn aside, near the statue of the General Beliard, you look down four flights of broad stone steps upon the Rue d'Isabelle. The chimneys of the houses in it are below your feet. Opposite to the lowest flight of steps, there is a large old mansion facing you, with a spacious walled garden behind—and to the right of it. In front of this garden, on the same side as the mansion, and with great boughs of trees sweeping over their lowly roofs, is a row of small, picturesque, old-fashioned cottages, not unlike, in degree and uniformity, to the almshouses so often seen in an English country town. The Rue d'Isabelle looks as though it had been untouched by the innovations of the builder for the last three centuries; and yet any one might drop a stone into it from the back windows of the grand modern hotels in the Rue Royale, built and furnished in the newest Parisian fashion.

In the thirteenth century, the Rue d'Isabelle was called the Fossé-aux-Chiens; and the kennels for the ducal hounds occupied the place where Madame Héger's pensionnat now stands. A hospital (in the ancient large meaning of the word) succeeded to the kennel. The houseless and the poor, perhaps the leprous, were received, by the brethren of a religious order, in a building on this sheltered site; and what had been a fosse for defence, was filled up with herb-gardens and orchards for upwards of a hundred years. Then came the aristocratic guild of the cross-bow men—that company the members whereof were required to prove their noble descent—untainted for so many generations, before they could be admitted into the guild; and, being admitted, were required to swear a solemn oath, that no other pastime or exercise should take up any part of their leisure, the whole of which was to be devoted to the practice of the noble art of shooting with the cross-bow. Once a year a grand match was held, under the patronage of some saint, to whose church-steeple was affixed the bird, or semblance of a bird, to be hit by the victor. {5} The conqueror in the game was Roi des Arbalétriers for the coming year, and received a jewelled decoration accordingly, which he was entitled to wear for twelve months; after which he restored it to the guild, to be again striven for. The family of him who died during the year that he was king, were bound to present the decoration to the church of the patron saint of the guild, and to furnish a similar prize to be contended for afresh. These noble cross-bow men of the middle ages formed a sort of armed guard to the powers in existence, and almost invariably took the aristocratic, in preference to the democratic side, in the numerous civil dissensions of the Flemish towns. Hence they were protected by the authorities, and easily obtained favourable and sheltered sites for their exercise-ground. And thus they came to occupy the old fosse, and took possession of the great orchard of the hospital, lying tranquil and sunny in the hollow below the rampart.

But, in the sixteenth century, it became necessary to construct a street through the exercise-ground of the "Arbalétriers du Grand Serment," and, after much delay, the company were induced by the beloved Infanta Isabella to give up the requisite plot of ground. In recompense for this, Isabella—who herself was a member of the guild, and had even shot down the bird, and been queen in 1615—made many presents to the arbalétriers; and, in return, the grateful city, which had long wanted a nearer road to St. Gudule, but been baffled by the noble archers, called the street after her name. She, as a sort of indemnification to the arbalétriers, caused a "great mansion" to be built for their accommodation in the new Rue d'Isabelle. This mansion was placed in front of their exercise-ground, and was of a square shape. On a remote part of the walls, may still be read—

PHILLIPPO IIII. HISPAN. REGE. ISABELLA-CLARA-
EUGENIA HISPAN. INFANS. MAGNÆ GULDÆ REGINA
GULDÆ FRATRIBUS POSUIT.

In that mansion were held all the splendid feasts of the Grand Serment des Arbalétriers. The master-archer lived there constantly, in order to be ever at hand to render his services to the guild. The great saloon was also used for the court balls and festivals, when the archers were not admitted. The Infanta caused other and smaller houses to be built in her new street, to serve as residences for her "garde noble;" and for her "garde bourgeoise," a small habitation each, some of which still remain, to remind us of English almshouses. The "great mansion," with its quadrangular form; the spacious saloon—once used for the archducal balls, where the dark, grave Spaniards mixed with the blond nobility of Brabant and Flanders—now a schoolroom for Belgian girls; the cross-bow men's archery-ground—all are there—the pensionnat of Madame Héger.

This lady was assisted in the work of instruction by her husband—a kindly, wise, good, and religious man—whose acquaintance I am glad to have made, and who has furnished me with some interesting details, from his wife's recollections and his own, of the two Miss Brontës during their residence in Brussels. He had the better opportunities of watching them, from his giving lessons in the French language and literature in the school. A short extract from a letter, written to me by a French lady resident in Brussels, and well qualified to judge, will help to show the estimation in which he is held.

"Je ne connais pas personnellement M. Héger, mais je sais qu'il est peu de caractères aussi nobles, aussi admirables que le sien. Il est un des membres les plus zélés de cette Société de S. Vincent de Paul dont je t'ai déjà parlé, et ne se contente pas de servir les pauvres et les malades, mais leur consacre encore les soirées. Après des journées absorbées tout entières par les devoirs que sa place lui impose, il réunit les pauvres, les ouvriers, leur donne des cours gratuits, et trouve encore le moyen de les amuser en les instruisant. Ce dévouement te dira assez que M. Héger est profondement et ouvertement religieux. Il a des manières franches et avenantes; il se fait aimer de tous ceux qui l'approchent, et surtout des enfants. Il a la parole facile, et possde à un haut degré l'éloquence du bon sens et du coeur. Il n'est point auteur. Homme de zèle et de conscience, il vient de se démettre des fonctions élevées et lucratives qu'il exerçait à l'Athénée, celles de Préfet des Etudes, parce qu'il ne peut y réaliser le bien qu'il avait espéré, introduire l'enseignement religieux dans le programme des études. J'ai vu une fois Madame Héger, qui a quelque chose de froid et de compassé dans son maintien, et qui prévient peu en sa faveur. Je la crois pourtant aimée et appréciée par ses élèves."

There were from eighty to a hundred pupils in the pensionnat, when Charlotte and Emily Brontë entered in February 1842.

M. Héger's account is that they knew nothing of French. I suspect they knew as much (or as little), for all conversational purposes, as any English girls do, who have never been abroad, and have only learnt the idioms and pronunciation from an Englishwoman. The two sisters clung together, and kept apart from the herd of happy, boisterous, well-befriended Belgian girls, who, in their turn, thought the new English pupils wild and scared-looking, with strange, odd, insular ideas about dress; for Emily had taken a fancy to the fashion, ugly and preposterous even during its reign, of gigot sleves, and persisted in wearing them long after they were "gone out." Her petticoats, too, had not a curve or a wave in them, but hung down straight and long, clinging to her lank figure. The sisters spoke to no one but from necessity. They were too full of earnest thought, and of the exile's sick yearning, to be ready for careless conversation or merry game. M. Héger, who had done little but observe, during the few first weeks of their residence in the Rue d'Isabelle, perceived that with their unusual characters, and extraordinary talents, a different mode must be adopted from that in which he generally taught French to English girls. He seems to have rated Emily's genius as something even higher than Charlotte's; and her estimation of their relative powers was the same. Emily had a head for logic, and a capability of argument, unusual in a man, and rare indeed in a woman, according to M. Héger. Impairing the force of this gift, was a stubborn tenacity of will, which rendered her obtuse to all reasoning where her own wishes, or her own sense of right, was concerned. "She should have been a man—a great navigator," said M. Héger in speaking of her. "Her powerful reason would have deduced new spheres of discovery from the knowledge of the old; and her strong imperious will would never have been daunted by opposition or difficulty; never have given way but with life." And yet, moreover, her faculty of imagination was such that, if she had written a history, her view of scenes and characters would have been so vivid, and so powerfully expressed, and supported by such a show of argument, that it would have dominated over the reader, whatever might have been his previous opinions, or his cooler perceptions of its truth. But she appeared egotistical and exacting compared to Charlotte, who was always unselfish (this is M. Héger's testimony); and in the anxiety of the elder to make her younger sister contented she allowed her to exercise a kind of unconscious tyranny over her.

After consulting with his wife, M. Héger told them that he meant to dispense with the old method of grounding in grammar, vocabulary, &c., and to proceed on a new plan—something similar to what he had occasionally adopted with the elder among his French and Belgian pupils. He proposed to read to them some of the master-pieces of the most celebrated French authors (such as Casimir de la Vigne's poem on the "Death of Joan of Arc," parts of Bossuet, the admirable translation of the noble letter of St. Ignatius to the Roman Christians in the "Bibliothèque Choisie des Pères de l'Eglise," &c.), and after having thus impressed the complete effect of the whole, to analyse the parts with them, pointing out in what such or such an author excelled, and where were the blemishes. He believed that he had to do with pupils capable, from their ready sympathy with the intellectual, the refined, the polished, or the noble, of catching the echo of a style, and so reproducing their own thoughts in a somewhat similar manner.

After explaining his plan to them, he awaited their reply. Emily spoke first; and said that she saw no good to be derived from it; and that, by adopting it, they should lose all originality of thought and expression. She would have entered into an argument on the subject, but for this, M. Héger had no time. Charlotte then spoke; she also doubted the success of the plan; but she would follow out M. Héger's advice, because she was bound to obey him while she was his pupil. Before speaking of the results, it may be desirable to give an extract from one of her letters, which shows some of her first impressions of her new life.

"Brussels, 1842 (May?).

"I was twenty-six years old a week or two since; and at this ripe time of life I am a school-girl, and, on the whole, very happy in that capacity. It felt very strange at first to submit to authority instead of exercising it—to obey orders instead of giving them; but I like that state of things. I returned to it with the same avidity that a cow, that has long been kept on dry hay, returns to fresh grass. Don't laugh at my simile. It is natural to me to submit, and very unnatural to command.

"This is a large school, in which there are about forty externes, or day pupils, and twelve pensionnaires, or boarders. Madame Héger, the head, is a lady of precisely the same cast of mind, degree of cultivation, and quality of intellect as Miss ---. I think the severe points are a little softened, because she has not been disappointed, and consequently soured. In a word, she is a married instead of a maiden lady. There are three teachers in the school—Mademoiselle Blanche, Mademoiselle Sophie, and Mademoiselle Marie. The two first have no particular character. One is an old maid, and the other will be one. Mademoiselle Marie is talented and original, but of repulsive and arbitrary manners, which have made the whole school, except myself and Emily, her bitter enemies. No less than seven masters attend, to teach the different branches of education—French, Drawing, Music, Singing, Writing, Arithmetic, and German. All in the house are Catholics except ourselves, one other girl, and the gouvernante of Madame's children, an Englishwoman, in rank something between a lady's maid and a nursery governess. The difference in country and religion makes a broad line of demarcation between us and all the rest. We are completely isolated in the midst of numbers. Yet I think I am never unhappy; my present life is so delightful, so congenial to my own nature, compared to that of a governess. My time, constantly occupied, passes too rapidly. Hitherto both Emily and I have had good health, and therefore we have been able to work well. There is one individual of whom I have not yet spoken—M. Héger, the husband of Madame. He is professor of rhetoric, a man of power as to mind, but very choleric and irritable in temperament. He is very angry with me just at present, because I have written a translation which he chose to stigmatize as '*peu correct.*' He did not tell me so, but wrote the word on the margin of my book, and asked, in brief stern phrase, how it happened that my compositions were always better than my translations? adding that the thing seemed to him inexplicable. The fact is, some weeks ago, in a high-flown humour, he forbade me to use either dictionary or grammar in translating the most difficult English compositions into French. This makes the task rather arduous, and compels me every now and then to introduce an English word, which nearly plucks the eyes out of his head when he sees it. Emily and he don't draw well together at all. Emily works like a horse, and she has had great difficulties to contend with—far greater than I have had. Indeed, those who come to a French school for instruction ought previously to have acquired a considerable knowledge of the French language, otherwise they will lose a great deal of time, for the course of instruction is adapted to natives and not to foreigners; and in these large establishments they will not change their ordinary course for one or two strangers. The few private lessons that M. Héger has vouchsafed to give us, are, I suppose, to be considered a great favour; and I can perceive they have already excited much spite and jealousy in the school.

"You will abuse this letter for being short and dreary, and there are a hundred things which I want to tell you, but I have not time. Brussels is a beautiful city. The Belgians hate the English. Their external morality is more rigid than ours. To lace the stays without a handkerchief on the neck is considered a disgusting piece of indelicacy."

The passage in this letter where M. Héger is represented as prohibiting the use of dictionary or grammar, refers, I imagine, to the time I have mentioned, when he determined to adopt a new method of instruction in the French language, of which they were to catch the spirit and rhythm rather from the ear and the heart, as its noblest accents fell upon them, than by over-careful and anxious study of its grammatical rules. It seems to me a daring experiment on the part of their teacher; but, doubtless, he knew his ground; and that it answered is evident in the composition of some of Charlotte's *devoirs*, written about this time. I am tempted, in illustration of this season of mental culture, to recur to a conversation which I had with M. Héger on the manner in which he formed his pupils' style, and to give a proof of his success, by copying a *devoir* of Charlotte's with his remarks upon it.

He told me that one day this summer (when the Brontës had been for about four months receiving instruction from him) he read to them Victor Hugo's celebrated portrait of Mirabeau, "mais, dans ma leçon je me bornais à ce qui concerne *Mirabeau orateur.* C'est après l'analyse de ce morceau, considéré surtout du point de vue du fond, de la disposition de ce qu'on pourrait appeler *la charpente* qu'ont été faits les deux portraits que je vous donne." He went on to say that he had pointed out to them the fault in Victor Hugo's style as being exaggeration in conception, and, at the same time, he had made them notice the extreme beauty of his "nuances" of expression. They were then dismissed to choose the subject of a similar kind of portrait. This selection M. Héger always left to them; for "it is necessary," he observed, "before sitting down to write on a subject, to have thoughts and feelings about it. I cannot tell on what subject your heart and mind have been excited. I must leave that to you." The marginal comments, I need hardly say, are M. Héger's; the words in italics are Charlotte's, for which he substitutes a better form of expression, which is placed between brackets. {6}

IMITATION.

"Le 31 Juillet, 1842.

PORTRAIT DE PIERRE L'HERMITE. CHARLOTTE BRONTË

"De temps en temps, il paraît sur la terre des hommes destinés à être les instruments [prédestinés] {Pourquoi cette suppression?} de grands changements moraux ou politiques. Quelquefois c'est un conquérant, un Alexandre ou un Attila, qui passe comme un ouragan, et purifie l'atmosphère moral, comme l'orage purifie l'atmosphère physique; quelquefois, c'est un révolutionnaire, un Cromwell, ou un Robespierre, qui fait expier par un roi {les fautes et} les vices de toute une dynastie; quelquefois c'est un enthousiaste religieux comme Mahomet, ou Pierre l'Hermite, qui, avec le seul levier de la pensée, soulève des nations entières, les déracine et les transplante dans des climats nouveaux, *peuplant l'Asie avec les habitants de l'Europe*. Pierre l'Hermite était gentilhomme de Picardie, en France, {Invtile, quand vous ecrivez er français} pourquoi donc n'a-t-il passé sa vie comma les autres gentilhommes, ses contemporains, ont passé la leur, à table, à la chasse, dans son lit, sans s'inquiéter de Saladin, ou de ses Sarrasins? N'est-ce pas, parce qu'il y a dans certaines natures, *une ardour*[un foyer d'activité] indomptable qui ne leur permet pas de rester inactives, *qui les force à se remuer afin d'exercer les facultes puissantes, qui même en dormant sont prêtes, comme Sampson, à briser les noeuds qui les retiennent*?

{Vous avez commencé à parler de Pierre: vous êtes entrée dans le sujet: marchez au but.}

"Pierre prit la profession des armes; *si son ardeur avait été de cette espèce* [s'il n'avait eu que cette ardeur vulgaire] qui provient d'une robuste santé, *il aurait* [c'eut] été un brave militaire, et rien de plus; mais son ardeur était celle de l'âme, sa flamme était pure et elle s'élevait vers le ciel.

"*Sans doute* [Il est vrai que] la jeunesse de Pierre *était* [fét] troublée par passions orageuses; les natures puissantes sont extrèmes en tout, elles ne connaissent la tiédeur ni dans le bien, ni dans le mal; Pierre donc chercha d'abord avidement la gloire qui se flétrit et les plaisirs qui trompent, mais *il fit bientôt la découverte* [bientôt il s'aperçut] que ce qu'il poursuivait n'etait qe'une illusion à laquelle il ne pourrait jamais atteindre; {Vnutile, quand vous avez dit illusion} il retourna donc sur ses pas, il recommença le voyage de la vie, mais cette fois il évita le chemin spacieux qui mène à la perdition et il prit le chemin étroit qui mène à la vie; *puisque* [comme] le trajet était long et difficile il jeta la casque et les armes du soldat, et se vêtit de l'habit simple du moine. A la vie militaire succéda la vie monastique, car les extrêmes se touchent, et *chez l'homme sincère* la sincérité du repentir amène [nécessairement à la suite] *avec lui* la rigueur de la pénitence. [Voilà donc Pierre devenu moine!]

"Mais *Pierre* [il] avait en lui un principe qui l'empêchait de rester long-temps inactif, ses idées, sur quel sujet *qu'il soit* [que ce fût] ne pouvaient pas être bornées; il ne lui suffisait pas que lui-même fût religieux, que lui-même fût convaincu de la réalité de Christianismé (sic), il fallait que toute l'Europe, que toute l'Asie, partageât sa conviction et professât la croyance de la Croix. La Piété [fervente] élevée par la Génie, nourrie par la Solitude, *fit naître une espèce d'inspiration* [exalta son âme jusqu'à l'inspiration] *dans son ame*, et lorsqu'il quitta sa cellule et reparut dans le monde, il portait comme Moïse l'empreinte de la Divinité sur son front, et *tout* [tous] reconnurent en lui la véritable apôtre de la Croix.

"Mahomet n'avait jamais remué les molles nations de l'Orient comme alors Pierre remua les peuples austères de l'Occident; il fallait que cette éloquence fût d'une force presque miraculeuse *qui pouvait* [presqu'elle] persuad*er* [ait] aux rois de vendre leurs royaumes *afin de procurer* [pour avoir] des armes et des soldats *pour aider* [à offrir] à Pierre dans la guerre sainte qu'il voulait livrer aux infidèles. La puissance de Pierre [l'Hermite] n'était nullement une puissance physique, car la nature, ou pour mieux dire, Dieu est impartial dans la distribution de ses dons; il accorde à l'un de ses enfants la grâce, la beauté, les perfections corporelles, à l'autre l'esprit, la grandeur morale. Pierre donc était un homme petit, d'une physionomie peu agréable; mais il avait ce courage, cette constance, cet enthousiasme, cette énergie de sentiment qui écrase toute opposition, et qui fait que la volonté d'un seul homme devient la loi de toute une nation. Pour se former une juste idée de l'influence qu'exerça cet homme sur les *caractères* [choses] et les idées de son temps, il faut se le représenter au milieu de l'armée des croisées dans son double rôle de prophète et de guerrier; le pauvre hermite, vêtu *du pauvre* [de l'humble] habit gris est là plus puissant qieun roi; il est entouré *d'une* [de la] multitude [avide] une multitude qui ne voit que lui, tandis qui lui, il ne voit que le ciel; ses yeux levés semblent dire, 'Je vois Dieu et les anges, et j'ai perdu de vue la terre!'

"*Dans ce moment le* [mais ce] pauvre *habit* [froc] gris est pour lui comme le manteau d'Elijah; il l'enveloppe d'inspiration; *il* [Pierre] lit dans l'avenir; il voit Jérusalem délivrée; [il voit] le saint sépulcre libre; il voit le Croissant argent est arraché du Temple, et l'Oriflamme et la Croix rouge sont établi à sa place; non-seulement Pierre voit ces merveilles, mais il les fait voir à tous ceux qui l'entourent; il ravive l'espérance et le courage dans [tous ces corps épuisés de fatigues et de privations]. La bataille ne sera livrée que demain, mais la victoire est décidée ce soir. Pierre a promis; et les Croisés se fient à sa parole, comme les Israëlites se fiaient à celle de Moïse et de Josué."

As a companion portrait to this, Emily chose to depict Harold on the eve of the battle of Hastings. It appears to me that her *devoir* is superior to Charlotte's in power and in imagination, and fully equal to it in language; and that this, in both cases, considering how little practical knowledge of French they had when they arrived at Brussels in February, and that they wrote without the aid of dictionary or grammar, is unusual and remarkable. We shall see the progress Charlotte had made, in ease and grace of style, a year later.

In the choice of subjects left to her selection, she frequently took characters and scenes from the Old Testament, with which all her writings show that she was especially familiar. The picturesqueness and colour (if I may so express it), the grandeur and breadth of its narrations, impressed her deeply. To use M. Héger's expression, "Elle était nourrie de la Bible." After he had read De la Vigne's poem on Joan of Arc, she chose the "Vision and Death of Moses on Mount Nebo" to write about; and, in looking over this *devoir*, I was much struck with one or two of M. Héger's remarks. After describing, in a quiet and simple manner, the circumstances under which Moses took leave of the Israelites, her imagination becomes warmed, and she launches out into a noble strain, depicting the glorious futurity of the Chosen People, as, looking down upon the Promised Land, he sees their prosperity in prophetic vision. But, before reaching the middle of this glowing description, she interrupts herself to discuss for a moment the doubts that have been thrown on the miraculous relations of the Old Testament. M. Héger remarks, "When you are writing, place your argument first in cool, prosaic language; but when you have thrown the reins on the neck of your imagination, do not pull her up to reason." Again, in the vision of Moses, he sees the maidens leading forth their flocks to the wells at eventide, and they are described as wearing flowery garlands. Here the writer is reminded of the necessity of preserving a certain verisimilitude: Moses might from his elevation see mountains and plains, groups of maidens and herds of cattle, but could hardly perceive the details of dress, or the ornaments of the head.

When they had made further progress, M. Héger took up a more advanced plan, that of synthetical teaching. He would read to them various accounts of the same person or event, and make them notice the points of agreement and disagreement. Where they were different, he would make them seek the origin of that difference by causing them to examine well into the character and position of each separate writer, and how they would be likely to affect his conception of truth. For instance, take Cromwell. He would read Bossuet's description of him in the "Oraison Funèbre de la Reine d'Angleterre," and show how in this he was considered entirely from the religious point of view, as an instrument in the hands of God, preordained to His work. Then he would make them read Guizot, and see how, in this view, Cromwell was endowed with the utmost power of free-will, but governed by no higher motive than that of expediency; while Carlyle regarded him as a character regulated by a strong and conscientious desire to do the will of the Lord. Then he would desire them to remember that the Royalist and Commonwealth men had each their different opinions of the great Protector. And from these conflicting characters, he would require them to sift and collect the elements of truth, and try to unite them into a perfect whole.

This kind of exercise delighted Charlotte. It called into play her powers of analysis, which were extraordinary, and she very soon excelled in it.

Wherever the Brontës could be national they were so, with the same tenacity of attachment which made them suffer as they did whenever they left Haworth. They were Protestant to the backbone in other things beside their religion, but pre-eminently so in that. Touched as Charlotte was by the letter of St. Ignatius before alluded to, she claimed equal self-devotion, and from as high a motive, for some of the missionaries of the English Church sent out to toil and to perish on the poisonous African coast, and wrote as an "imitation," "Lettre d'un Missionnaire, Sierra Léone, Afrique."

Something of her feeling, too, appears in the following letter:—

"Brussels, 1842.

"I consider it doubtful whether I shall come home in September or not. Madame Héger has made a proposal for both me and Emily to stay another half-year, offering to dismiss her English master, and take me as English teacher; also to employ Emily some part of each day in teaching music to a certain number of the pupils. For these services we are to be allowed to continue our studies in French and German, and to have board, &c., without paying for it; no salaries, however, are offered. The proposal is kind, and in a great selfish city like Brussels, and a great selfish school, containing nearly ninety pupils (boarders and day pupils included), implies a degree of interest which demands gratitude in return. I am inclined to accept it. What think you? I don't deny I sometimes wish to be in England, or that I have brief attacks of home sickness; but, on the whole, I have borne a very valiant heart so far; and I have been happy in Brussels, because I have always been fully occupied with the employments that I like. Emily is making rapid progress in French, German, music, and drawing. Monsieur and Madame Héger begin to recognise the valuable parts of her character, under her singularities.

"If the national character of the Belgians is to be measured by the character of most of the girls is this school, it in a character singularly cold, selfish, animal, and inferior. They are very mutinous and difficult for the teachers to manage; and their principles are rotten to the core. We avoid them, which it is not difficult to do, as we have the brand of Protestantism and Anglicism upon us. People talk of the danger which Protestants expose themselves to in going to reside in Catholic countries, and thereby running the chance of changing their faith. My advice to all Protestants who are tempted to do anything so besotted as turn Catholics, is, to walk over the sea on to the Continent; to attend mass sedulously for a time; to note well the mummeries thereof; also the idiotic, mercenary aspect of all the priests; and then, if they are still disposed to consider Papistry in any other light than a most feeble, childish piece of humbug, let them turn Papists at once—that's all. I consider Methodism, Quakerism, and the extremes of High and Low Churchism foolish, but Roman Catholicism beats them all. At the same time, allow me to tell you, that there are some Catholics who are as good as any Christians can be to whom the Bible is a sealed book, and much better than many Protestants."

When the Brontës first went to Brussels, it was with the intention of remaining there for six months, or until the *grandes vacances* began in September. The duties of the school were then suspended for six weeks or two months, and it seemed a desirable period for their return. But the proposal mentioned in the foregoing letter altered their plans. Besides, they were happy in the feeling that they were making progress in all the knowledge they had so long been yearning to acquire. They were happy, too, in possessing friends whose society had been for years congenial to them, and in occasional meetings with these, they could have the inexpressible solace to residents in a foreign country—and peculiarly such to the Brontës—of talking over the intelligence received from their respective homes—referring to past, or planning for future days. "Mary" and her sister, the bright, dancing, laughing Martha, were parlour-boarders in an establishment just beyond the barriers of Brussels. Again, the cousins of these friends were resident in the town; and at their house Charlotte and Emily were always welcome, though their overpowering shyness prevented their more valuable qualities from being known, and generally kept them silent. They spent their weekly holiday with this family, for many months; but at the end of the time, Emily was as impenetrable to friendly advances as at the beginning; while Charlotte was too physically weak (as "Mary" has expressed it) to "gather up her forces" sufficiently to express any difference or opposition of opinion, and had consequently an assenting and deferential manner, strangely at variance with what they knew of her remarkable talents and decided character. At this house, the T.'s and the Brontës could look forward to meeting each other pretty frequently. There was another English family where Charlotte soon became a welcome guest, and where, I suspect, she felt herself more at her ease than either at Mrs. Jenkins', or the friends whom I have first mentioned.

An English physician, with a large family of daughters, went to reside at Brussels, for the sake of their education. He placed them at Madame Héger's school in July, 1842, not a month before the beginning of the *grandes vacances* on August 15th. In order to make the most of their time, and become accustomed to the language, these English sisters went daily, through the holidays, to the pensionnat in the Rue d'Isabelle. Six or eight boarders remained, besides the Miss Brontës. They were there during the whole time, never even having the break to their monotonous life, which passing an occasional day with a friend would have afforded them; but devoting themselves with indefatigable diligence to the different studies in which they were engaged. Their position in the school appeared, to these new comers, analogous to what is often called that of a parlour-boarder. They prepared their French, drawing, German, and literature for their various masters; and to these occupations Emily added that of music, in which she was somewhat of a proficient; so much so as to be qualified to give instruction in it to the three younger sisters of my informant.

The school was divided into three classes. In the first were from fifteen to twenty pupils; in the second, sixty was about the average number—all foreigners, excepting the two Brontës and one other; in the third, there were from twenty to thirty pupils. The first and second classes occupied a long room, divided by a wooden partition; in each division were four long ranges of desks; and at the end was the *estrade*, or platform, for the presiding instructor. On the last row, in the quietest corner, sat Charlotte and Emily, side by side, so deeply absorbed in their studies as to be insensible to any noise or movement around them. The school-hours were from nine to twelve (the luncheon hour), when the boarders and half-boarders—perhaps two-and-thirty girls—went to the refectoire (a room with two long tables, having an oil-lamp suspended over each), to partake of bread and fruit; the *externes*, or morning pupils, who had brought their own refreshment with them, adjourning to eat it in the garden. From one to two, there was fancy-work—a pupil reading aloud some light literature in each room; from two to four, lessons again. At four, the externes left; and the remaining girls dined in the refectoire, M. and Madame Héger presiding. From five to six there was recreation, from six to seven, preparation for lessons; and, after that succeeded the *lecture pieuse*—Charlotte's nightmare. On rare occasions, M. Héger himself would come in, and substitute a book of a different and more interesting kind. At eight, there was a slight meal of water and *pistolets* (the delicious little Brussels rolls), which was immediately followed by prayers, and then to bed.

The principal bedroom was over the long classe, or schoolroom. There were six or eight narrow beds on each side of the apartment, every one enveloped in its white draping curtain; a long drawer, beneath each, served for a wardrobe, and between each was a stand for ewer, basin, and looking-glass. The beds of the two Miss Brontës were at the extreme end of the room, almost as private and retired as if they had been in a separate apartment.

During the hours of recreation, which were always spent in the garden, they invariably walked together, and generally kept a profound silence; Emily, though so much the taller, leaning on her sister. Charlotte would always answer when spoken to, taking the lead in replying to any remark addressed to both; Emily rarely spoke to any one. Charlotte's quiet, gentle manner never changed. She was never seen out of temper for a moment; and occasionally, when she herself had assumed the post of English teacher, and the impertinence or inattention of her pupils was most irritating, a slight increase of colour, a momentary sparkling of the eye, and more decided energy of manner, were the only outward tokens she gave of being conscious of the annoyance to which she was subjected. But this dignified endurance of hers subdued her pupils, in the long run, far more than the voluble tirades of the other mistresses. My informant adds:—"The effect of this manner was singular. I can speak from personal experience. I was at that time high-spirited and impetuous, not respecting the French mistresses; yet, to my own astonishment, at one word from her, I was perfectly tractable; so much so, that at length, M. and Madame Héger invariably preferred all their wishes to me through her; the other pupils did not, perhaps, love her as I did, she was so quiet and silent; but all respected her."

With the exception of that part which describes Charlotte's manner as English teacher—an office which she did not assume for some months later—all this description of the school life of the two Brontës refers to the commencement of the new scholastic year in October 1842; and the extracts I have given convey the first impression which the life at a foreign school, and the position of the two Miss Brontës therein, made upon an intelligent English girl of sixteen. I will make a quotation from "Mary's" letter referring to this time.

"The first part of her time at Brussels was not uninteresting. She spoke of new people and characters, and foreign ways of the pupils and teachers. She knew the hopes and prospects of the teachers, and mentioned one who was very anxious to marry, 'she was getting so old.' She used to get her father or brother (I forget which) to be the bearer of letters to different single men, who she thought might be persuaded to do her the favour, saying that her only resource was to become a sister of charity if her present employment failed and that she hated the idea. Charlotte naturally looked with curiosity to people of her own condition. This woman almost frightened her. 'She declares there is nothing she can turn to, and laughs at the idea of delicacy,—and she is only ten years older than I am!' I did not see the connection till she said, 'Well, Polly, I should hate being a sister of charity; I suppose that would shock some people, but I should.' I thought she would have as much feeling as a nurse as most people, and more than some. She said she did not know how people could bear the constant pressure of misery, and never to change except to a new form of it. It would be impossible to keep one's natural feelings. I promised her a better destiny than to go begging any one to marry her, or to lose her natural feelings as a sister of charity. She said, 'My youth is leaving me; I can never do better than I have done, and I have done nothing yet.' At such times she seemed to think that most human beings were destined by the pressure of worldly interests to lose one faculty and feeling after another 'till they went dead altogether. I hope I shall be put in my grave as soon as I'm dead; I don't want to walk about so.' Here we always differed. I thought the degradation of nature she feared was a consequence of poverty, and that she should give her attention to earning money. Sometimes she admitted this, but could find no means of earning money. At others she seemed afraid of letting her thoughts dwell on the subject, saying it brought on the worst palsy of all. Indeed, in her position, nothing less than entire constant absorption in petty money matters could have scraped together a provision.

"Of course artists and authors stood high with Charlotte, and the best thing after their works would have been their company. She used very inconsistently to rail at money and money-getting, and then wish she was able to visit all the large towns in Europe, see all the sights and know all the celebrities. This was her notion of literary fame,—a passport to the society of clever people . . . When she had become acquainted with the people and ways at Brussels her life became monotonous, and she fell into the same hopeless state as at Miss W---'s, though in a less degree. I wrote to her, urging her to go home or elsewhere; she had got what she wanted (French), and there was at least novelty in a new place, if no improvement. That if she sank into deeper gloom she would soon not have energy to go, and she was too far from home for her friends to hear of her condition and order her home as they had done from Miss W---'s. She wrote that I had done her a great service, that she should certainly follow my advice, and was much obliged to me. I have often wondered at this letter. Though she patiently tolerated advice, she could always quietly put it aside, and do as she thought fit. More than once afterwards she mentioned the 'service' I had done her. She sent me 10*l.* to New Zealand, on hearing some exaggerated accounts of my circumstances, and told me she hoped it would come in seasonably; it was a debt she owed me 'for the service I had done her.' I should think 10*l.* was a quarter of her income. The 'service' was mentioned as an apology, but kindness was the real motive."

The first break in this life of regular duties and employments came heavily and sadly. Martha—pretty, winning, mischievous, tricksome Martha—was taken ill suddenly at the Château de Koekelberg. Her sister tended her with devoted love; but it was all in vain; in a few days she died. Charlotte's own short account of this event is as follows:—

"Martha T.'s illness was unknown to me till the day before she died. I hastened to Koekelberg the next morning—unconscious that she was in great danger—and was told that it was finished. She had died in the night. Mary was taken away to Bruxelles. I have seen Mary frequently since. She is in no ways crushed by the event; but while Martha was ill, she was to her more than a mother—more than a sister: watching, nursing, cherishing her so tenderly, so unweariedly. She appears calm and serious now; no bursts of violent emotion; no exaggeration of distress. I have seen Martha's grave—the place where her ashes lie in a foreign country."

Who that has read "Shirley" does not remember the few lines—perhaps half a page—of sad recollection?

"He has no idea that little Jessy will die young, she is so gay, and chattering, and arch—original even now; passionate when provoked, but most affectionate if caressed; by turns gentle and rattling; exacting yet generous; fearless . . . yet reliant on any who will help her. Jessy, with her little piquant face, engaging prattle, and winning ways, is made to be a pet.

* * * * *

"Do you know this place? No, you never saw it; but you recognise the nature of these trees, this foliage—the cypress, the willow, the yew. Stone crosses like these are not unfamiliar to you, nor are these dim garlands of everlasting flowers. Here is the place: green sod and a grey marble head-stone—Jessy sleeps below. She lived through an April day; much loved was she, much loving. She often, in her brief life, shed tears—she had frequent sorrows; she smiled between, gladdening whatever saw her. Her death was tranquil and happy in Rose's guardian arms, for Rose had been her stay and defence through many trials; the dying and the watching English girls were at that hour alone in a foreign country, and the soil of that country gave Jessy a grave.

* * * * *

"But, Jessy, I will write about you no more. This is an autumn evening, wet and wild. There is only one cloud in the sky; but it curtains it from pole to pole. The wind cannot rest; it hurries sobbing over hills of sullen outline, colourless with twilight and mist. Rain has beat all day on that church tower" (Haworth): "it rises dark from the stony enclosure of its graveyard: the nettles, the long grass, and the tombs all drip with wet. This evening reminds me too forcibly of another evening some years ago: a howling, rainy autumn evening too—when certain who had that day performed a pilgrimage to a grave new made in a heretic cemetery, sat near a wood fire on the hearth of a foreign dwelling. They were merry and social, but they each knew that a gap, never to be filled, had been made in their circle. They knew they had lost something whose absence could never be quite atoned for, so long as they lived; and they knew that heavy falling rain was soaking into the wet earth which covered their lost darling; and that the sad, sighing gale was mourning above her buried head. The fire warmed them; Life and Friendship yet blessed them: but Jessy lay cold, coffined, solitary—only the sod screening her from the storm."

This was the first death that had occurred in the small circle of Charlotte's immediate and intimate friends since the loss of her two sisters long ago. She was still in the midst of her deep sympathy with "Mary," when word came from home that her aunt, Miss Branwell, was ailing—was very ill. Emily and Charlotte immediately resolved to go home straight, and hastily packed up for England, doubtful whether they should ever return to Brussels or not, leaving all their relations with M. and Madame Héger, and the pensionnat, uprooted, and uncertain of any future existence. Even before their departure, on the morning after they received the first intelligence of illness—when they were on the very point of starting—came a second letter, telling them of their aunt's death. It could not hasten their movements, for every arrangement had been made for speed. They sailed from Antwerp; they travelled night and day, and got home on a Tuesday morning. The funeral and all was over, and Mr. Brontë and Anne were sitting together, in quiet grief for the loss of one who had done her part well in their household for nearly twenty years, and earned the regard and respect of many who never knew how much they should miss her till she was gone. The small property which she had accumulated, by dint of personal frugality and self-denial, was bequeathed to her nieces. Branwell, her darling, was to have had his share; but his reckless expenditure had distressed the good old lady, and his name was omitted in her will.

When the first shock was over, the three sisters began to enjoy the full relish of meeting again, after the longest separation they had had in their lives. They had much to tell of the past, and much to settle for the future. Anne had been for some little time in a situation, to which she was to return at the end of the Christmas holidays. For another year or so they were again to be all three apart; and, after that, the happy vision of being together and opening a school was to be realised. Of course they did not now look forward to settling at Burlington, or any other place which would take them away from their father; but the small sum which they each independently possessed would enable them to effect such alterations in the parsonage-house at Haworth as would adapt it to the reception of pupils. Anne's plans for the interval were fixed. Emily quickly decided to be the daughter to remain at home. About Charlotte there was much deliberation and some discussion.

Even in all the haste of their sudden departure from Brussels, M. Héger had found time to write a letter of sympathy to Mr. Brontë on the loss which he had just sustained; a letter containing such a graceful appreciation of the daughters' characters, under the form of a tribute of respect to their father, that I should have been tempted to copy it, even had there not also been a proposal made in it respecting Charlotte, which deserves a place in the record of her life.

"Au Révérend Monsieur Brontë, Pasteur Évangélique, &c, &c.

"Samedi, 5 Obre.

"MONSIEUR,

"Un évènement bien triste décide mesdemoiselles vas filles à retourner brusquement en Angleterre, ce départ qui nous afflige beaucoup a cependant ma complète approbation; il est bien naturel qu'elles cherchent à vous consoler de ce que le ciel vient de vous ôter, on se serrant autour de vous, poui mieux vous faire apprécier ce que le ciel vous a donné et ce qu'il vous laisse encore. J'espère que vous me pardonnerez, Monsieur, de profiter de cette circonstance pour vous faire parvenir l'expression de mon respect; je n'ai pas l'honneur de vous connaître personnellement, et cependant j'éprouve pour votre personne un sentiment de sincère vénération, car en jugeant un père de famille par ses enfants on ne risque pas de se tromper, et sous ce rapport l'éducation et les sentiments que nous avons trouvés dans mesdemoiselles vos filles n'ont pu que nous donner une très-haute idée de votre mérite et de votre caractère. Vous apprendrez sans doute avec plaisir que vos enfants ont fait du progrès trèsremarquable dans toutes les branches de l'enseignenient, et que ces progrès sont entiérement dû à leur amour pour le travail et à leur persévérance; nous n'avons eu que bien peu à faire avec de pareilles éléves; leur avancement est votre œuvre bien plus que la nôtre; nous n'avons pas eu à leur apprendre le prix du temps et de l'instruction, elles avaient appris tout cela dans la maison paternelle, et nous n'avons eu, pour notre part, que le faible mérite de diriger leurs efforts et de fournir un aliment convenable à la louable activité que vos filles ont puisées dans votre exemple et dans vos leçons. Puissent les éloges méritées que nous donnons à vos enfants vous être de quelque consolation dans le malheur que vous afflige; c'est là notre espoir en vous écrivant, et ce sera, pour Mesdemoiselles Charlotte et Emily, une douce et belle récompense de leurs travaux.

"En perdant nos deux chéres éléves, nous ne devons pas vous cacher que nous éprouvons à la fois et du chagrin et de l'inquiétude; nous sommes affligés parce que cette brusque séparation vient briser l'affection presque paternelle que nous leur avons vouée, et notre peine s'augmente à la vue de tant de travaux interrompues, de tant de choses bien commencées, et qui ne demandent que quelque temps encore pour être menées à bonne fin. Dans un an, chacune de vos demoiselles eût été entièrement prémunie contre les éventualités de l'avenir; chacune d'elles acquérait à la fois et l'instruction et la science d'enseignement; Mlle Emily allait apprendre le piano; recevoir les leçons du meilleur professeur que nous ayons en Belgique, et déjà elle avait elle-même de petites élèves; elle perdait donc à la fois un reste d'ignorance et un reste plus gênant encore de timidité; Mlle Charlotte commençait à donner des leçons en français, et d'acquérir cette assurance, cet aplomb si nécessaire dans l'enseignement; encore un an tout au plus et l'œuvre était achevée et bien achevée. Alors nous aurions pu, si cela vous eût convenu, offrir à mesdemoiselles vos filles ou du moins à l'une des deux une position qui eût été dans ses goûts, et qui lui eût donné cette douce indépendance si difficile à trouver pour une jeune personne. Ce n'est pas, croyez le bien, Monsieur, ce n'est pas ici pour nous une question d'intérêt personnel, c'est une question d'affection; vous me pardonnerez si nous vous parlons de vos enfants, si nous nous occupons de leur avenir, comme si elles faisaient partie de notre famille; leurs qualités personnelles, leur bon vouloir, leur zèle extrême sont les seules causes qui nous poussent à nous hasarder de la sorte. Nous savons, Monsieur, que vous peserez plus mûrement et plus sagement que nous la conséquence qu'aurait pour l'avenir une interruption complète dans les études de vos deux filles; vous déciderez ce qu'il faut faire, et vous nous pardonnerez notre franchise, si vous daignez considérer que le motif qui nous fait agir est une affection bien désintéressée et qui s'affligerait beaucoup de devoir déjà se résigner à n'être plus utile à vos chers enfants.

"Agréez, je vous prie, Monsieur, l'expression respectueuse de mes sentiments de haute considération.

"C. HÉGER."

There was so much truth, as well as so much kindness in this letter—it was so obvious that a second year of instruction would be far more valuable than the first, that there was no long hesitation before it was decided that Charlotte should return to Brussels.

Meanwhile, they enjoyed their Christmas all together inexpressibly. Branwell was with them; that was always a pleasure at this time; whatever might be his faults, or even his vices, his sisters yet held him up as their family hope, as they trusted that he would some day be their family pride. They blinded themselves to the magnitude of the failings of which they were now and then told, by persuading themselves that such failings were common to all men of any strength of character; for, till sad experience taught them better, they fell into the usual error of confounding strong passions with strong character.

Charlotte's friend came over to see her, and she returned the visit. Her Brussels life must have seemed like a dream, so completely, in this short space of time, did she fall back into the old household ways; with more of household independence than she could ever have had during her aunt's lifetime. Winter though it was, the sisters took their accustomed walks on the snow-covered moors; or went often down the long road to Keighley, for such books as had been added to the library there during their absence from England.

CHAPTER XII

Towards the end of January, the time came for Charlotte to return to Brussels. Her journey thither was rather disastrous. She had to make her way alone; and the train from Leeds to London, which should have reached Euston-square early in the afternoon, was so much delayed that it did not get in till ten at night. She had intended to seek out the Chapter Coffee-house, where she had stayed before, and which would have been near the place where the steam-boats lay; but she appears to have been frightened by the idea of arriving at an hour which, to Yorkshire notions, was so late and unseemly; and taking a cab, therefore, at the station, she drove straight to the London Bridge Wharf, and desired a waterman to row her to the Ostend packet, which was to sail the next morning. She described to me, pretty much as she has since described it in "Villette," her sense of loneliness, and yet her strange pleasure in the excitement of the situation, as in the dead of that winter's night she went swiftly over the dark river to the black hull's side, and was at first refused leave to ascend to the deck. "No passengers might sleep on board," they said, with some appearance of disrespect. She looked back to the lights and subdued noises of London—that "Mighty Heart" in which she had no place—and, standing up in the rocking boat, she asked to speak to some one in authority on board the packet. He came, and her quiet simple statement of her wish, and her reason for it, quelled the feeling of sneering distrust in those who had first heard her request; and impressed the authority so favourably that he allowed her to come on board, and take possession of a berth. The next morning she sailed; and at seven on Sunday evening she reached the Rue d'Isabelle once more; having only left Haworth on Friday morning at an early hour.

Her salary was 16*l.* a year; out of which she had to pay for her German lessons, for which she was charged as much (the lessons being probably rated by time) as when Emily learnt with her and divided the expense, viz., ten francs a month. By Miss Brontë's own desire, she gave her English lessons in the *classe*, or schoolroom, without the supervision of Madame or M. Héger. They offered to be present, with a view to maintain order among the unruly Belgian girls; but she declined this, saying that she would rather enforce discipline by her own manner and character than be indebted for obedience to the presence of a *gendarme*. She ruled over a new schoolroom, which had been built on the space in the play-ground adjoining the house. Over that First Class she was *surveillante* at all hours; and henceforward she was called *Mademoiselle* Charlotte by M. Héger's orders. She continued her own studies, principally attending to German, and to Literature; and every Sunday she went alone to the German and English chapels. Her walks too were solitary, and principally taken in the allée défendue, where she was secure from intrusion. This solitude was a perilous luxury to one of her temperament; so liable as she was to morbid and acute mental suffering.

On March 6th, 1843, she writes thus:—

"I am settled by this time, of course. I am not too much overloaded with occupation; and besides teaching English, I have time to improve myself in German. I ought to consider myself well off, and to be thankful for my good fortunes. I hope I am thankful; and if I could always keep up my spirits and never feel lonely, or long for companionship, or friendship, or whatever they call it, I should do very well. As I told you before, M. and Madame Héger are the only two persons in the house for whom I really experience regard and esteem, and of course, I cannot be always with them, nor even very often. They told me, when I first returned, that I was to consider their sitting-room my sitting-room also, and to go there whenever I was not engaged in the schoolroom. This, however, I cannot do. In the daytime it is a public room, where music-masters and mistresses are constantly passing in and out; and in the evening, I will not, and ought not to intrude on M. and Madame Héger and their children. Thus I am a good deal by myself, out of school-hours; but that does not signify. I now regularly give English lessons to M. Héger and his brother-in-law. They get on with wonderful rapidity; especially the first. He already begins to speak English very decently. If you could see and hear the efforts I make to teach them to pronounce like Englishmen, and their unavailing attempts to imitate, you would laugh to all eternity.

"The Carnival is just over, and we have entered upon the gloom and abstinence of Lent. The first day of Lent we had coffee without milk for breakfast; vinegar and vegetables, with a very little salt fish, for dinner; and bread for supper. The Carnival was nothing but masking and mummery. M. Héger took me and one of the pupils into the town to see the masks. It was animating to see the immense crowds, and the general gaiety, but the masks were nothing. I have been twice to the D.'s" (those cousins of "Mary's" of whom I have before made mention). "When she leaves Bruxelles, I shall have nowhere to go to. I have had two letters from Mary. She does not tell me she has been ill, and she does not complain; but her letters are not the letters of a person in the enjoyment of great happiness. She has nobody to be as good to her as M. Héger is to me; to lend her books; to converse with her sometimes, &c.

"Good-bye. When I say so, it seems to me that you will hardly hear me; all the waves of the Channel heaving and roaring between must deaden the sound."

From the tone of this letter, it may easily be perceived that the

Brussels of 1843 was a different place from that of 1842. Then she had Emily for a daily and nightly solace and companion. She had the weekly variety of a visit to the family of the D.s; and she had the frequent happiness of seeing "Mary" and Martha. Now Emily was far away in Haworth—where she or any other loved one, might die, before Charlotte, with her utmost speed, could reach them, as experience, in her aunt's case, had taught her. The D.s were leaving Brussels; so, henceforth, her weekly holiday would have to be passed in the Rue d'Isabelle, or so she thought. "Mary" was gone off on her own independent course; Martha alone remained—still and quiet for ever, in the cemetery beyond the Porte de Louvain. The weather, too, for the first few weeks after Charlotte's return, had been piercingly cold; and her feeble constitution was always painfully sensitive to an inclement season. Mere bodily pain, however acute, she could always put aside; but too often ill-health assailed her in a part far more to be dreaded. Her depression of spirits, when she was not well, was pitiful in its extremity. She was aware that it was constitutional, and could reason about it; but no reasoning prevented her suffering mental agony, while the bodily cause remained in force.

The Hégers have discovered, since the publication of "Villette," that at this beginning of her career as English teacher in their school, the conduct of her pupils was often impertinent and mutinous in the highest degree. But of this they were unaware at the time, as she had declined their presence, and never made any complaint. Still it must have been a depressing thought to her at this period, that her joyous, healthy, obtuse pupils were so little answerable to the powers she could bring to bear upon them; and though from their own testimony, her patience, firmness, and resolution, at length obtained their just reward, yet with one so weak in health and spirits, the reaction after such struggles as she frequently had with her pupils, must have been very sad and painful.

She thus writes to her friend E.:—

"April, 1843.

"Is there any talk of your coming to Brussels? During the bitter cold weather we had through February, and the principal part of March, I did not regret that you had not accompanied me. If I had seen you shivering as I shivered myself, if I had seen your hands and feet as red and swelled as mine were, my discomfort would just have been doubled. I can do very well under this sort of thing; it does not fret me; it only makes me numb and silent; but if you were to pass a winter in Belgium, you would be ill. However, more genial weather is coming now, and I wish you were here. Yet I never have pressed you, and never would press you too warmly to come. There are privations and humiliations to submit to; there is monotony and uniformity of life; and, above all, there is a constant sense of solitude in the midst of numbers. The Protestant, the foreigner, is a solitary being, whether as teacher or pupil. I do not say this by way of complaining of my own lot; for though I acknowledge that there are certain disadvantages in my present position, what position on earth is without them? And, whenever I turn back to compare what I am with what I was—my place here with my place at Mrs. ---'s for instance—I am thankful. There was an observation in your last letter which excited, for a moment, my wrath. At first, I thought it would be folly to reply to it, and I would let it die. Afterwards, I determined to give one answer, once for all. 'Three or four people,' it seems, 'have the idea that the future *époux* of Mademoiselle Brontë is on the Continent.' These people are wiser than I am. They could not believe that I crossed the sea merely to return as teacher to Madame Hégers. I must have some more powerful motive than respect for my master and mistress, gratitude for their kindness, &c., to induce me to refuse a salary of 50*l*. in England, and accept one of 16*l*. in Belgium. I must, forsooth, have some remote hope of entrapping a husband somehow, or somewhere. If these charitable people knew the total seclusion of the life I lead,—that I never exchange a word with any other man than Monsieur Héger, and seldom indeed with him,—they would, perhaps, cease to suppose that any such chimerical and groundless notion had influenced my proceedings. Have I said enough to clear myself of so silly an imputation? Not that it is a crime to marry, or a crime to wish to be married; but it is an imbecility, which I reject with contempt, for women, who have neither fortune nor beauty, to make marriage the principal object of their wishes and hopes, and the aim of all their actions; not to be able to convince themselves that they are unattractive, and that they had better be quiet, and think of other things than wedlock."

The following is an extract, from one of the few letters which have been preserved, of her correspondence with her sister Emily:—

"May 29, 1843

"I get on here from day to day in a Robinson-Crusoe-like sort of way, very lonely, but that does not signify. In other respects, I have nothing substantial to complain of, nor is this a cause for complaint. I hope you are well. Walk out often on the moors. My love to Tabby. I hope she keeps well."

And about this time she wrote to her father,

"June 2nd, 1818,

"I was very glad to hear from home. I had begun to get low-spirited at not receiving any news, and to entertain indefinite fears that something was wrong. You do not say anything about your own health, but I hope you are well, and Emily also. I am afraid she will have a good deal of hard work to do now that Hannah" (a servant-girl who had been assisting Tabby) "is gone. I am exceedingly glad to hear that you still keep Tabby" (considerably upwards of seventy). "It is an act of great charity to her, and I do not think it will be unrewarded, for she is very faithful, and will always serve you, when she has occasion, to the best of her abilities; besides, she will be company for Emily, who, without her, would be very lonely."

I gave a *devoir*, written after she had been four months under M. Héger's tuition. I will now copy out another, written nearly a year later, during which the progress made appears to me very great.

"31 Mai, 1843.

"SUR LA MORT DE NAPOLÉON.

"Napoléon naquit en Corse et mourut à Ste. Hélène. Entre ces deux îles rien qu'un vaste et brûlant désert et l'océan immense. Il naquit fils d'un simple gentilhomme, et mourut empereur, mais sans couronne et dans les fers. Entre son berceau et sa tombe qu'y a-t-il? la carrière d'un soldat parvenu, des champs de bataille, une mer de sang, un trône, puis du sang encore, et des fers. Sa vie, c'est l'arc en ciel; les deux points extrêmes touchent la terre, la comble lumi-neuse mesure les cieux. Sur Napoléon au berceau une mère brillait; dans la maison paternelle il avait des frères et des soeurs; plus tard dans son palais il eut une femme qui l'aimait. Mais sur son lit de mort Napoléon est seul; plus de mère, ni de frère, ni de soeur, ni de femme, ni d'enfant!! D'autres ont dit et rediront ses exploits, moi, je m'arrête à contempler l'abandonnement de sa dernière heure!

"Il est là, exilé et captif, enchaîné sur un écueil. Nouveau Prométhée il subit le châtiment de son orgueil! Prométhée avait voulu être Dieu et Créateur; il déroba le feu du Ciel pour animer le corps qu'il avait formé. Et lui, Buonaparte, il a voulu créer, non pas un homme, mais un empire, et pour donner une existence, une âme, à son œuvre gigantesque, il n'a pas hésité à arracher la vie à des nations entières. Jupiter indigné de l'impiété de Prométhée, le riva vivant à la cime du Caucase. Ainsi, pour punir l'ambition rapace de Buonaparte, la Providence l'a enchaîné, jusqu'à ce que la mort s'en suivit, sur un roc isolé de l'Atlantique. Peut-être là aussi a-t-il senti lui fouillant le flanc cet insatiable vautour dont parle la fable, peut-être a-t-il souffert aussi cette soif du coeur, cette faim de l'âme, qui torturent l'exilé, loin de sa famille et de sa patrie. Mais parler ainsi n'est-ce pas attribuer gratuitement à Napoléon une humaine faiblesse qu'il n'éprouva jamais? Quand donc s'est-il laissé enchaîner par un lien d'affection? Sans doute d'autres conquérants ont hésité dans leur carrière de gloire, arrêtés par un obstacle d'amour ou d'amitié, retenus par la main d'une femme, rappéles par la voix d'un ami—lui, jamais! Il n'eut pas besoin, comme Ulysse, de se lier au mât du navire, ni de se boucher les oreilles avec de la cire; il ne redoutait pas le chant des Sirènes—il le dédaignait; il se fit marbre et fer pour exécuter ses grands projets. Napoléon ne se regardait pas comme un homme, mais comme l'incarnation d'un peuple. Il n'aimait pas; il ne considérait ses amis et ses proches que comme des instruments auxquels il tint, tant qu'ils furent utiles, et qu'il jeta de côté quand ils cessèrent de l'être. Qu'on ne se permette donc pas d'approcher du sépulcre du Corse avec sentiments de pitié, ou de souiller de larmes la pierre qui couvre ses restes, son âme répudierait tout cela. On a dit, je le sais, qu'elle fut cruelle la main qui le sépara de sa femme et de son enfant. Non, c'était une main qui, comme la sienne, ne tremblait ni de passion ni de crainte, c'était la main d'un homme froid, convaincu, qui avait su deviner Buonaparte; et voici ce que disait cet homme que la défaite n'a pu humilier, ni la victoire enorgueiller. 'Marie-Louise n'est pas la femme de Napoléon; c'est la France que Napoléon a épousée; c'est la France qu'il aime, leur union enfante la perte de l'Europe; voilà la divorce que je veux; voilà l'union qu'il faut briser.'

"La voix des timides et des traîtres protesta contre cette sentence. 'C'est abuser de droit de la victoire! C'est fouler aux pieds le vaincu! Que l'Angleterre se montre clémente, qu'elle ouvre ses bras pour recevoir comme hôte son ennemi désarmé.' L'Angleterre aurait peut-être écouté ce conseii, car partout et toujours il y a des âmes faibles et timorées bientôt séduites par la flatterie ou effrayées par le reproche. Mais la Providence permit qu'un homme se trouvât qui n'a jamais su ce que c'est que la crainte; qui aima sa patrie mieux que sa renommée; impénétrable devant les menaces, inaccessible aux louanges, il se présenta devant le conseil de la nation, et levant son front tranquille en haut, il osa dire: 'Que la trahison se taise! car c'est trahir que de conseiller de temporiser avec Buonaparte. Moi je sais ce que sont ces guerres dont l'Europe saigne encore, comme une victime sous le couteau du boucher. Il faut en finir avec Napoléon Buonaparte. Vous vous effrayez à tort d'un mot si dur! Je n'ai pas de magnanimité, dit-on? Soit! que m'importe ce qu'on dit de moi? Je n'ai pas ici à me faire une réputation de héros magnanime, mais à guérir, si la cure est possible, l'Europe qui se meurt, épuisée de ressources et de sang, l'Europe dont vous négligez les vrais intérêts, préoccupés que vous êtes d'une vaine renommée de clémence. Vous êtes faibles! Eh bien! je viens vous aider. Envoyez

Buonaparte à Ste. Hélène! n'hésitez pas, ne cherchez pas un autre endroit; c'ést le seul convenable. Je vous le dis, j'ai réfléchi pour vous; c'est là qu'il doit êtré et non pas ailleurs. Quant à Napoléon, homme, soldat, je n'ai rien contre lui; c'est un lion royal, auprès de qui vous n'ètes que des chacals. Mais Napoléon Empereur, c'est autre chose, je l'extirperai du sol de l'Europe.' Et celui qui parla ainsi toujours sut garder sa promesse, celle-là comme toutes les autres. Je l'ai dit, et je le répète, cet homme est l'égal de Napoléon par le génie; comme trempe de caractère, comme droiture, comme élévation de pensée et de but, il est d'une tout autre espèce. Napoléon Buonaparte était avide de renommée et de gloire; Arthur Wellesley ne se soucie ni de l'une ni de l'autre; l'opinion publique, la popularité, étaient choses de grand valeur aux yeux de Napoléon; pour Wellington l'opinion publique est une rumeur, un rien que le souffle de son inflexible volonté fait disparaître comme une bulle de savon. Napoléon flattait le peuple; Wellington le brusqne; l'un cherchait les applau-dissements, l'autre ne se soucie que du témoignage de sa conscience; quand elle approuve, c'est assez; toute autre louange l'obsède. Aussi ce peuple, qui adorait Buonaparte s'irritait, s'insurgeait contre la morgue de Wellington: parfois il lui témoigna sa colère et sa haine par des grognements, par des hurlements de bêtes fauves; et alors, avec une impassibilité de sénateur romain, le moderne Coriolan toisait du regard l'émeute furieuse; il croisait ses bras nerveux sur sa large poitrine, et seul, debout sur son seuil, il attendait, il bravait cette tempête populaire dont les flots venaient mourir à quelques pas de lui: et quand la foule, honteuse de sa rebellion, venait lécher les pieds du maître, le hautain patricien méprisait l'hommage d'aujourd'hui comme la haine d'hier, et dans les rues de Londres, et devant son palais ducal d'Apsley, il repoussait d'un genre plein de froid dédain l'incommode empressement du peuple enthousiaste.   Cette fierté néanmoins n'excluait pas en lui une rare modestie; partout il se soustrait à l'éloge; se dérobe au panégyrique; jamais il ne parle de ses exploits, et jamais il ne souffre qu'un autre lui en parle en sa présence. Son caractère égale en grandeur et surpasse en vérité celui de tout autre héros ancien ou moderne. La gloire de Napoléon crût en une nuit, comme la vigne de Jonas, et il suffit d'un jour pour la flétrir; la gloire de Wellington est comme les vieux chênes qui ombragent le château de ses pères sur les rives du Shannon; le chêne croît lentement; il lui faut du temps pour pousser vers le ciel ses branches noueuses, et pour enfoncer dans le sol ces racines profondes qui s'enchevêtrent dans les fondements solides de la terre; mais alors, l'arbre séculaire, inébranlable comme le roc où il a sa base, brave et la faux du temps et l'effort des vents et des tempêtes. Il faudra peut-être un siècle à l'Angleterre pour qu'elle connaise la valeur de son héros. Dans un siècle, l'Europe entière saura combien Wellington a des droits à sa reconnaissance."

How often in writing this paper "in a strange land," must Miss Brontë have thought of the old childish disputes in the kitchen of Haworth parsonage, touching the respective merits of Wellington and Buonaparte! Although the title given to her *devoir* is, "On the Death of Napoleon," she seems yet to have considered it a point of honour rather to sing praises to an English hero than to dwell on the character of a foreigner, placed as she was among those who cared little either for an England or for Wellington. She now felt that she had made great progress towards obtaining proficiency in the French language, which had been her main object in coming to Brussels. But to the zealous learner "Alps on Alps arise." No sooner is one difficulty surmounted than some other desirable attainment appears, and must be laboured after. A knowledge of German now became her object; and she resolved to compel herself to remain in Brussels till that was gained. The strong yearning to go home came upon her; the stronger self-denying will forbade. There was a great internal struggle; every fibre of her heart quivered in the strain to master her will; and, when she conquered herself, she remained, not like a victor calm and supreme on the throne, but like a panting, torn, and suffering victim. Her nerves and her spirits gave way. Her health became much shaken.

"Brussels, August 1st, 1843.

"If I complain in this letter, have mercy and don't blame me, for, I forewarn you, I am in low spirits, and that earth and heaven are dreary and empty to me at this moment. In a few days our vacation will begin; everybody is joyous and animated at the prospect, because everybody is to go home. I know that I am to stay here during the five weeks that the holidays last, and that I shall be much alone during that time, and consequently get downcast, and find both days and nights of a weary length. It is the first time in my life that I have really dreaded the vacation. Alas! I can hardly write, I have such a dreary weight at my heart; and I do so wish to go home. Is not this childish? Pardon me, for I cannot help it. However, though I am not strong enough to bear up cheerfully, I can still bear up; and I will continue to stay (D. V.) some months longer, till I have acquired German; and then I hope to see all your faces again. Would that the vacation were well over! it will pass so slowly. Do have the Christian charity to write me a long, long letter; fill it with the minutest details; nothing will be uninteresting. Do not think it is because people are unkind to me that I wish to leave Belgium; nothing of the sort. Everybody is abundantly civil, but home-sickness keeps creeping over me. I cannot shake it off. Believe me, very merrily, vivaciously, gaily, yours,

"C.B."

The *grandes vacances* began soon after the date of this letter, when she was left in the great deserted pensionnat, with only one teacher for a companion. This teacher, a Frenchwoman, had always been uncongenial to her; but, left to each other's sole companionship, Charlotte soon discovered that her associate was more profligate, more steeped in a kind of cold, systematic sensuality, than she had before imagined it possible for a human being to be; and her whole nature revolted from this woman's society. A low nervous fever was gaining upon Miss Brontë. She had never been a good sleeper, but now she could not sleep at all. Whatever had been disagreeable, or obnoxious, to her during the day, was presented when it was over with exaggerated vividness to her disordered fancy. There were causes for distress and anxiety in the news from home, particularly as regarded Branwell. In the dead of the night, lying awake at the end of the long deserted dormitory, in the vast and silent house, every fear respecting those whom she loved, and who were so far off in another country, became a terrible reality, oppressing her and choking up the very life-blood in her heart. Those nights were times of sick, dreary, wakeful misery; precursors of many such in after years.

In the daytime, driven abroad by loathing of her companion and by the weak restlessness of fever, she tried to walk herself into such a state of bodily fatigue as would induce sleep. So she went out, and with weary steps would traverse the Boulevards and the streets, sometimes for hours together; faltering and resting occasionally on some of the many benches placed for the repose of happy groups, or for solitary wanderers like herself. Then up again—anywhere but to the pensionnat—out to the cemetery where Martha lay—out beyond it, to the hills whence there is nothing to be seen but fields as far as the horizon. The shades of evening made her retrace her footsteps—sick for want of food, but not hungry; fatigued with long continued exercise— yet restless still, and doomed to another weary, haunted night of sleeplessness. She would thread the streets in the neighbourhood of the Rue d'Isabelle, and yet avoid it and its occupant, till as late an hour as she dared be out. At last, she was compelled to keep her bed for some days, and this compulsory rest did her good. She was weak, but less depressed in spirits than she had been, when the school re-opened, and her positive practical duties recommenced.

She writes thus:—

"October 13th, 1843

"Mary is getting on well, as she deserves to do. I often hear from her. Her letters and yours are one of my few pleasures. She urges me very much to leave Brussels and go to her; but, at present, however tempted to take such a step, I should not feel justified in doing so. To leave a certainty for a complete uncertainty, would be to the last degree imprudent. Notwithstanding that, Brussels is indeed desolate to me now. Since the D.s left, I have had no friend. I had, indeed, some very kind acquaintances in the family of a Dr. ---, but they, too, are gone now. They left in the latter part of August, and I am completely alone. I cannot count the Belgians anything. It is a curious position to be so utterly solitary in the midst of numbers. Sometimes the solitude oppresses me to an excess. One day, lately, I felt as if I could bear it no longer, and I went to Madame Héger, and gave her notice. If it had depended on her, I should certainly have soon been at liberty; but M. Héger, having heard of what was in agitation, sent for me the day after, and pronounced with vehemence his decision, that I should not leave. I could not, at that time, have persevered in my intention without exciting him to anger; so I promised to stay a little while longer. How long that will be, I do not know. I should not like to return to England to do nothing. I am too old for that now; but if I could hear of a favourable opportunity for commencing a school, I think I should embrace it. We have as yet no fires here, and I suffer much from cold; otherwise, I am well in health. Mr. --- will take this letter to England. He is a pretty-looking and pretty behaved young man, apparently constructed without a backbone; by which I don't allude to his corporal spine, which is all right enough, but to his character.

"I get on here after a fashion; but now that Mary D. has left Brussels, I have nobody to speak to, for I count the Belgians as nothing. Sometimes I ask myself how long shall I stay here; but as yet I have only asked the question; I have not answered it. However, when I have acquired as much German as I think fit, I think I shall pack up bag and baggage and depart. Twinges of home-sickness cut me to the heart, every now and then. To-day the weather is glaring, and I am stupified with a bad cold and headache. I have nothing to tell you. One day is like another in this place. I know you, living in the country, can hardly believe it is possible life can be monotonous in the centre of a brilliant capital like Brussels; but so it is. I feel it most on holidays, when all the girls and teachers go out to visit, and it sometimes happens that I am left, during several hours, quite alone, with four great desolate schoolrooms at my disposition. I try to read, I try to write; but in vain. I then wander about from room to room, but the silence and loneliness of all the house weighs down one's spirits like lead. You will hardly believe that Madame Héger (good and kind as I have described her) never comes near me on these occasions. I own, I was astonished the first time I was left alone thus; when everybody else was enjoying the pleasures of a fête day with their friends, and she knew I was quite by myself, and never took the least notice of me. Yet, I understand, she praises me very much to everybody, and says what excellent lessons I give. She is not colder to me than she is to the other teachers; but they are less dependent on her than I am. They have relations and acquaintances in Bruxelles. You remember the letter she wrote me, when I was in England? How kind and affectionate that was? is it not odd? In the meantime, the complaints I make at present are a sort of relief which I permit myself. In all other respects I am well satisfied with my position, and you may say so to people who inquire after me (if any one does). Write to me, dear, whenever you can. You do a good deed when you send me a letter, for you comfort a very desolate heart."

One of the reasons for the silent estrangement between Madame Héger and Miss Brontë, in the second year of her residence at Brussels, is to be found in the fact, that the English Protestant's dislike of Romanism increased with her knowledge of it, and its effects upon those who professed it; and when occasion called for an expression of opinion from Charlotte Brontë, she was uncompromising truth. Madame Héger, on the opposite side, was not merely a Roman Catholic, she was *dévote*. Not of a warm or impulsive temperament, she was naturally governed by her conscience, rather than by her affections; and her conscience was in the hands of her religious guides. She considered any slight thrown upon her Church as blasphemy against the Holy Truth; and, though she was not given to open expression of her thoughts and feelings, yet her increasing coolness of behaviour showed how much her most cherished opinions had been wounded. Thus, although there was never any explanation of Madame Héger's change of manner, this may be given as one great reason why, about this time, Charlotte was made painfully conscious of a silent estrangement between them; an estrangement of which, perhaps, the former was hardly aware. I have before alluded to intelligence from home, calculated to distress Charlotte exceedingly with fears respecting Branwell, which I shall speak of more at large when the realisation of her worst apprehensions came to affect the daily life of herself and her sisters. I allude to the subject again here, in order that the reader may remember the gnawing, private cares, which she had to bury in her own heart; and the pain of which could only be smothered for a time under the diligent fulfilment of present duty. Another dim sorrow was faintly perceived at this time. Her father's eyesight began to fail; it was not unlikely that he might shortly become blind; more of his duty must devolve on a curate, and Mr. Brontë, always liberal, would have to pay at a higher rate than he had heretofore done for this assistance.

She wrote thus to Emily:—

"Dec.1st, 1843.

"This is Sunday morning. They are at their idolatrous 'messe,' and I am here, that is in the Refectoire. I should like uncommonly to be in the dining-room at home, or in the kitchen, or in the back kitchen. I should like even to be cutting up the hash, with the clerk and some register people at the other table, and you standing by, watching that I put enough flour, not too much pepper, and, above all, that I save the best pieces of the leg of mutton for Tiger and Keeper, the first of which personages would be jumping about the dish and carving-knife, and the latter standing like a devouring flame on the kitchen-floor. To complete the picture, Tabby blowing the fire, in order to boil the potatoes to a sort of vegetable glue! How divine are these recollections to me at this moment! Yet I have no thought of coming home just now. I lack a real pretext for doing so; it is true this place is dismal to me, but I cannot go home without a fixed prospect when I get there; and this prospect must not be a situation; that would be jumping out of the frying-pan into the fire. *You* call yourself idle! absurd, absurd! . . . Is papa well? Are you well? and Tabby? You ask about Queen Victoria's visit to Brussels. I saw her for an instant flashing through the Rue Royale in a carriage and six, surrounded by soldiers. She was laughing and talking very gaily. She looked a little stout, vivacious lady, very plainly dressed, not much dignity or pretension about her. The Belgians liked her very well on the whole. They said she enlivened the sombre court of King Leopold, which is usually as gloomy as a conventicle. Write to me again soon. Tell me whether papa really wants me very much to come home, and whether you do likewise. I have an idea that I should be of no use there—a sort of aged person upon the parish. I pray, with heart and soul, that all may continue well at Haworth; above all in our grey half-inhabited house. God bless the walls thereof! Safety, health, happiness, and prosperity to you, papa, and Tabby. Amen.

"C. B."

Towards the end of this year (1843) various reasons conspired with the causes of anxiety which have been mentioned, to make her feel that her presence was absolutely and imperatively required at home, while she had acquired all that she proposed to herself in coming to Brussels the second time; and was, moreover, no longer regarded with the former kindliness of feeling by Madame Héger. In consequence of this state of things, working down with sharp edge into a sensitive mind, she suddenly announced to that lady her immediate intention of returning to England. Both M. and Madame Héger agreed that it would be for the best, when they learnt only that part of the case which she could reveal to them—namely, Mr. Brontë's increasing blindness. But as the inevitable moment of separation from people and places, among which she had spent so many happy hours, drew near, her spirits gave way; she had the natural presentiment that she saw them all for the last time, and she received but a dead kind of comfort from being reminded by her friends that Brussels and Haworth were not so very far apart; that access from one place to the other was not so difficult or impracticable as her tears would seem to predicate; nay, there was some talk of one of Madame Héger's daughters being sent to her as a pupil, if she fulfilled her intention of trying to begin a school. To facilitate her success in this plan, should she ever engage in it, M. Héger gave her a kind of diploma, dated from, and sealed with the seal of the Athénée Royal de Bruxelles, certifying that she was perfectly capable of teaching the French language, having well studied the grammar and composition thereof, and, moreover, having prepared herself for teaching by studying and practising the best methods of instruction. This certificate is dated December 29th 1843, and on the 2nd of January, 1844, she arrived at Haworth.

On the 23rd of the month she writes as follows:—

"Every one asks me what I am going to do, now that I am returned home; and every one seems to expect that I should immediately commence a school. In truth, it is what I should wish to do. I desire it above all things. I have sufficient money for the undertaking, and I hope now sufficient qualifications to give me a fair chance of success; yet I cannot yet permit myself to enter upon life—to touch the object which seems now within my reach, and which I have been so long straining to attain. You will ask me why? It is on papa's account; he is now, as you know, getting old, and it grieves me to tell you that he is losing his sight. I have felt for some months that I ought not to be away from him; and I feel now that it would be too selfish to leave him (at least, as long as Branwell and Anne are absent), in order to pursue selfish interests of my own. With the help of God, I will try to deny myself in this matter, and to wait.

"I suffered much before I left Brussels. I think, however long I live, I shall not forget what the parting with M. Héger cost me. It grieved me so much to grieve him who has been so true, kind, and disinterested a friend. At parting he gave me a kind of diploma certifying my abilities as a teacher, sealed with the seal of the Athénée Royal, of which he is professor. I was surprised also at the degree of regret expressed by my Belgian pupils, when they knew I was going to leave. I did not think it had been in their phlegmatic nature . . . I do not know whether you feel as I do, but there are times now when it appears to me as if all my ideas and feelings, except a few friendships and affections, are changed from what they used to be; something in me, which used to be enthusiasm, is tamed down and broken. I have fewer illusions; what I wish for now is active exertion—a stake in life. Haworth seems such a lonely, quiet spot, buried away from the world. I no longer regard myself as young—indeed, I shall soon be twenty-eight; and it seems as if I ought to be working and braving the rough realities of the world, as other people do. It is, however, my duty to restrain this feeling at present, and I will endeavour to do so."

Of course her absent sister and brother obtained a holiday to welcome her return home, and in a few weeks she was spared to pay a visit to her friend at B. But she was far from well or strong, and the short journey of fourteen miles seems to have fatigued her greatly.

Soon after she came back to Haworth, in a letter to one of the household in which she had been staying, there occurs this passage:—"Our poor little cat has been ill two days, and is just dead. It is piteous to see even an animal lying lifeless. Emily is sorry." These few words relate to points in the characters of the two sisters, which I must dwell upon a little. Charlotte was more than commonly tender in her treatment of all dumb creatures, and they, with that fine instinct so often noticed, were invariably attracted towards her. The deep and exaggerated consciousness of her personal defects—the constitutional absence of hope, which made her slow to trust in human affection, and, consequently, slow to respond to any manifestation of it—made her manner shy and constrained to men and women, and even to children. We have seen something of this trembling distrust of her own capability of inspiring affection, in the grateful surprise she expresses at the regret felt by her Belgian pupils at her departure. But not merely were her actions kind, her words and tones were ever gentle and caressing, towards animals: and she quickly noticed the least want of care or tenderness on the part of others towards any poor brute creature. The readers of "Shirley" may remember that it is one of the tests which the heroine applies to her lover.

"Do you know what soothsayers I would consult?" . . . "The little Irish beggar that comes barefoot to my door; the mouse that steals out of the cranny in my wainscot; the bird in frost and snow that pecks at my window for a crumb; the dog that licks my hand and sits beside my knee. I know somebody to whose knee the black cat loves to climb, against whose shoulder and cheek it likes to purr. The old dog always comes out of his kennel and wags his tail, and whines affectionately when somebody passes." [For "somebody" and "he," read "Charlotte Brontë" and "she."] "He quietly strokes the cat, and lets her sit while he conveniently can; and when he must disturb her by rising, he puts her softly down, and never flings her from him roughly: he always whistles to the dog, and gives him a caress."

The feeling, which in Charlotte partook of something of the nature of an affection, was, with Emily, more of a passion. Some one speaking of her to me, in a careless kind of strength of expression, said, "she never showed regard to any human creature; all her love was reserved for animals." The helplessness of an animal was its passport to Charlotte's heart; the fierce, wild, intractability of its nature was what often recommended it to Emily. Speaking of her dead sister, the former told me that from her many traits in Shirley's character were taken; her way of sitting on the rug reading, with her arm round her rough bull-dog's neck; her calling to a strange dog, running past, with hanging head and lolling tongue, to give it a merciful draught of water, its maddened snap at her, her nobly stern presence of mind, going right into the kitchen, and taking up one of Tabby's red-hot Italian irons to sear the bitten place, and telling no one, till the danger was well-nigh over, for fear of the terrors that might beset their weaker minds. All this, looked upon as a well-invented fiction in "Shirley," was written down by Charlotte with streaming eyes; it was the literal true account of what Emily had done. The same tawny bull-dog (with his "strangled whistle"), called "Tartar" in "Shirley," was "Keeper" in Haworth parsonage; a gift to Emily. With the gift came a warning. Keeper was faithful to the depths of his nature as long as he was with friends; but he who struck him with a stick or whip, roused the relentless nature of the brute, who flew at his throat forthwith, and held him there till one or the other was at the point of death. Now Keeper's household fault was this. He loved to steal upstairs, and stretch his square, tawny limbs, on the comfortable beds, covered over with delicate white counterpanes. But the cleanliness of the parsonage arrangements was perfect; and this habit of Keeper's was so objectionable, that Emily, in reply to Tabby's remonstrances, declared that, if he was found again transgressing, she herself, in defiance of warning and his well-known ferocity of nature, would beat him so severely that he would never offend again. In the gathering dusk of an autumn evening, Tabby came, half-triumphantly, half-tremblingly, but in great wrath, to tell Emily that Keeper was lying on the best bed, in drowsy voluptuousness. Charlotte saw Emily's whitening face, and set mouth, but dared not speak to interfere; no one dared when Emily's eyes glowed in that manner out of the paleness of her face, and when her lips were so compressed into stone. She went upstairs, and Tabby and Charlotte stood in the gloomy passage below, full of the dark shadows of coming night. Downstairs came Emily, dragging after her the unwilling Keeper, his hind legs set in a heavy attitude of resistance, held by the "scuft of his neck," but growling low and savagely all the time. The watchers would fain have spoken, but durst not, for fear of taking off Emily's attention, and causing her to avert her head for a moment from the enraged brute. She let him go, planted in a dark corner at the bottom of the stairs; no time was there to fetch stick or rod, for fear of the strangling clutch at her throat—her bare clenched fist struck against his red fierce eyes, before he had time to make his spring, and, in the language of the turf, she "punished him" till his eyes were swelled up, and the half-blind, stupified beast was led to his accustomed lair, to have his swollen head fomented and cared for by the very Emily herself. The generous dog owed her no grudge; he loved her dearly ever after; he walked first among the mourners to her funeral; he slept moaning for nights at the door of her empty room, and never, so to speak, rejoiced, dog fashion, after her death. He, in his turn, was mourned over by the surviving sister. Let us somehow hope, in half Red Indian creed, that he follows Emily now; and, when he rests, sleeps on some soft white bed of dreams, unpunished when he awakens to the life of the land of shadows.

Now we can understand the force of the words, "Our poor little cat is dead. Emily is sorry."

CHAPTER XIII

The moors were a great resource this spring; Emily and Charlotte walked out on them perpetually, "to the great damage of our shoes, but I hope, to the benefit of our health." The old plan of school-keeping was often discussed in these rambles; but in-doors they set with vigour to shirt-making for the absent Branwell, and pondered in silence over their past and future life. At last they came to a determination.

"I have seriously entered into the enterprise of keeping a school—or rather, taking a limited number of pupils at home. That is, I have begun in good earnest to seek for pupils. I wrote to Mrs. --- " (the lady with whom she had lived as governess, just before going to Brussels), "not asking her for her daughter—I cannot do that—but informing her of my intention. I received an answer from Mr. --- expressive of, I believe, sincere regret that I had not informed them a month sooner, in which case, he said, they would gladly have sent me their own daughter, and also Colonel S.'s, but that now both were promised to Miss C. I was partly disappointed by this answer, and partly gratified; indeed, I derived quite an impulse of encouragement from the warm assurance that if I had but applied a little sooner they would certainly have sent me their daughter. I own I had misgivings that nobody would be willing to send a child for education to Haworth. These misgivings are partly done away with. I have written also to Mrs. B., and have enclosed the diploma which M. Héger gave me before I left Brussels. I have not yet received her answer, but I wait for it with some anxiety. I do not expect that she will send me any of her children, but if she would, I dare say she could recommend me other pupils. Unfortunately, she knows us only very slightly. As soon as I can get an assurance of only *one* pupil, I will have cards of terms printed, and will commence the repairs necessary in the house. I wish all that to be done before winter. I think of fixing the board and English education at 25*l*. per annum."

Again, at a later date, July 24th, in the same year, she writes:—

"I am driving on with my small matter as well as I can. I have written to all the friends on whom I have the slightest claim, and to some on whom I have no claim; Mrs. B., for example. On her, also, I have actually made bold to call. She was exceedingly polite; regretted that her children were already at school at Liverpool; thought the undertaking a most praiseworthy one, but feared I should have some difficulty in making it succeed on account of the *situation*. Such is the answer I receive from almost every one. I tell them the *retired situation* is, in some points of view, an advantage; that were it in the midst of a large town I could not pretend to take pupils on terms so moderate (Mrs. B. remarked that she thought the terms very moderate), but that, as it is, not having house-rent to pay, we can offer the same privileges of education that are to be had in expensive seminaries, at little more than half their price; and as our number must be limited, we can devote a large share of time and pains to each pupil. Thank you for the very pretty little purse you have sent me. I make to you a curious return in the shape of half a dozen cards of terms. Make such use of them as your judgment shall dictate. You will see that I have fixed the sum at 35*l*., which I think is the just medium, considering advantages and disadvantages."

This was written in July; August, September, and October passed away, and no pupils were to be heard of. Day after day, there was a little hope felt by the sisters until the post came in. But Haworth village was wild and lonely, and the Brontës but little known, owing to their want of connections. Charlotte writes on the subject, in the early winter months, to this effect—

"I, Emily, and Anne, are truly obliged to you for the efforts you have made in our behalf; and if you have not been successful, you are only like ourselves. Every one wishes us well; but there are no pupils to be had. We have no present intention, however, of breaking our hearts on the subject, still less of feeling mortified at defeat. The effort must be beneficial, whatever the result may be, because it teaches us experience, and an additional knowledge of this world. I send you two more circulars."

A month later, she says:—

"We have made no alterations yet in our house. It would be folly to do so, while there is so little likelihood of our ever getting pupils. I fear you are giving yourself too much trouble on our account. Depend upon it, if you were to persuade a mamma to bring her child to Haworth, the aspect of the place would frighten her, and she would probably take the dear girl back with her, instanter. We are glad that we have made the attempt, and we will not be cast down because it has not succeeded."

There were, probably, growing up in each sister's heart, secret unacknowledged feelings of relief, that their plan had not succeeded. Yes! a dull sense of relief that their cherished project had been tried and had failed. For that house, which was to be regarded as an occasional home for their brother, could hardly be a fitting residence for the children of strangers. They had, in all likelihood, become silently aware that his habits were such as to render his society at times most undesirable. Possibly, too, they had, by this time, heard distressing rumours concerning the cause of that remorse and agony of mind, which at times made him restless and unnaturally merry, at times rendered him moody and irritable.

In January, 1845, Charlotte says:—"Branwell has been quieter and less irritable, on the whole, this time than he was in summer. Anne is, as usual, always good, mild, and patient." The deep-seated pain which he was to occasion to his relations had now taken a decided form, and pressed heavily on Charlotte's health and spirits. Early in this year, she went to H. to bid good-bye to her dear friend "Mary," who was leaving England for Australia.

Branwell, I have mentioned, had obtained the situation of a private tutor. Anne was also engaged as governess in the same family, and was thus a miserable witness to her brother's deterioration of character at this period. Of the causes of this deterioration I cannot speak; but the consequences were these. He went home for his holidays reluctantly, stayed there as short a time as possible, perplexing and distressing them all by his extraordinary conduct—at one time in the highest spirits, at another, in the deepest depression—accusing himself of blackest guilt and treachery, without specifying what they were; and altogether evincing an irritability of disposition bordering on insanity.

Charlotte and Emily suffered acutely from his mysterious behaviour. He expressed himself more than satisfied with his situation; he was remaining in it for a longer time than he had ever done in any kind of employment before; so that for some time they could not conjecture that anything there made him so wilful, and restless, and full of both levity and misery. But a sense of something wrong connected with him, sickened and oppressed them. They began to lose all hope in his future career. He was no longer the family pride; an indistinct dread, caused partly by his own conduct, partly by expressions of agonising suspicion in Anne's letters home, was creeping over their minds that he might turn out their deep disgrace. But, I believe, they shrank from any attempt to define their fears, and spoke of him to each other as little as possible. They could not help but think, and mourn, and wonder.

"Feb. 20th, 1845.

"I spent a week at H., not very pleasantly; headache, sickliness, and flatness of spirits, made me a poor companion, a sad drag on the vivacious and loquacious gaiety of all the other inmates of the house. I never was fortunate enough to be able to rally, for as much as a single hour, while I was there. I am sure all, with the exception perhaps of Mary, were very glad when I took my departure. I begin to perceive that I have too little life in me, now-a-days, to be fit company for any except very quiet people. Is it age, or what else, that changes me so?"

Alas! she hardly needed to have asked this question. How could she be otherwise than "flat-spirited," "a poor companion," and a "sad drag" on the gaiety of those who were light-hearted and happy! Her honest plan for earning her own livelihood had fallen away, crumbled to ashes; after all her preparations, not a pupil had offered herself; and, instead of being sorry that this wish of many years could not be realised, she had reason to be glad. Her poor father, nearly sightless, depended upon her cares in his blind helplessness; but this was a sacred pious charge, the duties of which she was blessed in fulfilling. The black gloom hung over what had once been the brightest hope of the family— over Branwell, and the mystery in which his wayward conduct was enveloped. Somehow and sometime, he would have to turn to his home as a hiding place for shame; such was the sad foreboding of his sisters. Then how could she be cheerful, when she was losing her dear and noble "Mary," for such a length of time and distance of space that her heart might well prophesy that it was "for ever"? Long before, she had written of Mary T., that she "was full of feelings noble, warm, generous, devoted, and profound. God bless her! I never hope to see in this world a character more truly noble. She would die willingly for one she loved. Her intellect and attainments are of the very highest standard." And this was the friend whom she was to lose! Hear that friend's account of their final interview:—

"When I last saw Charlotte (Jan. 1845), she told me she had quite decided to stay at home. She owned she did not like it. Her health was weak. She said she should like any change at first, as she had liked Brussels at first, and she thought that there must be some possibility for some people of having a life of more variety and more communion with human kind, but she saw none for her. I told her very warmly, that she ought not to stay at home; that to spend the next five years at home, in solitude and weak health, would ruin her; that she would never recover it. Such a dark shadow came over her face when I said, 'Think of what you'll be five years hence!' that I stopped, and said, 'Don't cry, Charlotte!' She did not cry, but went on walking up and down the room, and said in a little while, 'But I intend to stay, Polly.'"

A few weeks after she parted from Mary, she gives this account of her days at Haworth.

"March 24th, 1845.

"I can hardly tell you how time gets on at Haworth. There is no event whatever to mark its progress. One day resembles another; and all have heavy, lifeless physiognomies. Sunday, baking-day, and Saturday, are the only ones that have any distinctive mark. Meantime, life wears away. I shall soon be thirty; and I have done nothing yet. Sometimes I get melancholy at the prospect before and behind me. Yet it is wrong and foolish to repine. Undoubtedly, my duty directs me to stay at home for the present. There was a time when Haworth was a very pleasant place to me; it is not so now. I feel as if we were all buried here. I long to travel; to work; to live a life of action. Excuse me, dear, for troubling you with my fruitless wishes. I will put by the rest, and not trouble you with them. You must write to me. If you knew how welcome your letters are, you would write very often. Your letters, and the French newspapers, are the only messengers that come to me from the outer world beyond our moors; and very welcome messengers they are."

One of her daily employments was to read to her father, and it required a little gentle diplomacy on her part to effect this duty; for there were times when the offer of another to do what he had been so long accustomed to do for himself, only reminded him too painfully of the deprivation under which he was suffering. And, in secret, she, too, dreaded a similar loss for herself. Long-continued ill health, a deranged condition of the liver, her close application to minute drawing and writing in her younger days, her now habitual sleeplessness at nights, the many bitter noiseless tears she had shed over Branwell's mysterious and distressing conduct—all these causes were telling on her poor eyes; and about this time she thus writes to M. Héger:—

"Il n'y a rien que je crains comme le désoeuvrement, l'inertie, la léthargie des facultés. Quand le corps est paresseux l'esprit souffre cruellement; je ne connaîtrais pas cette léthargie, si je pouvais écrire. Autrefois je passais des journées, des semaines, des mois entiers à écrire, et pas tout-à-fait sans fruit, puisque Southey et Coleridge, deux de nos meilleurs auteurs, à qui j'ai envoyé certains manuscrits, en ont bien voulu témoigner leur approbation; mais à présent, j'ai la vue trop faible; si j'écrivais beaueoup je deviendrais aveugle. Cette faiblesse de vue est pour moi une terrible privation; sans cela, savez-vous ce que je ferais, Monsieur? J'écrirais un livre et je le dédierais à mon maître de littérature, au seul maître que j'aie jamais eu—à vous, Monsieur! Je vous ai dit souvent en français combien je vous respecte, combien je suis redevable à votre bonté, à vos conseils. Je voudrais le dire une fois en anglais. Cela ne se peut pas; il ne faut pas y penser. La carrière des lettres m'est fermée . . . N'oubliez pas de me dire comment vous vous portez, comment Madame et les enfants se portent. Je compte bientôt avoir de vos nouvelles; cette idée me souris, car le souvenir de vos bontés ne s'effacera jamais de ma mémoire, et tant que ce souvenir durera, le respect que vous m'avez inspiré durera aussi. Agréez, Monsieur," &c.

It is probable, that even her sisters and most intimate friends did not know of this dread of ultimate blindness which beset her at this period. What eyesight she had to spare she reserved for the use of her father. She did but little plain-sewing; not more writing than could be avoided, and employed herself principally in knitting.

"April 2nd, 1845.

"I see plainly it is proved to us that there is scarcely a draught of unmingled happiness to be had in this world. ---'s illness comes with ---'s marriage. Mary T. finds herself free, and on that path to adventure and exertion to which she has so long been seeking admission. Sickness, hardship, danger are her fellow travellers—her inseparable companions. She may have been out of the reach of these S. W. N. W. gales, before they began to blow, or they may have spent their fury on land, and not ruffled the sea much. If it has been otherwise, she has been sorely tossed, while we have been sleeping in our beds, or lying awake thinking about her. Yet these real, material dangers, when once past, leave in the mind the satisfaction of having struggled with difficulty, and overcome it. Strength, courage, and experience are their invariable results; whereas, I doubt whether suffering purely mental has any good result, unless it be to make us by comparison less sensitive to physical suffering... Ten years ago, I should have laughed at your account of the blunder you made in mistaking the bachelor doctor for a married man. I should have certainly thought you scrupulous over-much, and wondered how you could possibly regret being civil to a decent individual, merely because he happened to be single, instead of double. Now, however, I can perceive that your scruples are founded on common sense. I know that if women wish to escape the stigma of husband-seeking, they must act and look like marble or clay—cold, expressionless, bloodless; for every appearance of feeling, of joy, sorrow, friendliness, antipathy, admiration, disgust, are alike construed by the world into the attempt to hook a husband. Never mind! well-meaning women have their own consciences to comfort them after all. Do not, therefore, be too much afraid of showing yourself as you are, affectionate and good-hearted; do not too harshly repress sentiments and feelings excellent in themselves, because you fear that some puppy may fancy that you are letting them come out to fascinate him; do not condemn yourself to live only by halves, because if you showed too much animation some pragmatical thing in breeches might take it into his pate to imagine that you designed to dedicate your life to his inanity. Still, a composed, decent, equable deportment is a capital treasure to a woman, and that you possess. Write again soon, for I feel rather fierce, and want stroking down."

"June 13th, 1845.

"As to the Mrs. ---, who, you say, is like me, I somehow feel no leaning to her at all. I never do to people who are said to be like me, because I have always a notion that they are only like me in the disagreeable, outside, first-acquaintance part of my character; in those points which are obvious to the ordinary run of people, and which I know are not pleasing. You say she is 'clever'—'a clever person.' How I dislike the term! It means rather a shrewd, very ugly, meddling, talking woman . . . I feel reluctant to leave papa for a single day. His sight diminishes weekly; and can it be wondered at that, as he sees the most precious of his faculties leaving him, his spirits sometimes sink? It is so hard to feel that his few and scanty pleasures must all soon go. He has now the greatest difficulty in either reading or writing; and then he dreads the state of dependence to which blindness will inevitably reduce him. He fears that he will be nothing in his parish. I try to cheer him; sometimes I succeed temporarily, but no consolation can restore his sight, or atone for the want of it. Still he is never peevish; never impatient; only anxious and dejected."

For the reason just given, Charlotte declined an invitation to the only house to which she was now ever asked to come. In answer to her correspondent's reply to this letter, she says:—

"You thought I refused you coldly, did you? It was a queer

sort of coldness, when I would have given my ears to say Yes, and was obliged to say No. Matters, however, are now a little changed. Anne is come home, and her presence certainly makes me feel more at liberty. Then, if all be well, I will come and see you. Tell me only when I must come. Mention the week and the day. Have the kindness also to answer the following queries, if you can. How far is it from Leeds to Sheffield? Can you give me a notion of the cost? Of course, when I come, you will let me enjoy your own company in peace, and not drag me out a visiting. I have no desire at all to see your curate. I think he must be like all the other curates I have seen; and they seem to me a self-seeking, vain, empty race. At this blessed moment, we have no less than three of them in Haworth parish—and there is not one to mend another. The other day, they all three, accompanied by Mr. S., dropped, or rather rushed, in unexpectedly to tea. It was Monday (baking day), and I was hot and tired; still, if they had behaved quietly and decently, I would have served them out their tea in peace; but they began glorifying themselves, and abusing Dissenters in such a manner, that my temper lost its balance, and I pronounced a few sentences sharply and rapidly, which struck them all dumb. Papa was greatly horrified also, but I don't regret it."

On her return from this short visit to her friend, she travelled with a gentleman in the railway carriage, whose features and bearing betrayed him, in a moment, to be a Frenchman. She ventured to ask him if such was not the case; and, on his admitting it, she further inquired if he had not passed a considerable time in Germany, and was answered that he had; her quick ear detected something of the thick guttural pronunciation, which, Frenchmen say, they are able to discover even in the grandchildren of their countrymen who have lived any time beyond the Rhine. Charlotte had retained her skill in the language by the habit of which she thus speaks to M. Héger:—

"Je crains beaucoup d'oublier le français—j'apprends tous les jours une demie page de français par coeur, et j'ai grand plaisir à apprendre cette leçon, Veuillez presenter à Madame l'assurance de mon estime; je crains que Maria-Louise et Claire ne m'aient déjà oubliées; mais je vous reverrai un jour; aussitôt que j'aurais gagné assez d'argent pour alter à Bruxelles, j'y irai."

And so her journey back to Haworth, after the rare pleasure of this visit to her friend, was pleasantly beguiled by conversation with the French gentleman; and she arrived at home refreshed and happy. What to find there?

It was ten o'clock when she reached the parsonage. Branwell was there, unexpectedly, very ill. He had come home a day or two before, apparently for a holiday; in reality, I imagine, because some discovery had been made which rendered his absence imperatively desirable. The day of Charlotte's return, he had received a letter from Mr. ---, sternly dismissing him, intimating that his proceedings were discovered, characterising them as bad beyond expression, and charging him, on pain of exposure, to break off immediately, and for ever, all communication with every member of the family.

Whatever may have been the nature and depth of Branwell's sins,—whatever may have been his temptation, whatever his guilt,—there is no doubt of the suffering which his conduct entailed upon his poor father and his innocent sisters. The hopes and plans they had cherished long, and laboured hard to fulfil, were cruelly frustrated; henceforward their days were embittered and the natural rest of their nights destroyed by his paroxysms of remorse. Let us read of the misery caused to his poor sisters in Charlotte's own affecting words:—

"We have had sad work with Branwell. He thought of

nothing but stunning or drowning his agony of mind. No one in this house could have rest; and, at last, we have been obliged to send him from home for a week, with some one to look after him. He has written to me this morning, expressing some sense of contrition . . . but as long as he remains at home, I scarce dare hope for peace in the house. We must all, I fear, prepare for a season of distress and disquietude. When I left you, I was strongly impressed with the feeling that I was going back to sorrow."

"August, 1845.

"Things here at home are much as usual; not very bright as it regards Branwell, though his health, and consequently his temper, have been somewhat better this last day or two, because he is now *forced to* abstain."

"August 18th, 1845.

"I have delayed writing, because I have no good news to communicate. My hopes ebb low indeed about Branwell. I sometimes fear he will never be fit for much. The late blow to his prospects and feelings has quite made him reckless. It is only absolute want of means that acts as any check to him. One ought, indeed, to hope to the very last; and I try to do so, but occasionally hope in his case seems so fallacious."

"Nov. 4th, 1845.

"I hoped to be able to ask you to come to Haworth. It almost seemed as if Branwell had a chance of getting employment, and I waited to know the result of his efforts in order to say, dear ---, come and see us. But the place (a secretaryship to a railway committee) is given to another person. Branwell still remains at home; and while *he* is here, *you* shall not come. I am more confirmed in that resolution the more I see of him. I wish I could say one word to you in his favour, but I cannot. I will hold my tongue. We are all obliged to you for your kind suggestion about Leeds; but I think our school schemes are, for the present, at rest."

"Dec. 31st, 1845.

"You say well, in speaking of ---, that no sufferings are so awful as those brought on by dissipation; alas! I see the truth of this observation daily proved. —and—must have as weary and burdensome a life of it in waiting upon their unhappy brother. It seems grievous, indeed, that those who have not sinned should suffer so largely."

In fact, all their latter days blighted with the presence of cruel, shameful suffering,—the premature deaths of two at least of the sisters,—all the great possibilities of their earthly lives snapped short,—may be dated from Midsummer 1845.

For the last three years of Branwell's life, he took opium habitually, by way of stunning conscience; he drank moreover, whenever he could get the opportunity. The reader may say that I have mentioned his tendency to intemperance long before. It is true; but it did not become habitual, as far as I can learn, until after he was dismissed from his tutorship. He took opium, because it made him forget for a time more effectually than drink; and, besides, it was more portable. In procuring it he showed all the cunning of the opium-eater. He would steal out while the family were at church—to which he had professed himself too ill to go—and manage to cajole the village druggist out of a lump; or, it might be, the carrier had unsuspiciously brought him some in a packet from a distance. For some time before his death he had attacks of delirium tremens of the most frightful character; he slept in his father's room, and he would sometimes declare that either he or his father should be dead before the morning. The trembling sisters, sick with fright, would implore their father not to expose himself to this danger; but Mr. Brontë is no timid man, and perhaps he felt that he could possibly influence his son to some self-restraint, more by showing trust in him than by showing fear. The sisters often listened for the report of a pistol in the dead of the night, till watchful eye and hearkening ear grew heavy and dull with the perpetual strain upon their nerves. In the mornings young Brontë would saunter out, saying, with a drunkard's incontinence of speech, "The poor old man and I have had a terrible night of it; he does his best—the poor old man! but it's all over with me."

CHAPTER XIV

In the course of this sad autumn of 1845, a new interest came up; faint, indeed, and often lost sight of in the vivid pain and constant pressure of anxiety respecting their brother. In the biographical notice of her sisters, which Charlotte prefixed to the edition of "Wuthering Heights" and "Agnes Grey," published in 1850—a piece of writing unique, as far as I know, in its pathos and its power—she says:—

"One day in the autumn of 1845, I accidentally lighted on a MS. volume of verse, in my sister Emily's handwriting. Of course, I was not surprised, knowing that she could and did write verse: I looked it over, and something more than surprise seized me—a deep conviction that these were not common effusions, nor at all like the poetry women generally write. I thought them condensed and terse, vigorous and genuine. To my ear they had also a peculiar music, wild, melancholy, and elevating. My sister Emily was not a person of demonstrative character, nor one on the recesses of whose mind and feelings even those nearest and dearest to her could, with impunity, intrude unlicensed: it took hours to reconcile her to the discovery I had made, and days to persuade her that such poems merited publication . . . Meantime, my younger sister quietly produced some of her own compositions, intimating that since Emily's had given me pleasure, I might like to look at hers. I could not but be a partial judge, yet I thought that these verses too had a sweet sincere pathos of their own. We had very early cherished the dream of one day being authors. We agreed to arrange a small selection of our poems, and, if possible, get them printed. Averse to personal publicity, we veiled our own names under those of Currer, Ellis, and Acton Bell; the ambiguous choice being dictated by a sort of conscientious scruple at assuming Christian names, positively masculine, while we did not like to declare ourselves women, because—without at the time suspecting that our mode of writing and thinking was not what is called 'feminine,' we had a vague impression that authoresses are liable to be looked on with prejudice; we noticed how critics sometimes use for their chastisement the weapon of personality, and for their reward, a flattery, which is not true praise. The bringing out of our little book was hard work. As was to be expected, neither we nor our poems were at all wanted; but for this we had been prepared at the outset; though inexperienced ourselves, we had read the experience of others. The great puzzle lay in the difficulty of getting answers of any kind from the publishers to whom we applied. Being greatly harassed by this obstacle, I ventured to apply to the Messrs. Chambers, of Edinburgh, for a word of advice; *they* may have forgotten the circumstance, but *I* have not, for from them I received a brief and business-like, but civil and sensible reply, on which we acted, and at last made way."

I inquired from Mr. Robert Chambers, and found, as Miss Brontë conjectured, that he had entirely forgotten the application which had been made to him and his brother for advice; nor had they any copy or memorandum of the correspondence.

There is an intelligent man living in Haworth, who has given me some interesting particulars relating to the sisters about this period. He says:—

"I have known Miss Brontë, as Miss Brontë, a long time; indeed, ever since they came to Haworth in 1819. But I had not much acquaintance with the family till about 1843, when I began to do a little in the stationery line. Nothing of that kind could be had nearer than Keighley before I began. They used to buy a great deal of writing paper, and I used to wonder whatever they did with so much. I sometimes thought they contributed to the Magazines. When I was out of stock, I was always afraid of their coming; they seemed so distressed about it, if I had none. I have walked to Halifax (a distance of ten miles) many a time, for half a ream of paper, for fear of being without it when they came. I could not buy more at a time for want of capital. I was always short of that. I did so like them to come when I had anything for them; they were so much different to anybody else; so gentle and kind, and so very quiet. They never talked much. Charlotte sometimes would sit and inquire about our circumstances so kindly and feelingly! . . . Though I am a poor working man (which I have never felt to be any degradation), I could talk with her with the greatest freedom. I always felt quite at home with her. Though I never had any school education, I never felt the want of it in her company."

The publishers to whom she finally made a successful application for the production of "Currer, Ellis, and Acton Bell's poems," were Messrs. Aylott and Jones, Paternoster Row. Mr. Aylott has kindly placed the letters which she wrote to them on the subject at my disposal. The first is dated January 28th, 1846, and in it she inquires if they will publish one volume octavo of poems; if not at their own risk, on the author's account. It is signed "C. Brontë." They must have replied pretty speedily, for on January 31st she writes again:—

"GENTLEMEN,

"Since you agree to undertake the publication of the work respecting which I applied to you, I should wish now to know, as soon as possible, the cost of paper and printing. I will then send the necessary remittance, together with the manuscript. I should like it to be printed in one octavo volume, of the same quality of paper and size of type as Moxon's last edition of Wordsworth. The poems will occupy, I should think, from 200 to 250 pages. They are not the production of a clergyman, nor are they exclusively of a religious character; but I presume these circumstances will be immaterial. It will, perhaps, be necessary that you should see the manuscript, in order to calculate accurately the expense of publication; in that case I will send it immediately. I should like, however, previously, to have some idea of the probable cost; and if, from what I have said, you can make a rough calculation on the subject, I should be greatly obliged to you."

In her next letter, February 6th, she says:—

"You will perceive that the poems are the work of three persons, relatives—their separate pieces are distinguished by their respective signatures."

She writes again on February 15th; and on the 16th she says:—

"The MS. will certainly form a thinner volume than I had anticipated. I cannot name another model which I should like it precisely to resemble, yet, I think, a duodecimo form, and a somewhat reduced, though still *clear* type, would be preferable. I only stipulate for *clear* type, not too small, and good paper."

On February 21st she selects the "long primer type" for the poems, and will remit 31*l*. 10*s*. in a few days.

Minute as the details conveyed in these notes are, they are not trivial, because they afford such strong indications of character. If the volume was to be published at their own risk, it was necessary that the sister conducting the negotiation should make herself acquainted with the different kinds of type, and the various sizes of books. Accordingly she bought a small volume, from which to learn all she could on the subject of preparation for the press. No half-knowledge—no trusting to other people for decisions which she could make for herself; and yet a generous and full confidence, not misplaced, in the thorough probity of Messrs. Aylott and Jones. The caution in ascertaining the risk before embarking in the enterprise, and the prompt payment of the money required, even before it could be said to have assumed the shape of a debt, were both parts of a self-reliant and independent character. Self-contained also was she. During the whole time that the volume of poems was in the course of preparation and publication, no word was written telling anyone, out of the household circle, what was in progress.

I have had some of the letters placed in my hands, which she addressed to her old schoolmistress, Miss W-. They begin a little before this time. Acting on the conviction, which I have all along entertained, that where Charlotte Brontë's own words could be used, no others ought to take their place, I shall make extracts from this series, according to their dates.

"Jan. 30th, 1846.

"MY DEAR MISS W---,

"I have not yet paid my visit to ---; it is, indeed, more than a year since I was there, but I frequently hear from E., and she did not fail to tell me that you were gone into Worcestershire; she was unable, however, to give me your exact address. Had I known it, I should have written to you long since. I thought you would wonder how we were getting on, when you heard of the railway panic; and you may be sure that I am very glad to be able to answer your kind inquiries by the assurance that our small capital is as yet undiminished. The York and Midland is, as you say, a very good line, yet, I confess to you, I should wish, for my own part, to be wise in time. I cannot think that even the very best lines will continue for many years at their present premiums; and I have been most anxious for us to sell our shares ere it be too late, and to secure the proceeds in some safer, if, for the present, less profitable investment. I cannot, however, persuade my sisters to regard the affair precisely from my point of view; and I feel as if I would rather run the risk of loss than hurt Emily's feelings by acting in direct opposition to her opinion. She managed in a most handsome and able manner for me, when I was in Brussels, and prevented by distance from looking after my own interests; therefore, I will let her manage still, and take the consequences. Disinterested and energetic she certainly is; and if she be not quite so tractable or open to conviction as I could wish, I must remember perfection is not the lot of humanity; and as long as we can regard those we love, and to whom we are closely allied, with profound and never-shaken esteem, it is a small thing that they should vex us occasionally by what appear to us unreasonable and headstrong notions.

"You, my dear Miss W---, know, full as well as I do, the value of sisters' affection to each other; there is nothing like it in this world, I believe, when they are nearly equal in age, and similar in education, tastes, and sentiments. You ask about Branwell; he never thinks of seeking employment, and I begin to fear that he has rendered himself incapable of filling any respectable station in life; besides, if money were at his disposal, he would use it only to his own injury; the faculty of self-government is, I fear, almost destroyed in him. You ask me if I do not think that men are strange beings? I do, indeed. I have often thought so; and I think, too, that the mode of bringing them up is strange: they are not sufficiently guarded from temptation. Girls are protected as if they were something very frail or silly indeed, while boys are turned loose on the world, as if they, of all beings in existence, were the wisest and least liable to be led astray. I am glad you like Broomsgrove, though, I dare say, there are few places you would *not* like, with Mrs. M. for a companion. I always feel a peculiar satisfaction when I hear of your enjoying yourself, because it proves that there really is such a thing as retributive justice even in this world. You worked hard; you denied yourself all pleasure, almost all relaxation, in your youth, and in the prime of life; now you are free, and that while you have still, I hope, many years of vigour and health in which you can enjoy freedom. Besides, I have another and very egotistical motive for being pleased; it seems that even 'a lone woman' can be happy, as well as cherished wives and proud mothers. I am glad of that. I speculate much on the existence of unmarried and never-to-be-married women now-a-days; and I have already got to the point of considering that there is no more respectable character on this earth than an unmarried woman, who makes her own way through life quietly, perseveringly, without support of husband or brother; and who, having attained the age of forty-five or upwards, retains in her possession a well-regulated mind, a disposition to enjoy simple pleasures, and fortitude to support inevitably pains, sympathy with the sufferings of others, and willingness to relieve want as far as her means extend."

During the time that the negotiation with Messrs. Aylott and Co. was going on, Charlotte went to visit her old school-friend, with whom she was in such habits of confidential intimacy; but neither then nor afterwards, did she ever speak to her of the publication of the poems; nevertheless, this young lady suspected that the sisters wrote for Magazines; and in this idea she was confirmed when, on one of her visits to Haworth, she saw Anne with a number of "Chambers's Journal," and a gentle smile of pleasure stealing over her placid face as she read.

"What is the matter?" asked the friend. "Why do you smile?"

"Only because I see they have inserted one of my poems," was the quiet reply; and not a word more was said on the subject.

To this friend Charlotte addressed the following letters:—

"March 3rd, 1846.

"I reached home a little after two o'clock, all safe and right yesterday; I found papa very well; his sight much the same. Emily and Anne were going to Keighley to meet me; unfortunately, I had returned by the old road, while they were gone by the new, and we missed each other. They did not get home till half-past four, and were caught in the heavy shower of rain which fell in the afternoon. I am sorry to say Anne has taken a little cold in consequence, but I hope she will soon be well. Papa was much cheered by my report of Mr. C.'s opinion, and of old Mrs. E.'s experience; but I could perceive he caught gladly at the idea of deferring the operation a few months longer. I went into the room where Branwell was, to speak to him, about an hour after I got home: it was very forced work to address him. I might have spared myself the trouble, as he took no notice, and made no reply; he was stupified. My fears were not in vain. I hear that he got a sovereign while I have been away, under pretence of paying a pressing debt; he went immediately and changed it at a public-house, and has employed it as was to be expected. --- concluded her account by saying he was a 'hopeless being;' it is too true. In his present state it is scarcely possible to stay in the room where he is. What the future has in store I do not know."

"March 31st, 1846.

"Our poor old servant Tabby had a sort of fit, a fortnight since, but is nearly recovered now. Martha" (the girl they had to assist poor old Tabby, and who remains still the faithful servant at the parsonage,) "is ill with a swelling in her knee, and obliged to go home. I fear it will be long before she is in working condition again. I received the number of the 'Record' you sent . . . I read D'Aubigné's letter. It is clever, and in what he says about Catholicism very good. The Evangelical Alliance part is not very practicable, yet certainly it is more in accordance with the spirit of the Gospel to preach unity among Christians than to inculcate mutual intolerance and hatred. I am very glad I went to—when I did, for the changed weather has somewhat changed my health and strength since. How do you get on? I long for mild south and west winds. I am thankful papa continues pretty well, though often made very miserable by Branwell's wretched conduct. *There*—there is no change but for the worse."

Meanwhile the printing of the volume of poems was quietly proceeding. After some consultation and deliberation, the sisters had determined to correct the proofs themselves, Up to March 28th the publishers had addressed their correspondent as C. Brontë, Esq.; but at this time some "little mistake occurred," and she desired Messrs. Aylott and Co. in future to direct to her real address, "*Miss* Brontë," &c. She had, however, evidently left it to be implied that she was not acting on her own behalf, but as agent for the real authors, since in a note dated April 6th, she makes a proposal on behalf of "C., E., and A. Bell," which is to the following effect, that they are preparing for the press a work of fiction, consisting of three distinct and unconnected tales, which may be published either together, as a work of three volumes, of the ordinary novel size, or separately, as single volumes, as may be deemed most advisable. She states, in addition, that it is not their intention to publish these tales on their own account; but that the authors direct her to ask Messrs. Aylott and Co. whether they would be disposed to undertake the work, after having, of course, by due inspection of the MS., ascertained that its contents are such as to warrant an expectation of success. To this letter of inquiry the publishers replied speedily, and the tenor of their answer may be gathered from Charlotte's, dated April 11th.

"I beg to thank you, in the name of C., E., and A. Bell, for your obliging offer of advice. I will avail myself of it, to request information on two or three points. It is evident that unknown authors have great difficulties to contend with, before they can succeed in bringing their works before the public. Can you give me any hint as to the way in which these difficulties are best met? For instance, in the present case, where a work of fiction is in question, in what form would a publisher be most likely to accept the MS.? Whether offered as a work of three vols., or as tales which might be published in numbers, or as contributions to a periodical?

"What publishers would be most likely to receive favourably a proposal of this nature?

"Would it suffice to *write* to a publisher on the subject, or would it be necessary to have recourse to a personal interview?

"Your opinion and advice on these three points, or on any other which your experience may suggest as important, would be esteemed by us as a favour."

It is evident from the whole tenor of this correspondence, that the truthfulness and probity of the firm of publishers with whom she had to deal in this her first literary venture, were strongly impressed upon her mind, and was followed by the inevitable consequence of reliance on their suggestions. And the progress of the poems was not unreasonably lengthy or long drawn out. On April 20th she writes to desire that three copies may be sent to her, and that Messrs. Aylott will advise her as to the reviewers to whom copies ought to be sent.

I give the next letter as illustrating the ideas of these girls as to what periodical reviews or notices led public opinion.

"The poems to be neatly done up in cloth. Have the goodness to send copies and advertisements, *as early as possible*, to each of the undermentioned periodicals.

"'Colburn's New Monthly Magazine.'
"'Bentley's Magazine.'
"'Hood's Magazine.'
"'Jerrold's Shilling Magazine.'
"'Blackwood's Magazine.'
"'The Edinburgh Review.'
"'Tait's Edinburgh Magazine.'
"'The Dublin University Magazine.'
"Also to the 'Daily News' and to the 'Britannia' papers.
"If there are any other periodicals to which you have been in

the habit of sending copies of works, let them be supplied also with copies. I think those I have mentioned will suffice for advertising."

In compliance with this latter request, Messrs. Aylott suggest that copies and advertisements of the work should be sent to the "Athenæum," "Literary Gazette," "Critic," and "Times;" but in her reply Miss Brontë says, that she thinks the periodicals she first mentioned will be sufficient for advertising in at present, as the authors do not wish to lay out a larger sum than two pounds in advertising, esteeming the success of a work dependent more on the notice it receives from periodicals than on the quantity of advertisements. In case of any notice of the poems appearing, whether favourable or otherwise, Messrs. Aylott and Co. are requested to send her the name and number of those periodicals in which such notices appear; as otherwise, since she has not the opportunity of seeing periodicals regularly, she may miss reading the critique. "Should the poems be remarked upon favourably, it is my intention to appropriate a further sum for advertisements. If, on the other hand, they should pass unnoticed or be condemned, I consider it would be quite useless to advertise, as there is nothing, either in the title of the work, or the names of the authors, to attract attention from a single individual."

I suppose the little volume of poems was published some time about the end of May, 1846. It stole into life; some weeks passed over, without the mighty murmuring public discovering that three more voices were uttering their speech. And, meanwhile, the course of existence moved drearily along from day to day with the anxious sisters, who must have forgotten their sense of authorship in the vital care gnawing at their hearts. On June 17th, Charlotte writes:—

"Branwell declares that he neither can nor will do anything for himself; good situations have been offered him, for which, by a fortnight's work, he might have qualified himself, but he will do nothing except drink and make us all wretched."

In the "Athenæum" of July 4th, under the head of poetry for the million, came a short review of the poems of C., E., and A. Bell. The reviewer assigns to Ellis the highest rank of the three "brothers," as he supposes them to be; he calls Ellis "a fine, quaint spirit;" and speaks of "an evident power of wing that may reach heights not here attempted." Again, with some degree of penetration, the reviewer says, that the poems of Ellis "convey an impression of originality beyond what his contributions to these volumes embody." Currer is placed midway between Ellis and Acton. But there is little in the review to strain out, at this distance of time, as worth preserving. Still, we can fancy with what interest it was read at Haworth Parsonage, and how the sisters would endeavour to find out reasons for opinions, or hints for the future guidance of their talents.

I call particular attention to the following letter of Charlotte's, dated July 10th, 1846. To whom it was written, matters not; but the wholesome sense of duty in it—the sense of the supremacy of that duty which God, in placing us in families, has laid out for us, seems to deserve especial regard in these days.

"I see you are in a dilemma, and one of a peculiar and difficult nature. Two paths lie before you; you conscientiously wish to choose the right one, even though it be the most steep, strait, and rugged; but you do not know which is the right one; you cannot decide whether duty and religion command you to go out into the cold and friendless world, and there to earn your living by governess drudgery, or whether they enjoin your continued stay with your aged mother, neglecting, *for the present*, every prospect of independency for yourself, and putting up with daily inconvenience, sometimes even with privations. I can well imagine, that it is next to impossible for you to decide for yourself in this matter, so I will decide it for you. At least, I will tell you what is my earnest conviction on the subject; I will show you candidly how the question strikes me. The right path is that which necessitates the greatest sacrifice of self-interest—which implies the greatest good to others; and this path, steadily followed, will lead, I believe, in time, to prosperity and to happiness, though it may seem, at the outset, to tend quite in a contrary direction. Your mother is both old and infirm; old and infirm people have but few sources of happiness—fewer almost than the comparatively young and healthy can conceive; to deprive them of one of these is cruel. If your mother is more composed when you are with her, stay with her. If she would be unhappy in case you left her, stay with her. It will not apparently, as far as short-sighted humanity can see, be for your advantage to remain at ---, nor will you be praised and admired for remaining at home to comfort your mother; yet, probably, your own conscience will approve, and if it does, stay with her. I recommend you to do what I am trying to do myself."

The remainder of this letter is only interesting to the reader as it conveys a peremptory disclaimer of the report that the writer was engaged to be married to her father's curate—the very same gentleman to whom, eight years afterwards, she was united; and who, probably, even now, although she was unconscious of the fact, had begun his service to her, in the same tender and faithful spirit as that in which Jacob served for Rachel. Others may have noticed this, though she did not.

A few more notes remain of her correspondence "on behalf of the Messrs. Bell" with Mr. Aylott. On July 15th she says, "I suppose, as you have not written, no other notices have yet appeared, nor has the demand for the work increased. Will you favour me with a line stating whether *any*, or how many copies have yet been sold?"

But few, I fear; for, three days later, she wrote the following:—

"The Messrs. Bell desire me to thank you for your suggestion respecting the advertisements. They agree with you that, since the season is unfavourable, advertising had better be deferred.

They are obliged to you for the information respecting the number of copies sold."

On July 23rd she writes to the Messrs. Aylott:—

"The Messrs. Bell would be obliged to you to post the enclosed note in London. It is an answer to the letter you forwarded, which contained an application for their autographs from a person who professed to have read and admired their poems. I think I before intimated, that the Messrs. Bell are desirous for the present of remaining unknown, for which reason they prefer having the note posted in London to sending it direct, in order to avoid giving any clue to residence, or identity by post-mark, &c."

Once more, in September, she writes, "As the work has received no further notice from any periodical, I presume the demand for it has not greatly increased."

In the biographical notice of her sisters, she thus speaks of the failure of the modest hopes vested in this publication. "The book was printed; it is scarcely known, and all of it that merits to be known are the poems of Ellis Bell.

"The fixed conviction I held, and hold, of the worth of these poems, has not, indeed, received the confirmation of much favourable criticism; but I must retain it notwithstanding."

FOOTNOTES:

{1} A reviewer pointed out the discrepancy between the age (twenty-seven years) assigned, on the mural tablet, to Anne Brontë at the time of her death in 1849, and the alleged fact that she was born at Thornton, from which place Mr. Brontë removed on February 25th, 1820. I was aware of the discrepancy, but I did not think it of sufficient consequence to be rectified by an examination of the register of births. Mr. Brontë's own words, on which I grounded my statement as to the time of Anne Brontë's birth, are as follows:—

"In Thornton, Charlotte, Patrick Branwell, Emily Jane, and Anne were born." And such of the inhabitants of Haworth as have spoken on the subject say that all the children of Mr. and Mrs. Brontë were born before they removed to Haworth. There is probably some mistake in the inscription on the tablet.

{2} In the month of April 1858, a neat mural tablet was erected within the Communion railing of the Church at Haworth, to the memory of the deceased members of the Brontë family. The tablet is of white Carrara marble on a ground of dove-coloured marble, with a cornice surmounted by an ornamental pediment of chaste design. Between the brackets which support the tablet, is inscribed the sacred monogram I.H.S., in old English letters. In Memory of Maria, wife of the Rev. P. Brontë, A.B., Minister of Haworth, She died Sept. 15th, 1821, in the 39th year of her age. Also, of Maria, their daughter, who died May 6th, 1825, in the 12th year of her age. Also, of Elizabeth, their daughter, who died June 15th, 1825, in the 11th year of her age. Also, of Patrick Branwell, their son, who died Sept. 24th, 1848, aged 31 years. Also, of Emily Jane, their daughter, who died Dec. 19th, 1848, aged 30 years. Also, of Anne, their daughter, who died May 28th, 1849, aged 29 years. She was buried at the Old Church, Scarborough.

Also, of Charlotte, their daughter, wife of the Rev. A. B. Nicholls, B.A. She died March 31st, 1855, in the 39th year of her age. "The sting of death is sin, and the strength of sin is the law, but thanks be to God which giveth us the victory through our Lord Jesus Christ."—1 Cor. xv. 56, 57.

{3} With regard to my own opinion of the present school, I can only give it as formed after what was merely a cursory and superficial inspection, as I do not believe that I was in the house above half an hour; but it was and is this,—that the house at Casterton seemed thoroughly healthy and well kept, and is situated in a lovely spot; that the pupils looked bright, happy, and well, and that the lady superintendent was a most prepossessing looking person, who, on my making some inquiry as to the accomplishments taught to the pupils, said that the scheme of education was materially changed since the school had been opened. I would have inserted this testimony in the first edition, had I believed that any weight could be attached to an opinion formed on such slight and superficial grounds.

{4} "Jane Eyre," vol. I., page 20.

{5} Scott describes the sport, "Shooting at the Popinjay," "as an ancient game formerly practised with archery, but at this period (1679) with firearms. This was the figure of a bird decked with parti-coloured feathers, so as to resemble a popinjay or parrot. It was suspended to a pole, and served for a mark at which the competitors discharged their fusees and carbines in rotation, at the distance of seventy paces. He whose ball brought down the mark held the proud title of Captain of the Popinjay for the remainder of the day, and was usually escorted in triumph to the most respectable change-house in the neighbourhood, where the evening was closed with conviviality, conducted under his auspices, and if he was able to maintain it, at his expense."—Old Mortality.

{6} In this Gutenberg eBook M. Héger's comments are given in {} at approximately the place where they occur—DP.

www.ingramcontent.com/pod-product-compliance
Lightning Source LLC
Chambersburg PA
CBHW020326170426
43200CB00006B/287